Revelations

LESSONS FROM
A MUTHA,
AUNTIE,
BESTIE

BEVY SMITH

Andy Cohen Books
Henry Holt and Company
New York

Andy Cohen Books
Henry Holt and Company
Publishers since 1866
120 Broadway
New York, New York 10271
www.henryholt.com

Andy Cohen Books® and ▉® are registered trademarks of
Macmillan Publishing Group, LLC.

Andy Cohen logo caricature by Robert Risko

Library of Congress Cataloging-in-Publication data is available.

ISBN: 9781250311788

Our books may be purchased in bulk for promotional, educational,
or business use. Please contact your local bookseller or the Macmillan
Corporate and Premium Sales Department at (800) 221-7945, extension
5442, or by e-mail at MacmillanSpecialMarkets@macmillan.com.

First Edition 2021

Designed by Meryl Sussman Levavi

Printed in the United States of America

1 3 5 7 9 10 8 6 4 2

To the household of 2813 Eighth Avenue, Apt. 4G,

Mommy, Daddy, Gerry, and Stephanie,

thank you for loving and nurturing me.

It Gets Greater Later.

—Bevy Smith,
talking to every Lil' Brown Bevy

Contents

Revelations

Evolution of a Grown-Ass Woman

I WOKE UP WITH FRANK SINATRA'S "MY WAY" BLASTING IN MY head. Today was the day, after ten months at a flashy six-figure job as a fashion advertising exec at *Rolling Stone* magazine, that I was going to quit. I had been counting down the days to this departure ever since I accepted the position. In my mind, *Rolling Stone* was the ultimate temp job: do the work, secure the bag (the *money* bag), and get to the business of living my *real life*.

It was a crisp January morning in 2005. In my boss's sunlit office, his head was down—he was studying some papers, probably sales projections for the upcoming issues. When you're a salesperson, that's all you're ever doing: studying the numbers, trying to figure out how you can make your quota and get a bonus, KA-CHING! When he heard my footsteps, he looked up and gave a wry smile. We got along incredibly well, and I genuinely liked him. He was like me, a smart, scrappy outsider—from Staten Island, in his case; I count him and Wu-Tang Clan as good things produced there—who had managed to make it into the hallowed halls of magazine publishing. Lots of folks were intimidated by him. He didn't suffer fools, and he didn't hold his tongue. Thankfully, I was his Golden Girl (Blanche, of course). He'd brought me onto this team to shore up fashion advertising in *Rolling Stone*, and in just ten short months, I had delivered, so we had a real love affair going on—so much so that we had a nickname: we were "Bevy and the Boss."

Bevy of "Bevy and the Boss" entered the office and sat down. The Boss asked what was up, and I launched into an anxiety-fueled, rambling monologue about how much I adored working with him and what an impactful learning experience it had been (it solidified that I never wanted to do sales ever again) but it was time for me to move on. "I'm quitting to lead a creative life," I said, "to act, sing, to just be." He told me I was having a midlife crisis. How dare he! ("Midlife crisis: an emotional crisis of identity and self-confidence that can occur in early middle age.") He clearly didn't know what he was talking about, and I rebutted his theory immediately. My narrative won't be mansplained. As a Black woman from Harlem—*pre-gentrification* Harlem—I couldn't have *that* be my story. I didn't have time for a midlife crisis.

I suspect there are currently a slew of folks at the Whole Foods on 125th Street or the Bikram Yoga place on 145th (a location that was formerly a crack house) who can identify with having a midlife crisis, but not I. In fact it was the opposite—when I decided to quit *Rolling Stone*, I'd found real clarity, about not only who I was at that moment, but who I wanted to end up being in life. In traditional self-help books, this would be described as "finding your purpose."

Now, before you think I'm going to go all Zen Bevy on you, be clear that I had no fucking idea *how* I was going to achieve this abstract concept of living my life's purpose. I didn't have a crystal

ball. But I did have enough of the spirit of the beloved Iyanla Vanzant to know that I had to "fix my life," and I couldn't do that with
a nine-to-five. Being tethered to a career I had outgrown was like
standing for two hours in a pair of six-inch spike heels: it looked
good, but my feet (and spirit) were swollen and in agony!

But, of course, no one knew it by looking at me. If social media
had been around in the late nineties and early aughts, the trolls
might have played armchair psychiatrists trying to dissect my life.
More than a decade before Instagram, I was living the Instagram life—a fierce, shapely woman pictured frequently in exotic
locales; hanging with beautiful, famous people; wearing designer
outfits; and excelling at her corporate job. Mine was a grown and
sexy lifestyle on steroids. I was a "Samantha"—if this reference is
unfamiliar, google *Sex and the City* and thank me later—thirty-
eight years old with a small but mighty roster of lovers and the
aforementioned cushy job.

When I proclaimed to anyone who would listen (friends, enemies, lovers, the *Rolling Stone* security guard, my mailman, my
eight-year-old nephew) that I was quitting my job, it seemed to
many of them that my leaving was coming out of nowhere—and
that's just the way I planned it. Who publicizes that, for the past
five years, they were unfulfilled in their career?

What's ironic is that even if I had told folks about my plans, they
probably wouldn't have believed me. You see, I really was a bona
fide rock star in the fashion advertising world then. (Of course,
this was back when folks still read magazines.) And my job came
with perks: I had an expense account so ample that I never paid for
meals. (I didn't come out my wallet even on the weekends, thanks
to my lovers.) I had become accustomed to flying first class, having a car and driver twenty hours a day while I attended European
fashion shows, and my fave perk of all time: Christmas gifts! My
assistants would groan about the holiday season because of all the

gifts I received. (Okay, if I'm being honest, my assistants groaned a lot anyway; I was a tough boss.) Every Christmas, my office would look like a photo shoot for the Neiman Marcus holiday catalog (pre-fifty-dollar collard greens), filled with gifts from every major design house, from Armani to Yves Saint Laurent, and these would be *exclusive* items. My haul of swag would include bags, shoes, jewelry, champagne—things that money literally couldn't buy because these items were *given*, and only to those with access. Here's a Bevelation for you: True luxury is *access*, and as a fashion and beauty advertising director, I'd worked for two decades to earn that access. Who willingly gives that up? Who walks away from a job that pays well, a bona fide good thing? I'll tell you who: someone looking for a *great* thing, an *inspiring* thing, a *creative* thing, a feeling of freedom, a new dream. In 2002, I wrote in my journal, "I want to live differently, explore and create!" That was more than two years before I actually went ahead and did just that.

Teddy Pendergrass used to sing, "You can't hide from yourself, / Everywhere you go, there you are." Well, I proved Teddy wrong: I hid from myself, and it was pretty darn easy to do. That version of my "self" was a character I was presenting, and everybody bought into her, including me. I was a top-tier customer who stanned for Beverly like she was the latest Supreme collaboration. I was obsessed with furthering the legend of this modern-day fashionista who had managed to claw her way into an industry that wasn't exactly clamoring to welcome curvy Black girls.

My entire thirties were dominated by the narrative that Beverly Smith, born and raised in Harlem, was a top-notch, self-made BAWSE, one who took no shit from anyone. She was a globetrotting, man-eating, designer garment–wearing vixen. To be clear, I'm aware that what I've just described sounds like the main character in a fabulous movie where I'm played by Angela Bassett— don't be shady; I know she would require padding—and everyone envies me. The real truth is that a "flashing lights" lifestyle takes its toll.

First off, when you work as hard as I did, it's hard to develop, much less maintain, intimate relationships, unless you count your vibrator. I dated a lot during that era, but nothing managed to stick. I remember my bestie Renee Billy, aka Nay Nay Billy, advising me to stop telling prospective boyfriends my travel schedule in advance. She said, "Why would a guy try to establish a relationship with a woman who is literally *never* around?" When she said it, I got all indignant. I thought she was advising me to lie, to hide my fabulous life from some basic guy. Nope. Instead, she was advising me to get to know a person, to date him more than a few times before submitting my travel itinerary. Hindsight is 20/20, but back then, I clearly needed eye surgery as my vision was blurred.

It wasn't just romantic relationships that were challenged by my high-powered job. I also wasn't as present for friends and family as I would have liked to be. Men's Fall/Winter Fashion Week takes place in Milan during the second week of January. My mom's birthday is on the eighth, my bestie Aimee Morris's is on the tenth; I missed both their birthdays a couple of times. But the event I most regret missing is my sister Stephanie's wedding. Her wedding took place during one of my sales trips to Europe, and although she didn't tell anyone she was getting married, I still felt guilty that I missed her special day. I tried to make it up to all of them by bringing back expensive gifts, but I now know that my mom and Aimee would have preferred to have me at their parties singing "Happy Birthday" in my trademark baritone voice, and my sister would have liked my being there acting hysterical about every little detail of her courthouse wedding.

Here's a Bevelation: When it comes to healthy relationships, nothing beats being there. Your presence is the ultimate present.

Back then, I simply wasn't evolved enough—and as a Scorpio,

I was more than just a little self-absorbed—so I felt justified in missing out on such events. I had a career in a very competitive space, and that was my justification. It was a space where I had made real inroads and gained clout, but there was always someone with more, especially from the general market—aka white fashion magazines. Working in fashion and advertising in the nineties while Black meant being constantly reminded that, to borrow the old *Sesame Street* song, one of these things (me) is *not* like the others, and I was determined not only to meet but to *exceed* expectations. And it wasn't just that I was Black. It was the way I showed up as a Black *woman*.

Let me paint the picture: showing up in elite and austere fashion spaces looking bawdy-licious, wearing brightly hued clothes that showcased my curves, rocking short haircuts or, sometimes (*clutch the pearls!*), braids—this was seen as daring and, yes, *brave*. (Can we have a moment and finally decree the death of the word *brave* to describe a woman who dares to break the "rules" and deviate from what mainstream society dictates is "beauty"?) I wasn't attempting to be brave when I wore braids instead of a long, silky weave. (I actually started wearing them after I caused a minor blackout while using my million-watt curling iron at my luxury hotel in Milan.) Even so, I understood that my braids were seen as a statement, part of my racial identity, and I didn't shy away from that. But braids were only a small part of my look. I took real pleasure in being audacious when it came to my garments, too. Clothing is a calling card, and I wanted to announce, without saying a word, that a Harlem girl was entering the room. I was drawn to clothes that most girls from the paler side of fashion wouldn't have dared try to pull off. Wearing all white in the middle of winter? Why not? My suntan is year-round. A Dolce & Gabbana corset dress in fuchsia? Lace me up and pray I don't have to go to the bathroom!

I received a lot of attention, and I appreciated it, but I was also very clear that my entire look had been cribbed from the women in my neighborhood. My look was bold, daring, even *brave* (ugh) in Europe, but in Harlem, it was just a Saturday-night look.

◆ ◆ ◆

Wherever I went out in the world, my goal always was (and always will be) to represent Harlem, my community. I felt accomplished while in the spotlight because I had learned to play the game and to play it my way, leading with swagger, going against the status quo, and, in return, garnering nice financial results. For a time, it felt like I was winning. But I didn't realize what a toll it was taking on me and my spirit. My wardrobe and attitude were a shield, protecting me from reality and signaling to all that I was living a fab life, but it soon began to feel less like protection and more like a weapon of my own making turned against me.

By the time I announced I was quitting, I was weary of the dog and pony show that is sales. Initially, I loved wining and dining clients, having "spa days" versus being in the office, going to fashion showrooms and selecting items fresh off the runway and not paying a dime for them. However, as with every good thing, there's always a price to pay. As I mentioned earlier, I missed important events in my loved ones' lives. And the more that continued to happen, the more I felt I was drowning in a shallow life, and the more I resented my "dream job." Sales is an intimate business, centered on developing client relationships, and I was great at it. But singing for my supper to meet my sales quota—treating folks to concerts, spa treatments, dinners—meant entertaining clients whom, if they hadn't been in control of advertising budgets, I would never have had a coffee with, much less a three-hour dinner followed by late-night cocktails. Knowing I only tolerated these people for the check, I started feeling disingenuous in my encounters with them. There were times when I did enjoy my work, when a client outing wasn't a chore and I didn't feel like a whore (yass, rhymes), and some clients became my friends, and still are to this day. However, for every genuine connection, there were ten forced relationships with snobs, insecure mean girls, and needy people who thought I was some kind of magical Negro who could advise them on everything from their love life to their career. Their brand of self-absorption and obliviousness began to wear on my nerves. I was frazzled, but it wasn't only being in service to clients that wore my smile down to a grimace; ultimately, I was exhausted from being in service to the persona I had created for myself. When I finally came to the realization that continuing to go down this path meant perhaps never knowing where the character ended and the real me began, I knew I had to tender my resignation.

I'll bet you're reading this right now and thinking, *I'd love to have those kinds of problems.* That's what you think . . . until you meet a woman like the one I was. Better yet, try *working* for one of us, and you'll be like, "Too short!" and your favorite word will be *beeyatch.* It's not entirely our fault that we get so caught up in playing the role of tough woman. We've been hardened by years of climbing the corporate ladder and watching mediocre men sprint ahead simply because of what swung between their legs or, in the case of many power-hungry men, barely dangled. Women often feel they have to take on a tough exterior; this often alienates everyone around us, especially those who try to get close. For many women, everyone is the competition, even our friends and subordinates. Just like those objects in the side-view mirror looking farther away than they really are, tough women often appear more secure than they really are. But when you get up on us, often the most powerful, aloof, unbothered-by-what-anyone-thinks-or-says among us are masking insecurities. That's me. I'm *us*—or at least I was.

Many folks thought I was prescient because I got out of magazine publishing before the glamorous perks were cut off. Here's the part where I should say, "Yes, that's right. I saw the fall coming," but that wouldn't be true, and writing a memoir is tricky enough—regarding your truth versus their truth versus the real truth—without complicating it with blatant untruths, aka lies. No, my reasons for getting out were different. Frankly, I witnessed that lifestyle up close, and it scared me. I was on a career trajectory, ascending rapidly, and I realized that very few people at the top of the heap were actually happy. Yes, they had "everything"—all the adoring fans, the not-so-adoring team, the perks—but many of them were miserable. In the early 2000s, I had a few friends who quit fashion. I was especially inspired by the PR fashion girl who became a yogi and the luxury marketer who quit to travel the world. Their stories inspired me, but I thought it was easy for them—they were young and thin and white, and if the thing they ran away to do didn't work out, fashion would welcome them back with open arms and free samples. That wasn't my story. Then, one day, I realized that while I wasn't young, white, or sample size, I was smart, Black, and savvy, and that, too, had value, so I woke the fuck up! I lived this story. Want to hear it? Here it goes . . .

The Ugly Side of
My Beautiful Life

I T WAS 1999. I WAS THE BEAUTY AND FASHION ADVERTISING director at *Vibe* magazine, and I'd landed at Milan's Malpensa Airport for the men's shows. That divinely crisp Sunday morning, I strutted into the terminal in six-inch heels with a porter struggling under the weight of my four suitcases. My regular driver, Giovanni, was waiting for me as I exited customs. Giovanni was dark-haired, swarthy, and fine, with that swagged-out Italian sex appeal. As he kissed me on both cheeks, I began to remember why this city had felt like a second home for so many years. His car was idling curb-side, which I'm sure was illegal (and horrible for the environment), but, hey, la dolce vita is a mindset. It's a good life indeed! I let my golden-brown mink slip off my shoulders onto the plush leather seats of the Mercedes sedan. Stretching out in comfort, I enjoyed the ride through the quiet streets of Milan, hearing nothing but what sounded like ten thousand church bells chiming in harmony.

We reached the iconic Principe di Savoia hotel, where I was a regular guest, and I was greeted by what seemed like the entire staff. "Buon giorno, Princess Smith," everyone said. Yaas, I was indeed feeling royal.

I was escorted to my regular room, a beautiful buttercup-yellow corner suite. It was filled with gifts from the major fashion houses: Cavalli (RIP), Versace, Missoni—you know, all the designers with names that end in a vowel. I went straight to the window, and as I opened the drapes, I caught the sunlight just right and I swear I heard "Ave Maria" playing on a loop. Suffice it to say, I was a long way from Harlem's 150th Street and Eighth Avenue. #MommaIMadeIt.

The bellman kissed my hand. I tipped him fifty bucks, a reimbursable expense, and he bowed out of the room backward, closing the door behind him. And I collapsed on the bed, sobbing into fifteen hundred dollars' worth of Frette sheets.

It seemed I had it all—but Houston, we had a problem.

At the time, though, I had no idea what that problem could be. I knew I was experiencing malaise. (Yes, I could have called it depression, but *malaise* sounds exotic and luxurious.) Just like Solange—well, before Solange, who was only sixteen then—I had tried to sex it away, shop it away, drink it away, eat it away, sex it away. (Mentioning sex twice isn't a typo; that was my favorite escape.) I was self-medicating, and for a while, each of these remedies had worked. But when they stopped quelling my despair, I felt worse than I did before—especially after rounds of meaningless sex with a well-hung and sweet-but-daft lover. Some of you ladies who have low numbers in the romance department may wonder why I didn't stop having sex when I knew it wasn't making me feel any better. Well, I don't know about you, but I was going to keep trying. No one calls me a quitter!

I know now that sexcapades can often be more trouble than they're worth. Yes, I practiced safe sex, but herpes is skin-to-skin.

There's also HPV, an oldie but a goodie, and crabs (though, fear of bedbugs may have replaced fear of crabs). So, you have this romp, and then you worry about disease. And itching. And what about pregnancy? Yes, again, you practice safe sex, but are you practicing it *correctly*!? After he ejaculates, he's supposed to get up and get something—preferably a flute of champagne and a warm, soapy washcloth; you know, for a cleanup in aisle five. He's not supposed to lounge around in my lady parts with the condom still on, letting his sperm imitate Michael Phelps! Damn, why was there so much angst around something that was supposed to be casual and fun?

My other drug of choice was shopping. I know I'm not alone in recovery. (Can I get an amen?) Out of all my addictions—this Scorpio has had a few—being a shopaholic was the toughest to kick because it's been glorified in pop culture. In fact, for many women, it's a badge of honor. Ladies, I'm telling you, it's not! It's a marketing hoax. Go online and type "shopaholic" into your search engine. Pages of garbage (I mean, items) will come up, most of them in pink—marketers know that women in crisis are suckers for pink. I'm sure you think the "Shop Till You Drop" mugs or the "I'm Not a Shopaholic, I'm Helping the Economy" T-shirts are cute and benign. They're *not*! As the sage and always up-front self-help goddess Iyanla Vanzant would say, "Call a thing, a thing." I mean, did you really need to purchase *three* Goyard bags at once, to the tune of ten thousand dollars? (True story, and the only highlight is that I was able to sell one when I went broke. More on that later.)

Back to Milan and the tear-soaked Frette bed linens. So, I was spiraling out of control and couldn't see my way around that feeling. I was unable to craft a strategy to solve my problem because I didn't know what was wrong, I knew only that something was definitely not right. Meanwhile, it was 9 a.m. on a Sunday in Milan, which meant it was only 3 a.m. in New York. Usually, when I'm feeling low, I call one of my besties—Renee, Aimee, or my sister, Stephanie. However, if I'd called any of them at 3 a.m. from Italy and admitted that I was crying in a luxury hotel suite, they would have freaked out, so I quickly ruled out transatlantic dialing. If I had been home, I could have made a booty call and avoided my feelings by having sex. I *did* think about calling Giovanni the driver—we had quite the flirtation going—but even in my sorry state, I retained my morals. (He's a married man, so off-limits.)

Unable to talk it out or sex it away, I just had to wallow in it, feeling every single emotion rise up. I didn't have a clue where to put all those feelings, so I sat with them—and they started nagging me, asking intrusive questions like "Don't you want more?" "Is this who you really want to be?" "How can you sustain this life?" and the hardest one, which wasn't even a question but a harsh declaration: "You know, there's a reason you've had ten assistants in five years. You're a bitch." Okay, maybe that last one was what an assistant said to me as she was exiting the building with her boxes, but it had obvi struck a chord and replayed in my head all the way to Italy.

It's true, my emotions were probably colored that morning by exhaustion, a combo of jet lag and a hangover from all the champagne I'd drunk on the flight—yes, I know you shouldn't drink on flights, but it's free, and this was before first class had Wi-Fi and lie-flat seats, so I needed to find some form of entertainment. But I knew there was more to my feelings than mere exhaustion.

This was the pre-internet era, when hotels still provided paper and envelopes to write letters to loved ones or, in my case, radical manifestos (very Tom Cruise in *Jerry Maguire*!). So, I grabbed some hotel stationery and wrote down all the times in my life I'd felt most inadequate and inauthentic. Then I listed the times when I'd hidden my true self, my best self, in order to serve the character of the high-flying fashionista. Next, I wrote down my feelings, how I no longer wanted to be in service to a superficial business, a multibillion-dollar business, whose sole goal often seemed to be making women doubt themselves, making them feel like shit unless they bought this face cream or that dress, the "It" handbag. I wrote down that I was spiraling, moving farther and farther away from the person I wanted, and had the potential, to be. I recently found a journal entry from that era that read, "As a person I think I'm a 5.5. I would like to be at least a 7." I had started seeing a pattern, and I realized I was living my life for the applause, the approval of others. I was addicted to the popularity and to the character I had created, but I wasn't being true to myself, to my core.

One of the first things I jotted down was "FASHION KILLS." Being a part of fashion brought out the worst of my insecurities, made me competitive and snarky. I already told you that the women with the toughest exteriors are usually the most insecure, right? Imagine working in a field where that behavior is not only a natural state of being, but is *rewarded*.

Lean in. I want to share a Bevelation: The fashion business thrives on women's insecurities. The fashion industry is marketing its wares to the running list we all keep in our heads about what's wrong with us. They know we hate our chubby elbows, that frown line on our chin (is that even a thing?), our naturally curly/kinky hair, our flat or big booty. And then they convince us that we are blessed because they have just the remedy for it—*for purchase*.

Well, that message—that something is wrong with you and it can be fixed only if you buy the product they just happen to be selling—is amplified when you're on the inside of the business. In an industry focused on highlighting the fantastic and fabulous, why do so many gatekeepers seem miserable? Sure, many of them are "hangry"—you know, carbohydrates are seen as the devil's work, along with capri pants and knockoff designer handbags. However, I believe many people who work in fashion are suffering from impostor syndrome and are judging themselves far more harshly than they judge consumers. We buy into playing a role: the morose Fashion Designer, he doesn't speak, the clothes speak for him; the Fashion Editor, eccentric diva, arrogant, prone to histrionics; the Fashionista, works in fashion but isn't a "creative," has a powerful job in PR or marketing, is often a "daughter/spouse of" or is a scrappy upstart who clawed their way to the middle/top and is in service to the aforementioned personalities (that would be me). Each role comes with its own set of challenges, but the one thing they all have in common is a fear of not fitting sample sizes, not fitting in, and hearing Heidi Klum say, "Either you're in or you're out. And you're out." Heavy is the head that wears a Philip Treacy crown, *le sigh*.

Another item on my hotel stationery list: I was no longer challenged by my job. I'm not one to rest on my laurels, and once I achieve a goal, I'm a firm believer in KIM, as in "Keep It Moving." When I arrived at *Vibe*, I was told by other salespeople and a few folks in management that I wouldn't be able to secure luxury fashion advertising. Those naysayers were just the fuel I needed to set out to prove them wrong—and boy, did I! I set fire to all their doubts by securing ads, along with my partner in crime, our European Advertising representative, Jeffrey Byrnes, from almost every luxury brand in fashion. Jeffrey and I were quite the duo. He was a blond California cutie with incredible style, and I was . . . well, *me*! A big part of the reason luxury brands bought pages was just because they liked to meet with us. Being a good salesperson requires a strong likability factor; no one spends money with people they hate. Where other magazine salespeople were straitlaced and stodgy with their power suits and their PowerPoints, we were hip-hop at its finest. Imagine a Mary J. Blige duet with Justin Timberlake (before he sold Janet Damita Jo Jackson out) singing the hook, and Blige in head-to-toe, monogram, fresh-off-the-runway looks. Jeffrey and I booked major business, which fed my ego (and my ego at that time had a ravenous appetite), put me on the map in my field, and paid me a handsome six-figure salary. I was *haute* shit. Yaas, she did that! (She is me.) But once I did it a thousand times, the thrill began to wear off, and booking all that business became like Groundhog Day. (Clearly, I was a much cuter version of Bill Murray.)

Another item on my list? I had made it all the way to this (glam) career destination only to ask myself, *Is this it?* I couldn't believe I had worked for *decades* to achieve my place in fashion advertising only to find that it wasn't the magic elixir I thought it would be. It didn't solve my issues; if anything, it exacerbated them. This was like that time when I got a weave to give my hair a rest—it was supposedly a "protective style"—but when I took it out three months later, my hair looked worse than it did before. (Jesus, be Jamaican castor oil.)

I'd experienced this feeling of disappointment in so many facets of my life, not just with that bad weave, but also in romantic relationships. In that hotel room, I realized I could no longer cover up what was wrong or use a quick sexcapade to pick myself up. I had to peel back the layers of the character I had built up, take off the "protective style," and do the work to get to happy, or at least excited, about my future. I had to find out what would fulfill me—and I couldn't be afraid to blow up the life I had painstakingly built for decades.

That was the Bevelation: I had to change my life, right away.

So, I called my boss and I quit my job, right? Wrong. But for fun, I did work out a film version of how I'd quit. It goes like this:

I dramatically get myself off the floor of my suite and, after blowing kisses to the adoring hotel staff, head outside. I do my soul-searching at the historic Duomo di Milano, wearing a Dolce & Gabbana veil, a totally inappropriate-for-church Versace mini-dress, and Gucci stilettos. Though the priest is conducting Mass in Italian, I understand every word he is saying, and I'm moved to tears, which I wipe away ever so gently with an antique Irish lace handkerchief. After Mass, I jump up and run out of the Duomo and into the square. Yes, I'm running in my six-inch heels because . . . movie magic. I pull out my cell phone—even though it's 1999 and you could not make transatlantic calls on cells, but more movie magic—and call my boss. I tell him, "Take this job and shove it, / I ain't working here no more" (which, in case you're younger than fifty or not a fan of watered-down country music, are lines from a very popular 1981 country song sung by Johnny Paycheck). My boss wishes me well and does not mention that, because of the six-hour time difference, I have woken him up at 3 a.m. Days later, after enjoying the best of Milan, I fly home and begin my new creative life as host of my own national TV show.

It's a good story, right? However, that ain't the way it went down. The real story is a lot less dramatic and did not involve a veil or a Johnny Paycheck–themed resignation. Instead, it involved dubious financial planning, finding new friends who believed in my dreams while dumping old ones who were wedded to the success I was trying to divorce, and getting over my fear of not being known. This was before social media influencers, but in my space of fashion and advertising, I was definitely a blue-check-mark kind of gal. And after a childhood of being bullied, I still felt the need to be verified, to have my decisions cosigned by others. That's why the real plan took five years to execute.

Parisian Bevy at a Belgian restaurant wearing
Italian designers. Globe-trotter!

#DoTheWork

As is the case for most folks, quitting outright wasn't an option for me. Even if it had been financially feasible, I wouldn't have resigned right away because I wasn't at all ready to let go of the identity I'd worked so hard to build. I still wanted to be Beverly who could get a reservation at any hot-spot restaurant in town, day of. I still wanted to be invited to sit front row at fashion shows, and I loved that my access extended beyond fashion. Super Bowl, NBA All-Star, the U.S. Open—just so we're clear, I don't like sports, but I enjoy fancy sporting events where lots of successful Black men congregate—if it was an extravaganza, a scene to be seen, I was there!

Most of us are so committed to our titles that they become the sum total of who we are, not just what we do. As much I would love to revise history and say that I was so confident in who I was back then that I threw caution to the wind, that's fake news. No, I took baby steps. After my initial Milanese breakdown, I managed to pull it together somewhat, but that trip featured a lot fewer costume changes than usual and almost no discotheques. (I love that even in 1999, Milan was still calling clubs "discos.") Instead, I brooded in my luxurious suite a lot, doing the work to strategize my new life.

◆ ◆ ◆

While I was sitting on the floor surrounded by fancy shopping bags in my plush Principe suite, it came to me: I would become Bevy Smith! I chose that name because "Bev Smith" had already been taken by an iconic journalist who had a talk show on BET when I was a kid, and "B. Smith" by the legendary restaurateur and lifestyle maverick (RIP). While I admired both those women, I wanted no confusion. Also, Bevy sounded right to me—it's unique, saucy. It evokes a gal who is a lot of fun, and it's easy to spell. (Once a marketer, always a marketer.) The inspiration to change my name actually came from a fellow Scorpio, the man formerly known as Diddy, Puff Daddy, Puffy, Brother Love, Sean Combs, and Sean John. Puff—that's what I call him, no matter how many times he changes his name—knows there's power in what people call you, especially when the name change is your directive.

Upon my return from Italy, I took a huge step. I decided I would no longer allow folks to introduce me as "Beverly Smith, who runs fashion at *Vibe* magazine." That descriptor would no longer do; I was focused on not being that person anymore. I had to start preparing for the day I wouldn't have a business card to usher me into rooms. What could be my new identity, one that wasn't tied to my job or any outside entity? What could I own for myself? What identity would proclaim that a remix was coming? First, I strategized on how I could begin the process of putting folks on notice that I was changing, morphing into something and someone new.

The post-Milan period found me restless, but I had a plan. I was going to tiptoe into changing my life. Nothing too radical, because initially I had no desire to leave *Vibe*. Instead, over the course of two to three years, I began trying to create different positions for myself within the brand. One of my more inspired ideas was to create a *Vibe* "travel agency," taking Black and Brown stylists to Fashion Week around the world and giving them access. I know this may not sound like a big deal in 2021, but fifteen years ago, there were very few stylists of color who had the clout to attend fashion shows. But when I proposed the idea to the higher-ups at *Vibe*, they basically gave me a blank stare and told me to stick to selling fashion advertising. Later on in my journey to becoming Bevy Smith, TV personality, I actually created a business where I was paid to take music artists and their teams to fashion shows; so, it turns out my idea was solid. However, many businesses, the fashion industry included, don't want mavericks; they want folks who fit into a corporate structure, execute what's in their job description, and cash the check.

Of course, being a salesperson means not taking no for an answer, so I pitched another idea: a liaison between fashion brands and the fashion editorial staff. I had a great relationship with our fashion editors, and of course the luxury brands wanted to build their relationships with the editors. I thought I could be a match-maker of sorts. That idea was met with a quizzical look that seemed to say, *What's your problem? Just cash the check and misuse your expense account—as a salesperson, it's your God-given right!* It was suggested I take a day off for a spa treatment (which, due to my dream job's expense account, I didn't have to pay for), to relax, relate, release, and get my mind back to business—the lucrative business at hand of selling advertising space for *Vibe*. It was then that I realized that as much as I loved *Vibe*, it didn't love me. Nope, I was a cog in its wheel. It wasn't personal; it was strictly business.

Ever notice that whenever anyone says that to you, it *feels* incredibly personal?

Time for a Bevelation: No matter what your corporate culture—I don't care if you work at a company with free breakfast, lunch, dinner, and premium snacks, or if there's a nap pod on the premises and they allow you to bring your emotional support peacock to work—most companies aren't truly invested in your personal development unless that personal development helps their bottom line and aligns with their corporate ethos. Your journey to fulfillment can't interfere with the bottom line, because as the great West Coast poet DJ Quik said, "If it don't make dollars, it don't make sense."

At the time, I was devastated to realize that my happiness wasn't of paramount importance to *Vibe*. We were a family, right? Didn't my "family" want to see me happy, even if that meant I would no longer be bringing in millions of dollars in advertising? Clearly, based on the number of people who sue their families over money, I should have known the answer would be no. It's true, the ideas I'd pitched them wouldn't bring in nearly the same amount of money, at least not immediately. But now, of course, no magazine actually sells ad pages; it sells experiential marketing, and those ideas fit right into a media company's brand strategy (like the Essence Festival and the New Yorker Festival). *New York Magazine*'s The Cut sells the items you read about in that column, and *Condé Nast Traveler* makes money if you click on a link that takes you to the hotel room featured in their website and you book the room. Look at me being a marketing visionary, ahead of my time!

In 2004, a dear friend of mine, Heather Vandenberghe, who ran a luxury brand, mentioned to me that *Rolling Stone* was looking for a senior fashion director. When the publisher had asked her about smart and connected advertising salespeople, she told him they should hire me but would probably not be able to lure me away from *Vibe*. It was then that I came up with the idea that changed the trajectory of my life. I said I was willing to meet with *Rolling Stone*. My plan was to use their job offer as bait to *Vibe*'s president! I figured there was no way he would let me go to the competition, right? Well, obvi I was wrong! I interviewed for the *Rolling Stone* job, got the offer, took it to *Vibe*'s management—and they didn't counter. Instead, they thanked me for my service.

Really? I know. I'm still shocked. What isn't shocking is that when I left *Vibe*, most of their luxury fashion advertising left with me. It still brings me great joy because I'm Petty LaBelle, Tom Petty and the Heartbreakers, and I live in Petty-coat Junction.

So, I took the job at *Rolling Stone*. It wasn't an easy decision. I'm like most folks: change is scary for me. I didn't want to leave the family I had created at *Vibe*. I certainly didn't think I would be able to recreate it at *Rolling Stone*. The magazine had a bit of reputation in the industry, a reputation for paying well because the work environment was so toxic. Lots of yelling and micromanaging. Of particular concern to me: you could count on one hand the Black or Brown people working there. That's why shockwaves rattled through the industry when I went to work for *Rolling Stone*. I was closely identified with the *Vibe* brand, and no one had any idea that I was less than thrilled to be a salesperson; no one saw my defection coming. When the news hit that I was going to *Rolling Stone*, many of my Black peers thought of this as a win for all of us: Beverly Smith from *Vibe*, an "urban culture" magazine (aka a Black magazine) going to a brand that would rather feature rock stars who hadn't charted in over two decades on its cover than a living Black superstar. (The Beatles have been on the cover of *Rolling Stone* about thirty times!)

I know. If you're reading this and you're under the age of thirty-five, you probably can't fathom a time when there hasn't been an Elaine Welteroth (former editor in chief of *Teen Vogue*) or an Edward Enninfull (first Black editor in chief of British *Vogue*). But there were few Black and Brown people on the editorial side then, and on the publishing side (the money side) it was even worse. When I went to *Rolling Stone* in the early 2000s, the magazine had had only one other Black person on its sales team, the divine Samantha Fennell, who also predated me at *Vibe*—for a time, I was literally following in her footsteps.

The idea of moving to a company where I would be "the only one" and have to continually prove myself wasn't attractive. Although I grew up loving sixties rock music (Janis Joplin, the Beatles, the Rolling Stones) and fancied myself a flower child, I knew that oftentimes white mainstream media loves our rhythm but not our blues. And my stint at *Rolling Stone* was definitely not one big sixties love-in. It seemed the owners loved the counterculture revolution of the sixties—hippies; burn your bra; take acid to turn on, tune in, and drop out—but had no use for civil rights and integration. The magazine may have been founded on the music of the Summer of Love, but the environment was more like a cold spring—frigid, actually. I'm a friendly kind of gal, and I created a few friendships there, but I forged a real sisterhood with a lovely, spirited young Italian American woman, Lea Melone, at the time, a feisty assistant. We bonded over hip-hop and our mutual dislike of *Rolling Stone* and its outright disdain for hip-hop.

The entire time I was there, it felt like doing penance, and I couldn't figure out why I was being tested in this way. I wanted to repent for my sins, but other than making liberal use of my T&E account at *Vibe*, I couldn't figure out what I had done to deserve this punishment. One bright side was that I wasn't emotionally invested in the brand. For the first time in a decade, I was able to leave work at 6 p.m. and not look back.

Time for another Bevelation: One of the most valuable lessons I learned at *Rolling Stone* is that sometimes a job is just a job. That's right. Unfortunately, not every career opportunity will be life-changing in a positive way. Oftentimes you won't feel connected; you may not find your "tribe." Sometimes it's just a paycheck, and a stepping-stone (pun intended).

There was a five-year gap between my meltdown in Milan and my work at *Rolling Stone*, five years between anointing myself Bevy Smith and actually embracing what the name symbolized for me. Those five years were filled with fear: fear of what others would think, fear of failure, fear of who I was if I didn't have a company's name attached to mine. I'm sure a few of you know what I mean. As women, we contort our very beings to make it in the corporate arena. If you add being Black to the equation, there is also the pressure of constantly proving that you actually are qualified for the job.

Those five years were filled with lots of fumbles and false starts, which I will go into later in the book—I'm such a tease—but by the time I arrived at *Rolling Stone*, I was committed to changing my life. I had everything I needed and a few things I didn't, like too much confidence and the half-baked plan I had begun to lay out in Milan. Fortunately, I also had a tenacious don't-take-no-for-an-answer spirit and the work ethic of Smitty and Lolly (my parentals), mixed with the knowledge that I had already succeeded to a degree beyond what many people expected I would or even could. So, I allowed my former wins to fuel my future successes. The plan was simple: save the significant pay increase I received from leaving *Vibe* to go to *Rolling Stone*, secure a five-figure bonus at the new magazine, and then run like I'd robbed the joint.

So, yes, the *Rolling Stone* job was a stopgap measure—you know, like when you're looking for Mr. Right but you settle for dating Mr. Right Now? *Rolling Stone* was Mr. Right Now. Each day, I reported to work, sat in my cubicle—at *Vibe*, I had an office, but *RS* ran in a much more "seemingly" democratic manner—looked at my calendar, and crossed off the day. Kind of like prison, but with a much better commissary—Felicity Huffman's version of prison versus the *Scared Straight* variety. Then I went through the motions of selling ad space, taking meetings, and trying to learn to appreciate Maroon 5. (PJ Morton's artistry helped with that.) But I was sleepwalking, dreaming of the time when the alarm clock would go off and I would awaken to my authentic, creative life.

In an effort to get ready for my creative abundance, I was obsessed with self-help books, especially *The Four Agreements*, by Miguel Ruiz, and Julia Cameron's *The Artist's Way*. Initially, I was put off by the idea of writing "morning pages," step one in *The Artist's Way*. The book asks you to put down three pages of stream-of-consciousness writing first thing in the morning, every morning. All I wanted to do upon waking up was go to the bathroom and check missed calls from the various suitors I was entertaining. But once I gave into the idea of really committing to *The Artist's Way*, writing my morning pages became the best part of my day. I gained clarity, and I soon declared that no one could call me before 8 a.m., while I was working on my pages.

My morning pages are a big part of why I was able to write this book. I've just cribbed notes from those journals. (You think I can remember all these details?) However, it wasn't all New Age affirmations and chants of "You go, girl" dancing in my head those mornings. I understood that I was taking a big risk by blowing up a life that many folks desired, a career that I had dreamed of since I was an eighteen-year-old receptionist at an advertising agency. Although I was two decades older and had made significant financial strides, I was still a Brown girl from Harlem, specifically from 150th Street and Frederick Douglass Boulevard. The median annual household income in the community where I grew up is currently $38,621 for a family of four. Please believe me when I say I was acutely aware of how well I was doing. Unlike many of my peers,

I worked with the knowledge that my success was not guaranteed; nor did I take for granted that I was most assuredly #Blessed.

The Four Agreements was another game changer in my life. The book has four simple "rules":

> *Be impeccable with your word.* There are many ways to translate this, depending on where you are in your life, but for me it meant being *kind* with my words, especially as they applied to me. Once I learned this rule, I no longer put barriers around what I could do, and I began to speak about myself in a positive manner. I also vowed to get out of the habit I had honed working in fashion of being catty, throwing out underhand comments, and engaging in plain old meanness for the sake of telling it like it is. Honestly, I've gotten better, but I'm definitely still a work in progress. Though I do temper my words, I know many people wouldn't necessarily agree, and to them I say, GET OVER IT. (Just kidding. I told y'all, I'm a work in progress.)
>
> *Don't take anything personally.* Rule two was incredibly helpful because when trying to change your life, folks are going to advise you against it. They will offer up myriad reasons you shouldn't do what you plan on doing. Now, some folks would call such people "haters," but I don't believe that. I think most times they are simply projecting their own limitations onto you. So, keep your own counsel. If you are authentically yourself, you can become your best adviser. What others say or do has *nothing* to do with you; that's their own nightmare—you don't have to share in it just like they don't have to share in your dream! This rule is especially helpful in these stressful times of social media trolling. This is a hard lesson to learn and even harder to apply, but try not to look for validation from outsiders, especially strangers on

a computer who don't even use their own photos as their social media avatars. If you can master that, you'll be able to accept the "likes" with a grain of salt when you post your fab vacation photos and not be devastated when you post about your new meditation practice and no one cares other than your mother and that weird white guy with locs who lives in Vermont. (What? I have eclectic followers.)

Don't make assumptions. Instead of assuming what someone means when they say something, or say nothing at all, ask for clarification! This saves you time and aggravation, especially when it comes to dating. As a single woman, I used to play that game of not wanting to ask a guy what we were doing. You feel like his girlfriend, he takes you out, introduces you to his friends—hell, you even meet his mom (by mistake, when she drops off his laundry, but still, you meet her)— but you still feel you're in the gray area. Instead of asking, you hope that one day he will just tell you, "Bess, you is my woman now." (I love musicals. Although problematic, *Porgy and Bess* is one of my faves.) That is, you *assume*— until he tells you he's engaged to someone else. Now, that never happened to me, because I'm a vengeful Scorpio and he wouldn't make it to his wedding day if he scorned me, okay! But I digress . . . a lot. Anyway, when you ask the hard questions, you may receive hard truths, but not knowing something doesn't make the issue go away. If you know exactly what you're dealing with, you can make adjustments and eventually right some wrongs, prevent small issues from morphing into colossal problems. So gird your loins, stop making assumptions, and ask.

Always do your best. My all-time favorite rule! This gives you an out, a way to not be so hard on yourself. Because sometimes you're going to "fail." Everything you do won't be genius, epic, or award-winning. But that's okay. As long as you actually did your *best*—this is the most important part (contrary to what your best friend, mother, or Vermont stalker says)—whatever *best* looks like in that moment, you're off the hook of feeling like a failure! Still a little too New Agey? Here's a real example: on March 12, 2020, I had an acting audition, right before New York City closed down in response to the coronavirus pandemic. I was very nervous about going to the audition, my anxiety was twofold, plus, I wasn't sure that I really knew and embodied my lines or the role. As a bonus case of the jitters, I was also terrified of being out and about and possibly contracting the virus. But, Still I Pushed Through (The Bevy Smith Story). I knew that even if I wasn't at my absolute best due to the pandemic and my fear of stinking up the joint with bad acting, I knew I owed it to myself to show up and be the best version of actress Bevy in a pandemic. I did the audition, had a few flubs but I don't think I was horrible, and left feeling like, okay, I did it, another acting audition under my belt. However, the very next day, New York shut down and so did the production. I don't know what will happen with that role, and I'm sure if there hadn't been a pandemic on the horizon or if I'd had more time to rehearse I would have done "better." But based on the circumstances, I know that I put what was 100 percent at that moment in time into my work. I'm comfortable sharing this story with you because I have already won, just by challenging myself to fight through my insecurities and my fear, knowing that I did my best.

◆ ◆ ◆

By the time I'd reached five years of planning and working on myself, I was a long way from that Milan hotel room. The confused, scared, codependent thirty-three-year-old had morphed into an emotionally evolved thirty-eight-year-old who was truly embracing her independence. I had begun to step out in faith and own my power as such. But, as you know, freethinking women with ideas of their own about what their lives should look like make folks uncomfortable. Women, especially Black women, with agency over their lives, who believe in their power and who aren't afraid to wield it in service to getting what they want, as opposed to accepting what others believe they should have, are seen as threatening to many people. Once I discovered my voice, I stopped living in the space of "I'm so lucky, people dream of this, be grateful" and decided that no one had the right to dictate to me what my version of a dream life looked like. Coming to the realization that I could count my blessings and live in gratitude (the hallmarks of a good girl) and still want more than I currently had—that was an explosive concept. When I began to understand that tapping into my true desires, aspirations that had long been hidden away, didn't make me a bad person but an enlightened, whole person, I went full throttle and embraced the GAW (Grown-Ass Woman) in me. (Thanks for the inspiration, Mary Mary.)

And it was the GAW in me who went into the *Rolling Stone* publisher's office and announced that she was quitting to pursue a "creative life." When the publisher asked, "What does that mean? What are you going to do exactly?" my response was, "Whatever I like. I'm going to write, act, sing, travel, do photography, deejay, paint, be a fire eater, and maybe even juggle"—all while giggling with euphoria. Now that I'm reflecting upon my vague list of goals, maybe that's why he thought I was having a midlife crisis.

Thankfully, due to my good ole *Four Agreements* lesson "Don't take anything personally," I really didn't care what he thought. As much as I respected him, I had clarity about my life, and it didn't entail sales quotas and cubicles or even a corner office. I was done with all the corporate trappings and giddy with excitement, even though I had absolutely no concrete plans other than to leave magazine publishing and live a life filled with creative expression. "Dear *Rolling Stone*, it's not you, it's me!" I was ready to leave before I even arrived.

I stayed at *Rolling Stone* for a whopping ten months. It was long enough to make a few friends; meet Tom Wolfe—tragically, I never asked him how he kept those white suits so clean, I thought I'd have more time; meet and hug Lenny Kravitz for a longer time than what was appropriate (what? he said to "let love rule," I was just following orders); and most important, receive a five-figure bonus for hitting my sales projections, a bonus that went toward building a new creative life for Bevy Smith. Yes, even though I dreaded going to work, I still wanted to excel at my job (pride/ego) and get my bonus check (bonus Bevelation/tip: Leave no money on the table), so I applied the work ethic that had been instilled in me by Smitty and Lolly, and I got the job done. I never wanted anyone at *Rolling Stone* to be able to say I didn't do a good job, that I was a slacker or, God forbid, lazy.

Unfortunately, when you're the only Black person in a company, you often feel you're representing the entire race. With no other Black employees on the business side of the magazine, how could I, as the senior director of fashion advertising, muck it up? I was acutely aware that if I didn't do a good job, I would make it that much harder for the next Black person who applied for the position to be considered. I'm always conscious of leaving the ladder down for the next person climbing up.

Gangs of New York: Paper *magazine shoot, Aimee, Micki, me,
Renee, and Minya. Designer labels, side ponytails,
and fierce attitudes, Harlem style!*

Uptown Girl

RACE FACTORS A LOT IN MY STORY, BUT WHAT CAN YOU expect? I grew up lower middle class (you couldn't have told me we weren't the Huxtables) in upper Manhattan, aka Harlem. The Harlem where I was raised isn't the Harlem of today, a neighborhood that was nearly renamed "SoHa" by gentrifiers. No, the Harlem of my childhood was an amalgamation of post–civil rights Black Power and drug-infused street life. Folks strutted around with beautiful Afros, quoting Malcolm X, wearing dashikis, and urging people to stay home from work and school on Black Solidarity Day. The flip side of that Harlem was "Junkie's Paradise," a strip of 116th Street between St. Nicholas Avenue and Lenox Avenue (now named Malcolm X Boulevard, but old-timers still call it Lenox), an open-air drug bazaar run by the notorious, flamboyantly well-dressed drug kingpin Nicky Barnes. Nicky's lifestyle was so fabulous that he was featured on the cover of the *New York Times Magazine* and later was the subject of a biopic starring Denzel Washington and Russell Crowe. I don't forgive him for pumping drugs into the community and destroying lives, but he also employed hundreds of people (the uneducated, people who served jail time, the underemployed) and sponsored community events, from block parties to funerals. For many people in Harlem, Barnes was a source of pride, an entrepreneur, a Robin Hood in slick suits, fur coats, and custom-made cars.

Our little family didn't fit into either category—we weren't political, and we weren't street. When we were invited to march with a community group for the African American Day Parade in 1975, my sister and I arrived in gingham dresses with our hair in plaits and ribbons, standing out like two Heidis among all the Aishas draped in African garb and sporting intricate cornrows or Afros. My parents were proud to be Black, but like many people born in the 1920s, they had no desire to go back to Africa, and they certainly weren't taking off work for Black Solidarity Day. Their solidarity was with the residents of 2813 Eighth Avenue, apartment 4G.

My parents were the unsung heroes of the Great Migration, the folks whom Jacob Lawrence painted, and whom many of the authors of the Harlem Renaissance didn't want to acknowledge. The Smittys (as they are affectionately known by their children's friends) weren't formally educated, but they were dedicated to working toward building a better life for their children. My dad was forty-one when I was born, and my mom was thirty-eight, making them on average ten to twenty years older than most of my friends' parents. My father woke up in the dark, in the wee hours of the morning, and went to work at a copper refinery plant five days a week. He commuted to Carteret, New Jersey—and by commute, I mean he took two trains and a New Jersey Transit bus to get to work. My mom cleaned houses and commuted as well, taking the A train to Penn Station, then catching the Long Island Railroad to her regular customers' homes.

Now, my mom would *kill* me if I left you with a tragic visual of her as a poor, plainly dressed, subservient character from the film *The Help*. Instead, think Willona from *Good Times* (well dressed, hair coiffed just so, and with a dynamite figure) meets no-nonsense Florence of *The Jeffersons*. My mother wore fabulous clothes on her commute to work and changed into an outfit—consisting of her old clothes, *not* a uniform—to clean houses. She was the kind of housekeeper who made the rules for how and when she would clean, never allowing the owners of the home underfoot. She enforced those rules, and if her clients didn't like it, she would leave. After all, she didn't *need* the money to survive—my dad paid all the household bills—but my mother was used to being an independent woman; she wasn't going to seek permission from my dad to furnish her elaborate wardrobe. #IGetItFromMyMomma.

We lived in a two-bedroom, fifth-floor walk-up at the aforementioned 2813 Eighth Avenue. It was five blocks from the legendary Polo Grounds, where the Yankees used to play, and across the street from the Dunbar Apartments, where a plethora of Talented Tenth–type Black people resided.

In our little home, the gender roles were flipped. My mom had a longer commute from Long Island than my dad did from Jersey. Also, she liked to occasionally stop at a bar after work with her girlfriends for a nightcap. That meant someone had to pick us kids up from our after-school programs, make dinner, and supervise homework. That somebody was my dad. Many of my friends didn't have fathers in the home, much less a dad who would cook for them every night, so we knew Smitty was special.

My mom was exceptional as well. She wasn't a hovering, overbearing type of mother. Instead, I learned from her through example. My mother was—and still is, at ninety-two years old—one of the most stylish women I knew. She's the reason I have always had such a passion for fashion and so much confidence in my personal style. When my mom walks into a room, she commands attention. She was so foxy that I had to ward off men, who would whistle at her in the street. I'd yell at them to leave my mother alone, like a tiny #TimesUp activist.

On weekends, she played music (Aretha Franklin, The Temptations, Otis Redding) and danced around in outrageous outfits, complete with costume and wig changes. It was like *RuPaul's Drag Race* in our little apartment, with my dad documenting it all with his Polaroid camera. There is one picture in the family photo album with my mom dressed in a short, sheer teddy, her two girls in pajamas on either side. My mother was proud of her shape, and she instilled that pride in us. To this day, because of her I can catalog my best physical attributes and know what to wear to accentuate the positives.

If Saturday nights were for my mom, Sundays were all about us kids. Without fail, after my mom made a feast of a dinner, the one meal of the week she was guaranteed to cook, we'd have a family outing. From Central Park and the Museum of Natural History to excursions on the Circle Line (with Smitty telling us what New York looked like when the Native Americans were the only ones here) to Coney Island on a graffiti-covered D train—there was always a weekend expedition. My mother was determined that we not feel confined or limited by growing up in Harlem.

I'm the youngest of three. My brother, Gerald, is eleven years older. He was the perfect big brother, teaching me and our sister, Stephanie, how to dance and giving us in-depth lessons on music from the sixties through the eighties. Gerald was a self-taught artist—he made fashion illustrations, celebrity portraits, abstract paintings—and he was a fly dresser, he went out dancing and/or roller-skating every single weekend. And, like my mom, he bought records every Friday when he got paid.

Just as my parents didn't quite fit in, neither did their kids. Gerry is gay, and back then that wasn't something that folks talked about. As a kid I had no idea about his sexuality—all I knew was that he wasn't like other guys his age on the block, aggressively trying to pick up girls while hanging out on the corner smoking marijuana. My brother had places to go and people to see; 150th Street held no sway over him. After he moved out, when he was twenty and I was nine, my sister and I missed him desperately; even though he was much older, he definitely was our best friend. However, because he took his duties as a big brother seriously, he often brought us to his studio apartment in Queens for sleepovers. His high-rise, LeFrak City, had elevators and big windows. Compared to our walk-up, with its small windows looking out onto a backyard, that little studio apartment with sunlight pouring in from every angle inspired me. I thought he had made it, and he inspired me to live in a high-rise when I got older.

My sister, Stephanie, a scant fifteen months older than me, has always been a mutha, auntie, and bestie, a self-professed "nerd girl." While our parents had no desire to "go back to Africa," Stephanie would gladly have booked passage on Marcus Garvey's Black Star Line. It was Stephanie who introduced me to the authors of the Harlem Renaissance, Black Panther teachings, and modern dance. She was her own rebel with a cause: she loved Black people and believed that one day we would overcome the shackles of the Man. She wore glasses from the time she was six years old, so what with her being called "four-eyed," and being a militant, you would think she wasn't popular, but that wasn't the case. Not only was Stephanie genuinely nice, helpful, and outgoing, but she also had a big ole butt. I'm talking *baby got back*! Problem was, she was still a baby—she had just started junior high, at age eleven—when she started receiving aggressive male attention. I imagine my sister would quote Angela Davis and Huey P. Newton while politely fending off the perverts on the block. (They knew exactly how young she was, but they still stared and occasionally even whispered to her as she walked past them.)

And then there was me, Lil' Brown Bevy. I was the quintessential baby of the family, a thumb sucker—I sucked my thumb until I lost my virginity; calling Dr. Freud!—and a crybaby. My poor parents couldn't leave me at a relative's home for a night out on the town because I would sob hysterically until they came to pick me up. Unfortunately, I carried this trait of crying when I felt abandoned into my romantic relationships. Initially, I thought it was cute, crying to get my way, but now I see it as manipulation, fueled by abandonment issues. Thank God for therapy.

Anyhoo, back to Lil' Brown Bevy. I was sensitive, polite, and studious. Outwardly, I was very shy, but I had a vivid imagination, so between my books and my sister, I didn't feel like a loner. I had myriad friends and adventures through the books I read—thanks also to my dad. A voracious reader with a fifth-grade education, he taught my sister and me to read before we attended elementary school, and he filled our house with his magazines and his books on world history and geography.

It was through reading that I began to dream up a different world. My sister and I would soak up the exotic locales in the oversize pages of *Life* magazine and read about the white stars we watched on TV and in the movies. *Natural Geographic* gave me an overview of the world, and was a companion piece to my dad's endless quizzes on geography, which took place most Sundays, sandwiched between reading the funnies and building a diorama in a shoebox.

My dad was obsessed with *National Geographic*, but *Ebony* magazine was my favorite. Representation, as we now know, is crucial for a child's development. In the post–civil rights era of the seventies, Black folks were ready to take their place in mainstream society, and many did, in arenas ranging from politics to entertainment. Yet, even the Black stars who crossed over, like Diana Ross, Flip Wilson, Lola Falana, Bill Cosby, and OJ Simpson—who would have thought those last two would later be convicted felons?— never shone as bright in those white magazines as they did in the pages of *Ebony*. Reading about my favorite celebs, getting a glimpse into their lives beyond the glitz and glam of their performances on TV, seeing their families, their homes—all this showed me that there were Black folks who lived like the Brady Bunch in a split-level ranch, Black families who owned mansions with dens and libraries like the rich white families on soap operas inhabited. *Ebony* taught me to dream and reinforced my pride in being Black.

We were a small family, especially after my brother moved out. My sister and I didn't have cousins close to our age because our parents had had us so late in life. My parents were from a different era, and that meant we weren't allowed to just hang outside on the stoop. Having older parents—a dad who made too much money for us to qualify for low-income after-school programs and a mother obsessed with making sure my sister and I dressed like young ladies, in knee socks, loafers, and pleated skirts versus the hip 1970s polyester looks that were on trend then—all these factors marked us as different in our neighborhood, but none of these differences really mattered until junior high school.

◆ ◆ ◆

On my first day at I.S. 10 (aka "the Dime"), I was walking to class, and a popular girl holding court with her crew passed me and said, "I like your shoes." I said thank you. And Miss Popularity burst out laughing and announced, "That bitch really thinks we like her shoes."

I was devastated, as I actually loved my shoes. They were brand-new, and my mom had told me they were good for my feet. I'm sure those Stride Rite full-leather uppers cost more than Miss Popularity's shoes. But stylish? Not so much. I found my sister at school and told her what had transpired. She vowed to persuade the Smittys to buy us stylish yet cheap shoes. True to her word, she did—and I still pay for that decision with bunions. (I know, not sexy.) That day marks not just the day I started making poor choices for my feet in a quest to be stylish, but also the beginning of my journey to become a Popular Girl.

Before junior high, I think most of my classmates would have described me as "nice." (Here's another Bevelation: *Nice* often just means forgettable and nondescript—in short, it's an overrated word.) After being in junior high for a week, I understood that "nice" wouldn't cut it. School was a battlefield. You know the saying "A closed mouth doesn't get fed"? Well, I was hungry for popularity, and the popular girls looked like they ate at the buffet each and every day. They were direct, vivacious, and yes, loud (in the best way—to this day I can't stand mealymouthed people, speak up when you have something to say); they seemed confident and bold. So, I had to adapt or starve.

When you're a nerd, you're naturally observant. You learn how to assess people—who they are, what makes them tick. In grade school, almost everyone is friendly, and cliques haven't really formed. Junior high is where I first discovered Mean Girls—and where I lost Lil' Brown Bevy.

I figured out early on what it took to be popular in my hood. You had to be stylish, witty—I mean, *sharp* zingers—a good dancer, and cute. Thanks to Stephanie, my wardrobe was a junior version of *Soul Train*. I'm one hell of a dancer thanks to my brother, and the Smitty genes took care of this cute little brown face. Who knows where my comedic timing came from, but if you've seen me on TV, you know I have it! The biggest challenge was learning to suppress Lil' Brown Bevy, the sensitive girl who liked to skip down the street, flip through 1950s health and nutrition journals, and, as an act of rebellion, read the liner notes to her big brother's albums. (We weren't even supposed to breathe on, much less touch, his extensive collection.)

If I could talk to my junior high self now, I would tell her, "Impostor syndrome is real, and it's exhausting. Instead of pretending, hone your particular gifts, and since nobody can be you BUT YOU, save the effort and just DO YOU!" Alas, it would take me decades to figure this out. My ignorance was bliss, and when

I began my quest to be a Popular Girl, I knew Lil' Brown Bevy couldn't come along for the ride.

First, I made sure my home life was kept separate from my social life, a habit I didn't drop for decades. I knew I had to do this when, one day, a grade-school friend came to my apartment unannounced and brought one of the Popular Girls along with her. Fortunately, I was only reading a magazine on the sofa and was quickly able to hide it. But what if my fifty-three-year-old, salt-and-pepper-haired dad, whom folks constantly mistook for my grandfather, had been in the room paring an apple with his pocketknife while building a diorama? I cringed when kids asked if he was my grandfather; that's why I loved when my mom picked us up. With her on-trend clothes, pretty face, and perfect shape, no one ever guessed she was old enough to be the grandmother of my peers.

After that first reaction to my sensible shoes, I shifted my demeanor. I no longer had such an easy smile, I learned to give attitude, and I practiced cursing. (It's true that practice makes perfect. I can swear with the best of them now.) Although my new appearance garnered attention, the Popular Girls remembered my original incarnation, NERD, and I was held in social purgatory for a while. I was in the clique but way down on the call sheet. I now think of my status as the fourth handmaiden-in-waiting to the Princess of Popularity, the equivalent to the lowest level of frequent flyer, the type of status that gives you an assigned seat (basic not premium) but charges you to check a bag or get a cocktail. I was allowed to sit with the Popular Girls at lunch, but I was on the outer edge of the table. When I was invited to hang out, I was told to bring money for snacks. Basically, I was being used.

My sister constantly pointed this out to me. She was very happy with her nerd girl clique and would tell me that my new friends were shallow, unintelligent losers. But I was like most people in abusive relationships—I thought that some attention was better than none, and that at least I had a seat at the table. Okay, it was a folding chair and I had to hold my plate on my lap, but hey, I was in the room.

By eighth grade, I started to realize that Stephanie was right. The Popular Girls were mean and not particularly clever about it. They were your basic Trumpian bullies. After a year of their hazing, I was fed up. So, I quietly started plotting my escape. In the New York City public school system, you're able to choose your high school. The Popular Girls had decreed Murry Bergtraum the one we would all attend. Meanwhile, I wanted to go to Norman Thomas, in Midtown Manhattan, which was housed in a skyscraper! (Rumor had it you had to take elevators and escalators to get to class.) Remember, I had been introduced to high-rise living by my brother, and now I had a chance to go to school in a skyscraper, and one on the East Side! I was literally moving on up, just like the Jeffersons.

Television put lots of notions in my head at the time. Norman Thomas High School specialized in marketing, a career I was introduced to by Darrin Stephens of *Bewitched*, a character who was an advertising executive. This alone would have been enough to sell me on Norman Thomas, but the biggest draw was the chance to start fresh. Sometimes you want to go where nobody knows your name. (Cheers to that!)

I applied to Norman Thomas and was accepted. I told no one until one fateful day in the cafeteria, when the Popular Queen began to discuss our strategy for taking over Murry Bergtraum. I let her finish her plans for world/high school domination before quietly announcing I was going somewhere else. She called me stupid (not for the first time, but certainly the last) and said I was going to be a lonely loser. If I'd had any doubts about my decision, they evaporated in that moment. For the first time (and also not the last!), I made a decision to change my life. When, after melting down in Milan, I started doing my introspective work, I realized that the decision I made when I was thirteen years old continues to inform many of my life choices. The moment I stood up for myself and refused to follow the crowd is one I look back on whenever I have to choose between doing what's popular and doing what I feel in my spirit is right for me. It was the first time that I bet on *me*—and it worked. That win gave me the courage to go out on a limb many times in my life. I bucked the system at thirteen, and for many years it was a decision I didn't regret. Unfortunately there was some collateral damage: I lacked the emotional maturity to understand I was leaving behind the very best part of me, Lil' Brown Bevy, in the process.

◆ ◆ ◆

I arrived at Norman Thomas knowing *exactly* how I wanted to be perceived, and I put my plan into action. My first order of business was, once again, to jettison Lil' Brown Bevy. No one knew me, so no one knew Nerd Girl Beverly, either. I seized my chance and welcomed MC Bev-Ski to the party! It was 1980. Hip-hop had supplanted disco as the music of my generation, and we all felt we had a stake in the movement. My specialty was freestyle rapping in the girls' bathroom. I also became a connoisseur of low-grade marijuana—I took great pride in being able to roll a very neat joint, not too tight, and in being an all-around fashionable Fly Girl.

The persona I crafted was a witty, street-smart, book-smart uptown girl—and it worked! I was instantly popular! However, I could never quite muster the Mean Girl feat of stepping on people less popular than me or bullying people for their lunch money, the traits needed to rule a clique. Instead, I made friends with lots of different cliques and befriended folks who reminded me of my nerdiest inner Lil' Brown Bevy self.

Another major breakthrough happened when I went to high school: I secured a boyfriend and lost my virginity. I'm going to fast-forward and spare you the details, but I will tell you I was fifteen years old, smoking copious amounts of "dirt weed," and it was on Palm Sunday. My first time was with the brother of my childhood best friend. He had a well-honed intellect and impeccable style—an all-around good guy who also knew how to fight. He was very popular, and he enhanced my status on the block. In fact, we were a power couple way before Jay-Z and Beyoncé. We stayed together for seven years. (There's more to the story, but even though Andy Cohen told me to put it all in this book, I'm going to do what feels right in my spirit and save our love story for another book, TV show, or Instagram Live.)

Anyhoo, back to high school.

So, I'm popular, having sex with my boyfriend, smoking weed, and playing hooky, which sometimes meant going to the Bronx to hang out with friends—very daring given that New Yorkers don't like to leave their boroughs. Another favorite haunt to play hooky in was the Mid-Manhattan Library, where I'd read business journals. I also loved visiting the main branch of the New York City Public Library, a Beaux-Arts architectural masterpiece. Remember the first *Sex and the City* movie, where Carrie plans an elaborate wedding in the library and gets left at the altar? Well, that's the gorgeous library where I would spend my afternoons reading books and looking up old newspaper articles on microfiche. Of course, I told none of my friends I was skipping school to visit the *library*; I didn't want them to think I was some nerd. NEVAH! But it's clear Lil' Brown Bevy never really left me. That's why I would take off and find solace at the library. I just needed some "me time," where I didn't have to be cool or funny, where I could have a little respite and be my most authentic self. To this day, I still do that; it's one of the reasons I travel so much by myself: sometimes I just want to be Lil' Brown Bevy, paint on the beach, listen to soft rock, and not have to entertain a soul except myself, just like in high school.

I wasn't the academic success I could have been, due to my playing so much hooky. I guess the bright side of that is I certainly didn't peak in high school, which is a good thing because then my whole mantra of #ItGetsGreaterLater wouldn't exist. After high school, some of my friends left for college, but there were many of us who either went to community college or started working. I was in the latter group, not because I didn't want to attend college but because I was in *love* with my boyfriend and, honestly, how could I ever leave him? This preoccupation with men would become a recurring theme, but for now, let's go with the anthem from *Dreamgirls*, "And I Am Telling You I'm Not Going." My parents were disappointed, but I immediately started seeking work, so I think they were relieved that I wasn't going to just lie around the house and sneak my boyfriend in for afternoon delights. Okay, I did that, too, but I also looked for a job. (Don't you judge me!)

During the eighties, if you could type fifty words per minute and presented like a nice young lady, you could become a temp secretary, the crème de la crème of temp work. However, having played hooky during typing class and having smoked weed in the bathroom while freestyle rapping about a teacher I suspected was a pervert, I never managed to type over thirty-five words a minute. Not fast enough to secure a secretarial gig, but sufficient to become a receptionist. I soon became a highly sought-after temp worker at the employment agencies. I was well groomed, dependable—the Smittys had passed that on to me—and as a daily *New York Times* and *Daily News* reader (never the *Post*), I was a sponge for pop culture, politics, and high-society news.

Even in the temp world there was a hierarchy, and very often the best assignments (in glamour industries, like advertising, fashion, and publishing) were given to girls with the "right" (or as it often seemed, *white*) look. I would sometimes get upset that even with my career gal wardrobe and professional demeanor, I had my share of overnight assignments (the bottom-rung jobs), which were not at all befitting of a girl who wore silk dresses and pumps and read *Forbes* for fun. I complained to my temp agency manager, and one fateful day, I was sent on what was supposed to be a week-long assignment at an advertising agency that specialized in fashion and luxury goods. Instead, I stayed for three years, and started my career in fashion advertising.

◆ ◆ ◆

Peter Rogers and Associates was owned by a charismatic, good-looking southern gay man, Peter Rogers. My first week as a temp, I met Oscar winner and screen legend Claudette Colbert and hair guru Vidal Sassoon—and that was enough for me. Honey, I'm home!

There was only one hitch. The firm was looking for a perma-nent replacement, a sophisticated, upscale greeter for their rich and famous clientele. I was eighteen and green, but at least I looked the part—my mother had been all too happy to buy me a plethora of silk blouses, pencil skirts, and classic pumps. I also had a knack for making people feel welcome, going the extra mile of hanging up clients' coats and remembering how they took their coffee, none of which was part of my job description. Working there, I began to devour *W* magazine (it was a broadsheet back then) and *Town & Country*, as many of the people captured in those pages came through the door of Peter Rogers, and it was my job to know who they were. To be clear, these responsibilities also weren't in my job description—all they'd specified in the job listing was that I answer phones on the first or second ring and keep my reception area neat and free of clutter—but I've always been the type to go above and beyond, and that habit has been key to my success.

My parents had instilled in us the idea that when it comes to your job, you always do your absolute best, no matter what the position entails. They'd never worked in an office, but thanks to watching TV shows and films where women were relegated to the secretarial pool, I had some insight into what was expected of me in an office environment. And I did my best to channel those fictional working girls' poise and confidence. I fell in love with the job, and I reveled in the glamour of being in a well-designed, sleek, mono-chromatic office that was the epitome of 1980s chic.

◆ ◆ ◆

Unfortunately, every other call I received on the Merlin telephone system, the 1980s version of a switchboard—it had a pager system and a Hold button; so Space Age!—seemed to be someone looking to apply for the job. *My* job. I knew I had to take my destiny into my hands, just like I did when I bucked the system and didn't attend the same high school the Popular Girls did. And I was confident I could do it again. Why wait for the powers that be to realize that I was the perfect receptionist? No, I had to take bold and slightly unethical action. So, when people called in to inquire about the position, I told them it had been filled. After a few weeks, the office manager, a gruff but sweet older white woman named Eleanor, said that they hadn't received many suitable applicants and would I be interested in staying on? Eleanor, thank you for considering me. Yes, I would like to stay and make $15,600 a year. And that is how I started my career in advertising.

In the 1980s, advertising was very much an old boys club—and *white* boys at that. Yes, there were famous Black advertising agencies, iconic houses like Uniworld, Burrell, and Carrol H. Williams Adver-tising, which created campaigns for mass brands (Pepsi, McDonald's, Procter & Gamble) that catered to Black consumers. I saw their ads on TV shows geared toward Black people, and in *Ebony*, but I never knew that agencies like theirs existed. I think one of the biggest disadvantages for children in Black and Brown communities is that we often don't know about all the various career opportunities in the world. To this day, when I speak at schools or after-school programs, I encounter so many kids who have no idea about careers outside of doctor, lawyer, accountant, and the usual entertainment/ sports fields. I have no regrets about working at Peter Rogers, but if I had been aware that there were agencies that created campaigns that resonated with me culturally, I would have finagled a way to become their temp receptionist and gotten *that* job.

Instead, I was at the fabulous world of Peter Rogers, where everyone was white except for the divinely flawless executive assistant to Peter Rogers, a woman named Blue. When Jay-Z and Beyoncé named their first daughter Blue Ivy, I knew that with a name like that, she was going to be an iconic young lady, just like Peter Rogers's Blue. Blue was gorgeous; she looked like a model, sexy and haughty, but not in a cold way, though she must have realized that familiarity breeds contempt, because she was clear about the power she wielded. Blue represented Peter; she was the gatekeeper. This meant that to get on Peter's calendar, you had to go through her. Of course, folks would curry favor with her to get close to him— lots of gifts and fawning smiles—but Blue wasn't charmed by any of it. This is how I learned that really good executive assistants often have more clout than upper management. They are the plug, the connector.

For a time, the only Black people at the agency were me and Blue, and while no one at Peter Rogers was overtly racist, there were lots of racist microaggressions to deal with. I became grateful for my mother having forced us to take outings outside the hood every Sunday. Those day trips meant being around people who didn't look or live like us. So, I wasn't intimidated around white folks, and, because of my Harlem Black Power education, I certainly didn't think they were better than me, just different.

One of the microaggressions I dealt with constantly was my white coworkers always wanting to know my story. Many, I suspect, regarded me as a liberal experiment. They would look on, horrified, when I told them I lived in Harlem, and would automatically assume I had a sob story about growing up hungry. Some of them even seemed downright disappointed once they realized they wouldn't have the opportunity to lift me out of some downtrodden ghetto experience.

The misplaced liberal do-gooders aside, for three years I was blessed to have not one but *four* mentors in the Peter Rogers orbit. The first person to notice me and truly engage me in conversation versus an interrogation—Dear White People, I know you think you're just asking questions, but many Black folks want to know why you're so nosy—was Keni Valenti. An Italian American from Queens, Keni was a downtown, avant-garde fashion designer. Keni would visit Peter Rogers to see his boyfriend, Jeff McKay, who was an art director there, and because Keni had working-class roots, he and I would laugh about the well-meaning, hand-wringing liberal brigade.

One day, Keni told Jeff that I didn't belong at the front desk, but in the back, where the real business of the agency was taking place. From that day on, Jeff, a WASP from Vevay, Indiana, a man so pale you could actually see the blue blood running through his veins—became my champion. I have no idea how Jeff became so open about race. After all, Indiana could have ranked in the "Top 10 Places to Visit If You're in the KKK." Yet, I never felt from him that cloying, patronizing behavior many folks demonstrated toward me at Peter Rogers. Out of all the amazing people I've met on my journey, Jeff was the one who believed in me the most, yet unlike so many lesser characters in my journey, he has never attempted to take any credit for my success. But to be clear, Jeff and Keni raised me professionally.

My other two mentors were media directors at the agency, Chuck Cohen and Gael Malloy. Chuck was a sarcastic, wicked-smart Vietnam vet from Brooklyn and a nonobservant Jew. Gael, a lapsed Irish Catholic, was a hippie with flaming red hair, a filthy mouth, and the biggest heart. They took me under their wing, sharing all their magazine subscriptions—as media directors, they received every magazine on the newsstand—and explaining to me the rudimentary workings of media planning. The role appealed to me because the media planner's job was to identify the best media platform to advertise a client's brand/product (radio, TV, magazines, newspapers, billboards, etc.). I got it instinctively—as a kid, I had read magazines like *Jet*, *Right On*, and of course *Ebony*, but I'd also read *Life*, *Time*, and *Good Housekeeping*. I knew I never saw the same ads that appeared in *Jet* in *Life*, and I understood on a very primary level that it was because the magazines targeted two different types of markets. But it all really made sense once Gael and Chuck taught me about audience demographics and the strategy behind placing ads to reach target markets.

Keni, Jeff, Chuck, and Gael were more than mentors; they became my family. But none of them shared my experiences—Keni was working class, but even he had the benefit of white privilege—and sometimes that made for a lonely experience in the workplace. Even so, I was open to their tutelage because my parents, my mom especially, would tell us that there is good and bad in everyone, so we shouldn't hate anyone based on their skin. I wanted to believe what my mom had told us, and having mentors like Keni, Jeff, Gael, and Chuck certainly made her words ring true.

By the time I was twenty-one, I had been working at Peter Rogers for three years and my champion, Jeff McKay, had left for Revlon; but he chafed under the corporate structure and quit. Then, with seed money from his Revlon contract, he opened up his own advertising agency. I was one of his first hires. The other hire was a handsome young gay man named Ali Hamed (aka David). We worked out of Jeff's one-bedroom apartment in the West Village. Ali was an art director, and I was the assistant, not to mention accounts payable and receivable, account services, and an all-around get-it-done gal. I was a terrible typist (damn you, MC Bev-Ski), but Jeff loved me and saw my potential. At one point, he asked what department I wanted to work in, and I said media planning. If it was good enough for Chuck and Gael, it was good enough for me. So, we added that to my list of projects. (We weren't big enough to have actual departments.)

Now that we're at the part of my story when I was starting to feel like I'd "made it," I'm going to start to dispense a little advice, a Bevelation.

Work for a start-up if you get the chance, especially if it's your goal to be an entrepreneur. You can learn from their wins and losses. I had no desire to be an entrepreneur. I came from two parents who worked *jobs*, and the only entrepreneurs I knew of in my community were people who owned a corner store or a beauty salon. Being at Jeff McKay Inc. on the ground floor taught me lessons about business that have served me well throughout my career, and probably the most important lesson was there's a difference between a *job* and a *career*.

No one in my immediate family had a career, so I didn't really comprehend the basic principles that separated a career from a job. In a job, you have set hours, and if you work past those hours, you receive overtime—this made sense because almost everyone around me had a job, and that was standard procedure. Most people I knew celebrated the opportunity to work overtime. In fact, I remember a few of my friends being offered the opportunity to become managers on their jobs and turning down the promotion because when you're a manager, you're no longer eligible for overtime pay. To many, that may seem like a shortsighted approach to work, but when no one around you has moved from being an hourly worker to management, where overtime pay is a drop in the bucket compared to what you can earn in bonuses, you have no way of knowing. My friends were shocked that I was paid the same amount of money whether I worked thirty-five or fifty hours. They thought I was a sucker—until I was five years into working at Jeff McKay and their pay had increased very minimally but my salary had risen by 30 percent. I had gone from gal Friday to an advertising executive.

Another important lesson I learned at Jeff McKay is that you have to be in the room where it happens. Jeff had a country home in Litchfield County, Connecticut, one of the most affluent areas of the country. One summer day, he invited the staff and a few of his friends that he worked with up for the weekend. Now, I loved Jeff and Ali, but this was the same weekend a popular "independent pharmaceutical salesperson" from my neighborhood, a real heavy-hitter, was hosting a trip to Great Adventure. Now the fifty-four-year-old Bevy would have told young Beverly to take her ass to Connecticut and risk contracting Lyme disease rather than sit in traffic for two hours on the Jersey Turnpike, drinking Pink Champale malt liquor and eating cold fried chicken (that actually still sounds good to me now, oh, life's simple pleasures). Then, I didn't have a mentor who could explain that opting for Great Adventure was the wrong move.

When I went back to work on Monday and my coworkers asked how my weekend was, I enthusiastically talked about riding roller-coasters, eating funnel cake, and getting an airbrushed piece of wood with my name on it (paid for by a guy who was trying to slip me "the wood"). When I asked about their weekend, they went on and on about what fun they had had, and mentioned the surprise guests who'd dropped in for drinks. They now had all kinds of inside jokes that, had I attended, I could have laughed at, too, experiences that strengthed their bond beyond the workplace.

Instead, at the same time they were drinking martinis in Litchfield, I was trying not to get my Salt & Pepa stack hairdo wet while riding the water flume.

That day, I learned that to truly thrive in a career, you can't just do a good job; relationships are paramount to success in the workplace, and often, shared extracurricular activities affect your career trajectory more than your work record. "Be in the room where it happens"—I only had to learn that lesson once. So, I put down the corn dog and picked up the croquet mallet! Much of my later success as an advertising executive stemmed from becoming a master at networking.

In seven years, Jeff McKay Inc. went from being a three-person shop in a one-bedroom apartment to being one of the hottest boutique fashion advertising agencies in New York. In that same time frame, I matured into a well-respected twenty-eight-year-old media director interacting with every major client, from media titan Tina Brown to legendary fashion designer Bill Blass. In between, I started a few projects I never finished, including attending New York University and getting engaged.

It was during that era that I really began to live life to the fullest. Lil' Brown Bevy was buried in my past. Honestly, I rarely ever thought about her because I had finally mastered the art of being the Popular Girl. I'd morphed from high school's MC Bev-Ski to living my twenties as Big Bev from Uptown.

◆ ◆ ◆

Big Bev from Uptown had a full-on secret life outside her advertising career. Like most Black people who work in primarily white environments, I was a master at code switching. I hid my "good in the hood" side from my white coworkers and my soaring career from my street friends. By the early nineties, hip-hop had gone mainstream, and I was a bona fide hip-hop hottie . . . on the low.

On the weekends, I'd be cavorting with icons like Biggie Smalls, Tupac, and Puff Daddy, and I'd still arrive at the agency on Monday morning ready to negotiate deals on behalf of my luxury clients.

In short, I was leading a double life. In the nineties, if you were Black, educated, dressed in suits, and carrying a briefcase to your well-paid "I'm the only Black person in the boardroom" corporate job, you fit the "Buppie" stereotype. If you were Black, street smart, and dressed in flashy, tight designer dresses for a city job with a side hustle, you would fall into the Ghetto Fabulous category, a term coined by the late, great music impresario Andre Harrell, who discovered Mary J. Blige and Puffy, two folks who epitomize this aesthetic. At work, I was a full-blown Buppie. But at night, I was in the streets hard, partying and cavorting five evenings a week. Me and Renee (Nay Nay Billy) even hosted parties under the name "Three the Hard Way"—and no one at Jeff McKay had any idea.

As a hip-hop party girl, I knew all the rappers and was invited to all the best parties, dinners, and trips—but unlike most of the hot girls in the club, I couldn't partake in the parties *after* the parties. With my career (not a job), I knew better than to take a guy up on an offer of leaving the club at 3 a.m. to head to Atlantic City or Virginia Beach for a quick mid-week beach romp. Nope, I would decline, saying I had to go to work the next morning. Some guys even offered to pay me for my day, thinking I had the type of job that would dock your pay if you missed a day. When I explained that that wouldn't work, saying, "You can't pay me for my day," they took umbrage at the implication that they didn't have enough money to pay me for a few days of work. (The male ego is often so very delicate.) The truth was they didn't. How can you put a price tag on missing a meeting with Tina Brown to go over the media strategy for a *Vanity Fair* magazine ad campaign? I knew that saying *that* would have been TMI, because then I would have had to explain who Tina was and that the *Vanity Fair* I was referring to was a magazine and not a bra company or a napkin brand. Instead, I learned to be tactful and offer up some excuse about my mother needing me to run an errand for her, which usually shut down any conversation. Black mothers and their errands reign supreme.

I wasn't the only one in my crew doing a juggling act. Most of my real friends from that scene were on a career path and/or pursuing advanced degrees, though, ironically, we never talked about it—except to complain about either how hungover we were at work or how we had to cram for a test because, instead of studying all week, we were at the Tunnel, Club USA, or the Red Zone. We were good-looking young women, and that was our commodity at the clubs, not our brains. We may not have bragged about our academic success or our careers, but we were smart enough never to get so caught up in our club lifestyle that we jeopardized what we had worked so hard to build in our other lives. My mother told us kids early on: no matter what you do at night, you get up and go to work the next day. Those words echoed in my vodka- and champagne-soaked brain, and I never forgot that success in my career depended on showing up at work, not calling in "sick" so I could go to Myrtle Beach.

Splitting my focus between being a party girl and building a career meant I really didn't have much use for Lil' Brown Bevy. What role would a thoughtful, sweet girl with a natural curiosity about the world play while I was trying to get Jay-Z and his cronies to give me a bottle of champagne for me and my girls? Most times she just didn't fit in, but one of the rare times Lil' Brown Bevy came out to play was when I hung out with Tupac.

We were introduced by Biggie—yes, children, Tupac and Biggie were friends before they were mortal enemies—at a spot on the Upper East Side called the Country Club, when Pac came to town to film *Above the Rim*. It was a common occurrence to meet celebs from out of town and just hang out, helping to show them a good time in the Big Apple. Guys took pride in introducing their homies from out of state to their city's finest, and I was a bona fide "hot girl." When we started hanging out, I met the Tupac of the "I Get Around" video, but eventually I was fortunate to also meet the man who wrote "A Rose Grew from Concrete."

By this point, I was in my mid-twenties and fully enmeshed in my Big Bev from Uptown lifestyle—and therefore, always surrounded by a bunch of gorgeous women. That's because I knew all the popular guys. We hung out at clubs until closing time (4 a.m.) and then piled into the guys' cars—and sometimes these people were complete strangers. (What? *You* get in Ubers and think nothing of it.) We'd head out for breakfast at classic New York City diners, where the guys would allow us to order anything on the menu except pork. (Nay Nay Billy would be upset because she craved bacon after the club.) Personally, I never even looked at the breakfast menu. Instead, I'd order the most expensive thing on the dinner menu. If you've ever wondered who eats the lobsters that sit in the tank at a coffee shop, that was me. My friends would tease me, but I learned early on that you have to teach folks how to treat you. If I expected you to wine and dine me, take me on nice trips (not just caravans to Virginia Beach), and buy me expensive handbags, I needed to start establishing that I was a girl who, even in the most basic of locations, had expensive tastes.

Pac never mocked me for my lobster-in-a-coffee-shop taste, though we were too busy talking, so maybe he didn't even notice. He was a philosopher and a revolutionary. We would talk about Black history (thanks, Stephanie) or interesting books we'd read. Pac got to know Lil' Brown Bevy, and I met Tupac Amaru Shakur. I think what connected us is that we both were hiding our more sensitive and precious selves from the cutthroat braggadocios of the nineties hip-hop scene. We recognized something special in each other.

Another rare moment when Big Bev from Uptown was usurped

by Lil' Brown Bevy was during my first trip to Paris. I was twenty-eight when Jeff sent me to Paris Fashion Week to pitch Kenzo, the legendary Japanese fashion designer. After years of attending New York Fashion Week and reading all about Paris (the architecture, the fashion, the food), I was ecstatic to go, even though the only French I knew was from "Lady Marmalade": *Voulez-vous coucher avec moi ce soir?* When translated, it means "Do you want to sleep with me tonight?" Probably not the best phrase to mutter around Paris, especially since Jeff was sending me alone.

The thought of being in a foreign country alone terrified me. Honestly, I thought about not going, but after a pep talk from my sister—she loved Paris because James Baldwin had lived there—and after I'd cobbled together a cute wardrobe from Barney's, Keni Valenti (he was selling vintage designer clothes by then), and the local spandex dress vendor on Third Avenue in the Bronx (high/low will always be the hallmark of great personal style), I went on my first international excursion.

Upon my arrival in Paris, I snagged a taxi—this was pre-Uber, pre-smartphones . . . shit, pre-*internet*—at the chic Charles de Gaulle Airport and rode into the city. And guess who showed up. Lil' Brown Bevy! It's impossible to act cool the first time you see the Arc de Triomphe and the Eiffel Tower. Skipping through Paris, even after almost getting mugged in the Tuileries Garden after gazing upon the Mona Lisa at the Louvre, I felt that nothing could squash my euphoria over being in Paris. At the Kenzo show, I met the legendary fashion editor André Leon Talley for the first time, and I've never forgotten how gracious he was in acknowledging me, a complete stranger, and moving me from a seat in the back to one at the front of the show. An entire set was built to resemble a train station, complete with smoking locomotive. To this day, I'm spoiled because of my first fabulous Paris Fashion Week experience; I can't abide a pedestrian fashion show.

◆ ◆ ◆

Shortly after that trip, I began to feel I was outgrowing the agency. You know the old song, "How Ya Gonna Keep 'Em Down on the Farm (After They've Seen Paree)?" Okay, I'm sure you don't, as it was made famous during World War I, and the only people who recognize the song now are fans of the 1998 cult classic *The Big Lebowski.* Either way the sentiment is real: travel broadens your horizons and teaches you things about yourself that you'll never have a chance to learn by "hugging your block." Now that's a Bevelation. Going on my first international trip alone, learning to navigate a foreign city without speaking the language, meeting fashion icon André Leon Talley, being trusted to conduct business, and warding off a mugger—all this had given me a real boost of confidence. I realized that Jeff McKay had gifted me with a strong foundation, but it was time to build something new on it.

The decision to leave Jeff McKay Inc. wasn't an easy one. Even though I was twenty-eight years old, it felt like leaving home for the first time. I was abandoning a safe haven, a friend, a father figure, someone who, like Smitty, had nurtured and protected me and who, like my mom, thought I was beautiful. (Jeff would buy me lovely gifts from Patrick Kelly, Vivienne Westwood, and other designer brands.) Unlike many so-called mentors, Jeff didn't want me to stay the little eighteen-year-old receptionist. He challenged me, pushed me to grow professionally and intellectually, and it was under his tutelage that I developed my passion for fine art and architecture. The doors he opened for me were normally the ones most securely bolted for Black people from Harlem, and to this day, I still use contacts I made through him. The best part is he never once asked for anything in return; he only wanted to see me walk through life successful and happy. There's a Bevelation: A true mentor sets you up to win with or without them.

Even with all that love and nurturing, I had to go—only, I didn't know where I was going or what I was quitting to do. The only thing I knew at that time was that whatever my next move was going to be, it wouldn't enjoy the safety net of Jeff McKay Inc.

I floated ideas about doing PR, perhaps becoming a writer, maybe event planning. At that point, I hadn't done the introspective work required to really figure out what I was passionate about. I was like so many people: saying that I wanted to make a change but, underneath it all, too scared to uproot myself from the stable life I had cultivated.

Still, the seeds of a Life with Vision began to take root when I quit Jeff McKay Inc.—not that I knew it at the time. All I knew was that based on my successful transition from nerdy, shy girl to Miss Popularity, and the more recent shift from receptionist to advertising executive, I would succeed at whatever came next. Even more crucial, I understood that it had been a long time since I had taken a chance and charted my own course, but that in order to grow, I had to get uncomfortable.

Here's another Bevelation: Becoming comfortable with being uncomfortable is a hallmark of every successful person's trajectory.

I began exploring a life that I couldn't have imagined pursuing when I was a kid growing up in Harlem, mainly because I didn't even know it was a possibility for me. For example, I knew that I wanted to be a world traveler—another spark that was lit while I was working at Jeff's. Smitty had shown me the world through books, and Jeff had secured me my first passport stamp. Now I felt I was ready to explore the globe.

Happily, my world had changed drastically in the ten years since I'd started out as a receptionist. When I resigned from Jeff McKay, I was a professional woman with a good wardrobe and a fashion/advertising pedigree I was proud of. Even the success of leading a dual life between my fashion advertising career and my Big Bev from Uptown shenanigans made me believe in myself. I felt I was ready for whatever the universe had in store for me.

I could never have guessed that it would be the persona I left behind, Lil' Brown Bevy, who would hold the key to true happiness.

Some of the Jeff McKay Inc. family after a night at the Apollo Theater: Jeff (kneeling, on the left), Jeff H (standing above me and Jeff), Nancy, Ali David, and Keni (on the phone)

Red Sole Proposition

I WAS TWENTY-TWO YEARS OLD WHEN I RECEIVED MY FIRST PAIR of Manolo Blahniks as a gift. Okay, it was more like they were being used on a shoot for an ad campaign and the stylist said I could take them home. Okay, a bag of them was left in a closet, and I took a pair. It was long ago; I can't remember the details—and after all, possession *is* nine-tenths of the law.

Anyhoo, however I obtained them, I was beyond excited to have a pair. Manolos retailed for four hundred dollars then, so they were super expensive, a status symbol. If you're thinking four hundred bucks isn't so much, just remember: this was 1988, and in today's money, that's over *eight hundred dollars*. Ka-ching! The price added to the shoe's cachet, but it was also *the* shoe of celebrities and rich women the world over. Eighties socialites like Bianca Jagger; supermodel Iman; the ultimate royal princess, Diana; and R&B diva Patti LaBelle all worshipped at the throne of Manolo Blahnik.

I'm going to go on about shoes for a while here, but there will be a point to all these high heels—wait for it!

My first pair of Blahniks were black peau de soie with an ankle strap—sexy, understated. The heel height was about 3.5 inches; that's practically a sneaker today. While they didn't scream, "Look at *me*," in the business of fashion, *everyone* looks at your handbag and shoes, and folks in the know knew when you were wearing Blahniks. I would walk into important rooms feeling uncomfortable and insecure, acutely aware that I was the only Black woman in the room. Then I would look down at my feet, and my Blahniks would instantly make me feel I had a right to be there. Like Dorothy's ruby slippers, they gave me strength, and they were the original power shoe for women, the shoe that told us we didn't have to sacrifice style and sex appeal to be taken seriously. I longed to be taken seriously, and wearing those shoes put me on the right path.

By the time I was thirty years old, I had been gone from Jeff McKay for two years and was clearing a path and creating my own lane. I went from being an assistant/office manager in her early twenties who thought exotic travel was a trip to Vegas for a boxing match; to being a twenty-eight-year-old meandering through various freelance assignments trying to figure out her life post Jeff McKay; to landing at *Vibe*, at twenty-nine, as a fashion advertising executive who traveled to Paris, Milan, and London for runway shows. And along the way, I amassed a collection of Blahniks.

One of the perks of being a fashion insider was being invited to the secret and extremely exclusive Blahnik sample sale. Being invited to that sale was a real badge of honor; it showed that you had arrived in the upper echelons of New York's high society. And one of the highlights of attending, besides bragging rights, was that the Fashion God and best friend to Monsieur Blahnik, the iconic André Leon Talley, held court there, advising women with his discerning taste and issuing proclamations about which shoes we *had* to have with his distinctive voice. That's why I was thoroughly pissed off when in the year of our Lord 2000, Carrie Bradshaw, an annoying-yet-inspiring character on *Sex and the City*, began making Blahniks popular with the masses. We'd barely recovered from Y2K hysteria, thinking that computers across the world were going to explode, and now some TV show was taking our discreetly chic power shoe and making it part of pop culture! Hadn't we suffered enough?

Soon, fashionistas were fretting that the popularity of *Sex and the City* was ruining the exclusivity of the shoe. Well, it turns out that it wasn't *Sex and the City* that put a chink in the armor of the Blahnik brand. It was a French designer who painted the sole of his sky-high stilettos red and gave me corns. (Yes, I have corns and bunions; podophiliacs, aka people with foot fetishes, aka fans of Instafeet, you need not darken my doorstep.) That designer was Christian Louboutin.

I was in my early thirties the first time I encountered Louboutin's shoes. I was in his Paris boutique, drawn into the store by the riot of color, the patterns, the textures, and the overall fabulosity! If Blahnik was classic and sensual, Louboutin was renegade and *sexual*, in your face and over the top. Every pair of shoes seemed like a character: it had personality, it made a statement, and it was *expensive*—kind of like a sophisticated party girl. Another point of difference was the price. I thought four hundred dollars was expensive for a pair of shoes, but when Louboutin came on the scene, he not only upped the sex ante and the heel of his stilettos, but he raised the price. Five hundred dollars for a plain black pump.

At age thirty-eight, when I quit *Rolling Stone*, I was no longer buying Blahniks, and I wasn't alone. Louboutins had usurped them as the international "It" shoes. Blahnik was still in business, but now the heel seemed too low, the patterns and fabrics not rare enough. I'm ashamed to say it, but I abandoned the shoe that had helped catapult Fashionista Beverly Smith in favor of Louboutins. Wearing Louboutins sent a signal that you were a boss babe, a fashion maverick who liked garnering attention and had a spare $1,100 to spend on a shoe with studs on it. And before you think about labeling me the worst turncoat and traitor, remember that even Carrie Bradshaw, a woman who had spent $40,000 on Blahniks even though she was a freelance magazine writer (hello, Fantasy Island), moved on to Louboutins in the *Sex and the City* movies.

Like Carrie, I spent a lot of money on shoes . . . and bags. Oh yeah, and on clothes. But I couldn't help it. I was surrounded by enablers, aka fellow shopaholics in the industry. They made it easy for me to be delusional and believe I *needed* to buy trendy clothes with absolutely no sustainability—not only would the style be dated within a year, but it was frowned upon to be a repeat offender and wear the same fabulous outfit twice. Somehow, I convinced myself that all this consumption was practically a business expense. After all, you *have* to make an entrance, and nothing says "I've arrived" quite like donning a new outfit for every day of the New York, London, Milan, and Paris Fashion Weeks, don't you agree? Of course, now I don't agree (and my bank account certainly doesn't either), but back then, it was easy to sell myself this bill of goods. I would have done anything not to acknowledge that I was miserable and that all this stuff I was acquiring was merely an over-the-counter ointment for the wound that was my shallow life. Of course, my life did not improve, no matter how many limited-edition items or "red bottoms" I bought.

My time as a shopaholic spanned from my early twenties to age thirty-eight. When I decided to pursue a new life in entertainment and resigned from *Rolling Stone*, I knew I couldn't afford to give in to my feelings of sadness or loneliness by shopping. But I was shocked when, a little over a year after leaving *Rolling Stone*, my savings ran out. Before you become Judge Judy or Suze Orman, know this: I wasn't frivolous with money. There were no shopping sprees during that one-year period. (I "shopped" my overstuffed closet.) And I don't regret how I spent most of my money: it went toward getting prepared for my new life.

First, I needed to cleanse my corporate outlook from my soul. I had been working in a structured office setting since age eighteen, so I needed to learn how to spend my days, create my life. I had to erase the old mindset of going to work, hitting my quota, and receiving a financial reward. Shortly after I resigned from *Rolling Stone*, I took my sepia version of *Eat, Pray, Love* and visited South Africa, Zambia, Brazil, and Costa Rica, places I had always dreamed of visiting. Experiencing other cultures reinforced in me that there was more than one way to live a good life. With each destination, I stopped judging myself against other versions of success and began to create my own definition. I also spent money on classes: acting, improv, stand-up, writing courses for one-woman shows, and fiction writing. I even took a course in screenwriting. I wanted to indulge that creative me who had been lying dormant for so long. I began making regular trips out to Los Angeles, for whatever exploratory meetings I could get with casting directors and agents. Flying back and forth to Los Angeles isn't cheap, especially back in the pre-Airbnb days, so I was spending—no, investing—thousands to establish a presence there.

Instead of panicking at my impoverished bank account, though, I looked at my closet and saw dollar signs, specifically in my shoes. One-of-a-kind, fresh-off-the-runway looks, gently worn. (That's consignment-speak.) In my new mindset of needing less stuff, it seemed logical that one of the first sacrifices I should make was my shoe collection. So, I sold my soles. No, that's not a typo. I actually sold my shoes, specifically those with that eye-catching red sole. Selling my Louboutins allowed me to pay more than a few bills. That basic black pump that had retailed for $500? Well, that pump could be resold for $250. Seeing the resale value of Louboutin inspired me, got me thinking about what I could do to become a Louboutin *in life*. What was my red sole?

Louboutin's success stemmed from marketing its red sole as an instantly recognizable status symbol. In my post–*Rolling Stone* life as a creative entrepreneur, I needed a point of differentiation. I knew that I had the ability to stand out in a crowd and connect with lots of different types of people, but I didn't know why, so I couldn't harness that power. A brand has to be covetable, instantly identifiable—and you in turn have to convince everyone that this certain something is unique to you, even if that's not exactly the case. Louboutin wasn't the first shoe designer to use a red sole, but it was the first to market it as something special. The brand convinced fashionistas, socialites, and celebrities that they *needed* a sexy shoe with a red sole, and it made the red sole signify passion and strength. I was a curvy, dark-skinned woman with short hair, a lisp, and a hard-core New York accent. Clearly, the entertainment business was just waiting for me . . . NOT! However, I knew from my popularity outside of the fashion world that what some would deem a negative could actually be a positive if I knew how to work it. From witnessing Louboutin's meteoric success, I knew that you can't come to the table demurely asking for a seat. You have to build a gorgeous throne, bring your "red sole" to the table, kick up your heels, and watch people clamber.

When I began my quest for a career in TV, I was competing with folks who had been in entertainment for years, women who had been groomed (many, since college) to be in front of a camera, women who "traditionally" looked the part. This is not to put myself down, but it's important to be realistic about your appearance— especially if you're entering a field where looks can often be the deciding factor in who gets the job. I knew I was attractive, but

I also understood that in the entertainment industry, my curves weren't desirable. Then again, they hadn't been coveted in the world of fashion advertising, either, a world where models who wear a size 4 are told to diet. Yet, I'd made my mark in that space. Entertainment would be no exception.

Going into entertainment at the age of thirty-eight, just as I started gaining weight, I had to have confidence in my appearance. As I began to gain weight, people started commenting on how "brave" I was. There's that silly phrase again! How is it *brave* to have a healthy self-image, to be body-positive and confident? It didn't and still doesn't make sense to me. Yes, my dress size had gone up, and I wore a good foundation under said dress, but I looked and felt sexy and vibrant. Not for nothing. In my community of Harlem, thick thighs have always saved lives, so why should I apologize or shroud myself in a muumuu because I've gained weight? Yes, I was heavier, but my curves hit in all the right places, and I wasn't going to put my dreams on layaway until I could fit some industry standard. America was going to have to learn to love (or at least accept) my curves on their TV screens.

My new curvy body could be an asset, but that alone couldn't be my "red sole." I needed to identify characteristics that were evergreen, not rooted in physicality, because looks fade, waistlines expand and contract (Jesus, be a Peloton or a Zumba class). To position myself as must-have talent, I had to create demand for who I was at my core. I had to learn to sell myself the same way I'd mastered selling ad pages and expensive shoes.

This part of my journey wasn't easy. Self-examination never is. But you know what I did find easy? Being unemployed. It was a pursuit at which I excelled. I'd always maintained that I didn't want to work, and those first months after leaving *RS*, before my money started getting funny, proved that I was born to be a lady of leisure. Having no job gave me an opportunity to create a morning ritual where I would take a long bath, write in my journal, paint with watercolors, and plot out what was next for me. Then, one day, after reading about ten self-help books in a row, it came to me: I knew how I was going to build a brand and create my own red sole. Out of all the self-help books I read, I kept coming back to *The Four Agreements*. It was a small book, and it got to straight to the point with four easy-to-decipher rules. Taking a note from that book, I also challenged myself to ask and answer three questions that helped me unearth not MC Bev-Ski, or Big Bev, or even Beverly Smith, fashion executive, but *the real me*.

1. Who Am I at My Core?

When I worked at Jeff McKay's ad agency, I was straddling two personas, Beverly Smith and Big Bev from Uptown—executive by day and "I won't miss a party" girl by night. Back then, this duality was the only way to live. The core of me, Lil' Brown Bevy, was never even a consideration at that time, with the exception of her cameo appearance with Tupac Amaru Shakur. By shunting her to the side, I'm sure I missed some incredible experiences. But I believe everything is as it should be. I can't deal in what-if scenarios. I won't be Lot's wife, looking back and turning into a pillar of salt, not even if it's Himalayan, pink, and from the sea. No, ma'am.

When I decided to take that earlier leap of faith and quit my Jeff McKay ad agency job, I went searching for my calling. I didn't know exactly what I wanted to do, but I was interested in publishing, PR, or journalism, and I wanted to merge my two worlds, my hometown of Harlem and the downtown, corporate world I had come to love. No more separation between my work life and my personal life. After drifting and taking on freelance assignments in the advertising marketing space, I was offered a sales job at *Essence*, but something in my spirit told me not to take it. Okay, it wasn't my spirit; it was common sense. I didn't know what I wanted exactly, but I knew I didn't want to hide who I was any longer. I had spent my entire career not letting Big Bev's party lifestyle infiltrate Beverly Smith's professional life, and I was over that juggling act.

Black women are not a monolith, so although *Essence* had an almost entirely Black team, it didn't necessarily mean those women and I were cut from the same cloth. I worshipped Susan Taylor, the former editor in chief of *Essence*, and she was always gracious, warm, and accepting of me, but some of the women who worked at the magazine didn't exactly welcome me with open arms when I came in to interview. Fortunately, that didn't matter. Once Susan decreed that she thought I should work there, she sent me directly to the sales director, for an advertising sales job. At the time, I believed I could never be a salesperson: I feared facing rejection day after day, and as a former media director, I was used to being on the buying side, the side with the power. Also, there was the matter of my fitting in at *Essence*: the women there were stylish, but a little conservative for my taste. I wanted to work at a place where no one would blink an eye when I wore a spandex dress and six-inch heels. Funny how things can change in a little over a decade. Now, if you go to the *Essence* office, you'll see women in everything from midriff tops paired with short skirts to power suits. However, back then, my look wasn't part of their corporate culture, and I craved a job where all of me—my Harlem swag, my fashion knowledge, my love of hip-hop, and my video vixen *bawdy*—would be accepted and celebrated.

That job ended up being as fashion ad director at *Vibe* magazine. It was that position that started me moving closer to my core. It forged a union between Big Bev and Beverly Smith, and let no man put that union asunder. I arrived at *Vibe* in 1998, and for five years, I found a home—and began to find myself. My friends Mimi Valdés and Emil Wilbekin worked at *Vibe*, and they had campaigned for me to become the fashion advertising director.

As a Black woman who had been a part of hip-hop culture since its infancy, I was excited to work at *Vibe*. I was a huge fan of the magazine. Started by music icon Quincy Jones, *Vibe* had much more of a global view of urban culture than any other hip-hop music magazine. The articles were longer, the photographs glossier, and the fashion—thanks to Emil Wilbekin—was on par with images you'd see in *GQ* or *Vogue*. And even with all that high-gloss shine, it still had the hip-hop grit. I felt at home there. In my mind, home was a place where I could wear an outfit that went from work to slay, date a rapper, and drink copious amounts of champagne at a work function and no one would say anything other than "Do you"!

I did me, and in the absolute best way. I worked hard, and I played even harder. Along with my Milan counterpart, the sublime Clyde to my Bonnie, Jeffrey Byrnes, I was responsible for breaking European luxury fashion brands as advertisers in the magazine. At that time, the task of securing urban fashion brands was done by a white woman from the Midwest, which some found counter-intuitive. She handled brands like Rocawear, Sean John, FUBU, and Enyce. Meanwhile, my clients were Prada, Gucci, Dior, and Armani. My job was challenging, but I relished it. I never felt like a salesperson. I thought of myself as a cultural liaison. Although, at meetings in Europe, I was often right back to being the "only one," it didn't feel oppressive. Each meeting I took with fashion brands, I brought along my culture, my community! I created lookbooks of partygoers in designer clothes, paired with shots by the famed Harlem Renaissance photographer James Van der Zee to illustrate that, as a people, Black folks have always had impeccable style. From Reconstruction to hip-hop, we have been style innovators, and we are the ultimate in repurposing clothing. How's *that* for "sustainable fashion"?

Also, at *Vibe*, for the first time, I was working in an office where the majority of the people were Black Ivy League, graduates of Historically Black Colleges. They were the cream of the crop. We didn't apologize for embracing and highlighting our culture. Being at *Vibe* meant that all the things that had made me an outsider at Peter Rogers or Jeff McKay made me the ultimate insider. Before *Vibe*, I had never had the opportunity to fully be myself in the workplace, and after more than a decade in the fashion advertising space, *Vibe* was home.

Experiencing that kind of freedom fueled me to think about my identity. This was pre–Bevy Smith; I was on my Beverly Smith persona—full-blown fashionista. Fashionista Beverly measured her success by how much money she made and how much access she garnered. She was unapologetically a boss, a tough but nurturing woman who wielded her power while displaying ample cleavage.

And then there was Big Bev from Uptown, who would not be sidelined. After all, I was working in the world of hip-hop, and that's Big Bev's domain, so I shouldn't have been surprised when I received a reminder of her a week into the job at *Vibe*. I was passing by the conference room where a guy I knew from the streets, a record executive (né hustler), was taking a meeting with the editors. When he saw me, he yelled, "Big Bev, what the fuck you doing up here?"

Remember, my Big Bev persona resided in the club, and she never let her club friends know she had a *career*. At first, I was a little taken aback. I thought about correcting the record exec ("Sir, you must address me as Beverly"), but then I realized that after so many years of tucking Big Bev away, I now had the chance to introduce her into my professional career.

I responded, "I'm the fashion and beauty advertising director."

He had this incredulous look on his face and said, "How the fuck did you get that job?"

I burst out laughing and told him to come by my office later so we could chop it up, and I'd fill him in.

Vibe was a life-changing experience for me. It was a place where I made contacts, created a family, and solidified my fashionista persona. However, all good things must come to an end, especially if you think of quitting jobs as a pastime.

Which brings me to *Rolling Stone*, aka prime-time Beverly Smith. I looked the part, and I could play the role in my sleep, but at this point in my life—I was thirty-seven years old (four years after my Milan hotel room epiphany)—I was over the whole fashion advertising world. I knew my worth, and I made sure that *RS* paid me accordingly.

At *Rolling Stone*, I went back to being the "only one." But not only was I the only Black person on the sales team; I was the only *woman*. This wasn't so long ago. It was 2005, and the only Black person working at *Rolling Stone*, besides the security and mailroom guys, was the writer Touré. I was so miserable at the job that my bestie Aimee had to talk me off a ledge almost every day. I walked into the building committed to exiting the *RS* job in ten months.

My brief tenure there is a reminder that money isn't everything. At *Rolling Stone*, I was making the most money I'd ever made in my career. For many people (even for me at that time), I should have been overjoyed: I'd come a long way from the receptionist with the annual salary of $15,600. But instead, I felt trapped, confined to a prison of my own creation. I used to give a side-eye whenever I heard people say money doesn't buy you happiness, but it's true. The increase in pay I received when I left *Vibe* for *Rolling Stone* in no way compensated for the loss of connection I felt.

In order to live a life I'd only begun to imagine, I knew I had to follow through with my plan and quit. In my journal entry for January 12, 2005, I wrote, "So, I resigned yesterday! This is what I need, the courage to see this journey through. I hope and pray that I'm strong enough to do this. To live creatively and to not go back to advertising, marketing, any of the old life, START ANEW. Now more than ever before I know that I must not freelance in the industry. I refuse to succumb. I know I feel good and I feel like I can be a better person and that's my goal in life—to do better."

My first days out of work were liberating. I realized that *this* was me: I was supposed to be one of those people you see at a coffee shop in the middle of the day, the ones who make you think, *Why the fuck aren't they at work?* Those first months reminded me of when I was a kid playing hooky at the library, but this time, instead of being ashamed of my nerdy pursuits, I knew I needed to come clean with the world about who I really was and rebrand myself. I also needed to cleanse, and not with a trendy green juice. I had to shed the personas I had created as protection. I was almost forty and had rarely shared with anyone the real me—if they did catch a glimpse, it was just that: a peek—before my insecurity of not being enough showed up and Big Bev or Fashionista Beverly made a special guest appearance and stole the show.

I realized that I was holding on to the hurt that had happened to me when I was in middle school. I was afraid, but it was time to release the narrative and the personas I had created along the way to hide the core of who I was: Lil' Brown Bevy.

So, here we go: who am I at my core? *At my core, I'm Lil' Brown Bevy.* She's curious, clever, adventurous, compassionate, funny, and also driven. She's a teacher, a guide, someone who will share her own personal stories of failure and disappointment so that you can learn from her mistakes, never worried that you may use them against her. She's a tenacious fighter, especially for what's important to her. Freedom is what she values most because she knows what it's like to feel trapped, even if it is by a platinum, diamond-encrusted cage of her own making. Best of all, she trusts her instincts; she doesn't live her life by consensus. All decisions, for better or worse, are made for her, by her—she has agency.

2. How Am I Perceived?

Once I understood my core, my next challenge was to figure out how I was being perceived. Some folks have referred to me as "bougie." Now I would never describe myself as such, because I hate the term. I believe anyone who says they're bougie probably isn't, kind of like people who proclaim themselves "very stable geniuses." I also hate that it's gone mainstream, like *bling bling*, which was originally attributed to Lil Wayne and is now used to sell everything from diamond jewelry to bedazzled water bottles. It pains me that *bougie* has gotten into the hands of blonde suburban moms everywhere. Personally, I say we let them keep the origin word, *bourgeois*, which is an insult. No one wants to be perceived as having "a marked concern for material interests and respectability with a tendency toward mediocrity" (the *Merriam-Webster* definition). *I* certainly don't. I've never seen the term *bougie* as cute, and it's certainly never anything I've wanted to emulate. (I will admit, I love the song "Bad and Boujee," although I've never cooked up dope with an Uzi. But, hey, if this book doesn't sell, who knows? Btw, why do they spell "boujee" that way? It's already slang, folks just be complicating things.)

Some of you may be reading this and thinking, *Who thinks Bevy is bougie?* (I'm talking about the shady ones who are here to hate-read, but, hey, as long as you purchased the book, keep going.) Here's the thing, though: it's all subjective. Some people think I'm bougie based on what they see of my life on social media, especially when it comes to my luxurious vacations. I may not showcase my closet, but I will give you a video of a gorgeous sunrise on the other side of the world. Others may have the impression, based on my work and proximity to celebrities, that I fancy myself a celeb, which is not true. I know I work with celebs, but I'm not one. Some mistake my self-confidence for arrogance, and that grates people.

It's important, as we advance in life, to be aware of the signals we give when we're dealing with people. Over my past few years as a media personality, a perception of me has emerged based on my straight, no chaser approach to everything, from fashion to pop culture to love to sex to money. Of course, some folks aren't fans, but others have told me they think of me as family, that I remind them of someone they know. That someone is usually their favorite mutha, auntie, or bestie. Although it's wonderful to be thought of as family, the flip side is not everyone loves their family.

With that in mind, I've learned to temper what I say, especially when dealing with the public. Folks will ask for your opinion, but they really don't want it; they want you to cosign what they believe about themselves. Now, the old me, the assertive, won't-back-down "Big Bev" me, would definitely tell folks what she thought and have little concern for hurting their feelings. After all, they'd asked me!

I'm no longer so cavalier about saying the "truth," especially if I believe it will hurt someone's feelings. Crushing someone's dreams with solely my opinion is not my ministry. That's what happened to me when I told people I wanted to do TV, and thank God I didn't listen because obviously they were wrong. Now Lil' Brown Bevy remembers the naysayers and shows up to encourage folks, even if I think they're going down an ill-fated path. I won't just tell them what they want to hear, but, instead of shooting down folks' hopes and dreams, I try to offer encouragement in a different direction.

I'm also aware that being blunt and truthful may cause a brawl, so now I take a beat and think, *If I say the wrong thing in the wrong way, this person who thinks she loves me could have a flashback to her combative relationship with her bestie/auntie/mother and want to molly wop me, all because I said she should probably pursue a career other than modeling.* Everyone who was ever told they were cute seems to think they can be a model, bless their hearts. Now I understand that when it comes to critiquing the public, less is more, and yes, you can be a model. You may not be Naomi but social media has broad criteria for folks who can be considered models . . .

When you're a media personality, people feel connected to the you they see on TV, and it disarms them when you connect with them in person and the assumptions they've held about you are dismantled. I've gone on quite a few auditions where they called me in because they'd seen the more comedic portions of my fashion commentary, but when I gave them my fashion background, along with a fashion history lesson, they were even more impressed. In 2019, I appeared in a Netflix documentary titled *The Remix: Hip Hop X Fashion*, and although I've appeared on TV discussing fashion for over a decade, many people didn't know about my fashion knowledge or my career trajectory. I love being discovered! I've also had auditions where Lil' Brown Bevy showed up and charmed the pants off the powers that be.

My favorite auditions aren't even the ones that ended in a booked job. I love that I'm so comfortable with who I truly am that when I go into a room, I'm not auditioning, really, but connecting with people. Some of the fulfilling relationships I've established in the entertainment field were created because I let people see the best part of me, Lil' Brown Bevy, in an audition.

When I finally started focusing on Lil' Brown Bevy, I wanted folks to get to know her, but I realized that she wasn't always showing up in my daily interactions. You know who showed up every day? Big Bev and Fashionista Beverly! Because they are tough, outspoken, and the ones who have protected Lil' Brown Bevy, they were my comfort zone. Still, their bravado was blocking my blessings, preventing the best of me, Lil' Brown Bevy, from entering the room, even when I wanted her to. Lil' Brown Bevy is far more nuanced, more textured than those other personas because she's human and vulnerable, and she owns that. So those other personas, which I created out of fear, were hampering Lil' Brown Bevy's shine. Ain't that a bitch! It's also a Bevelation: Sometimes the personas we create out of self-protection can actually dim our light, stymieing us from truly radiating.

Did I miss out on opportunities that would have been in alignment with my happiness all because I had those façades up? Was the title of my book going to be *She Never Had a Chance: The Story of Lil' Brown Bevy*? No, ma'am, that would not, could not, be my story. I had to change the way I was being thought of. I had been selling a narrative in my personal and professional life that was doing me more harm than good and stunting my spiritual growth!

To be clear, I haven't banished my alter egos. When I quit advertising and fashion to become a TV personality, I didn't just expunge all the knowledge I'd accumulated in those fields over the years, and I didn't totally dismiss Fashionista Beverly Smith and Big Bev from Uptown. They were still useful. There are times when I need that ferocious, assertive attitude that can only be embodied by Big Bev, and certainly Fashionista Beverly Smith, with her in-depth knowledge of style and her fully stamped passport, has come in handy in myriad ways, even on my last TV show, *Page Six TV*. Part of the reason I was hired for that gig is because of my luxury goods background and my passion for travel. When chatting about celebrity haunts all over the world, it helps to have a fashion professional/ world traveler with a pop culture point of view on camera.

I've learned that finding one's core, one's true self, doesn't need to be an all-or-nothing proposition. I don't need to erase my other identities. However, if folks' perceptions of who I am are in direct opposition to how I would like to be perceived, then perhaps it's time to tinker with the recipe. So, I've begun to bundle my personas up, into a gumbo of sorts, with Lil' Brown Bevy as the roux holding it all together.

3. How Would I Like to Be Perceived?

Rolling Stone did a lot to enhance my legend in the urban space of marketing and advertising. Once the word was out that I was no longer at the company, and I began appearing on TV shows as a lifestyle expert, brands that marketed to Black consumers began reaching out to me for speaking engagements. One of my most fulfilling speaking events was a tour of Historically Black Colleges and Universities (HBCUs) sponsored by Boost Mobile. One of my very successful girlfriends, Caralene Robinson, was a vice president at Boost. Caralene, whom I knew from my Big Bev days, when we were running the streets and not letting a soul know we were driven career girls, asked me to be a part of a panel consisting of five Black professionals from different fields.

Over the course of a few weeks, we shared with students at HBCUs the rewards and challenges of working in corporate America as a Black person. When I started the tour, it included professional public speakers, and from them, I learned . . . what *not* to do. Yes, they had impressive spiels, but they were just reciting a script, and that wasn't inspiring to me. By the second stop on the tour, I'd decided that I was going to strip down and really tell my story. All of it! Even the parts that weren't my best moments. And that decision was a game changer for me.

During that tour, I realized that being authentically me was the ultimate way to connect with people. Being fabulous like Fashionista Bevy will intrigue people, but most won't bother to look beyond the garments. The people drawn to Fashionista Beverly are drawn to the glitz and glam, but they aren't *inspired by her.* I didn't want my story to begin and end based on things I had purchased. Being a true inspiration to others comes from your core, not from a store. (That rhymes! Come on, MC Bev-Ski!)

So, I decided to start showing up on that college tour and lead with Lil' Brown Bevy. In fact, she was introduced to the public on that tour. For the first time since I was fourteen, I spoke about being bullied, being nerdy and passive. I spoke about my dreams and goals. I told the students that I didn't have it all figured out, and my transparency inspired them. I know that if I had shown up as fabulous Fashionista Beverly Smith, I would have attracted one very specific type of student: the flashy overachiever who garnered all the attention and was probably a bit of a bully. But by showing up with who I was at my core, I ended up attracting all types of students, from the quiet, closeted boys who dreamed of moving to New York City, to the junior diva who entered the event surrounded by adoring fans but asked for a one-on-one so she could let her guard down and confess that she really didn't have a clue about her career path and that she was nervous about graduating.

It was after that college tour that I began to be in demand as a motivational speaker, and those experiences were the foundation for Life with Vision, my seminars, where I help people discover their most authentic selves, their own Lil' Brown Bevys. Lil' Brown Bevy is how I would like to be perceived. She is an emotionally intelligent woman, in touch with her feelings and not afraid to show them—even if it leaves her open to being hurt, because she's learned that she's strong and that she will heal.

I'm passionate about doing well not just for myself, but for my family and community. It fills me with pride when I encounter people of various ages, races, and socioeconomic levels who tell me that they love seeing me on TV or listening to me on the radio because my presence, my ability to live my life out loud, motivates them to pursue their passions. And I'm convinced that I wouldn't have the diverse audience of folks who connect with me if I were still hiding behind Big Bev or Fashionista Beverly.

If you're reading this and want to embrace the real you, to unleash her/him/them into the world, but feel that time isn't on your side, please don't fall prey to that trap. I'm fifty-four, and I give thanks that I can say that number out loud with no hesitation—thanks to my mother's very modern outlook on aging. She's never been coy about telling people her age. As a matter of fact, she's the first one to announce her age without being asked. Yet again, I'm following my mom's lead; I've never worried about getting older. Why would I? My twenties were fun; my thirties were for soul searching; in my forties, I was laying the groundwork; but now, baby, I'm hitting my stride and am a living testament that life truly does get greater later.

◆ ◆ ◆

Answering those three questions allowed me to realize that *my* red sole is a mix of my curiosity and passion plus the chutzpah to go for whatever it is I desire, even if it makes no sense to anyone else: *my* red sole is the authentic, candid, passionate yet empathetic me. What I've gleaned over the years is that people love the idea of keeping it "real," but most folks never let you see anything behind the façade—especially if that's what's making them money or garnering them approval. I've learned enough to know that while folks like to hang with Big Bev from Uptown, it's Lil' Brown Bevy who wins folks over and forges real relationships.

Now, before you start to think I'm Bevpak Chopra, this is fifty-four-year-old Bevy talking. But back at age thirty-eight, right after leaving *Rolling Stone*, I wasn't nearly as clear about what my red sole was. My plans *appeared* to be mapped out: quit job, travel for clarity, come back, and become a TV star. But fifteen years after the fact, I realize I didn't have a clue about what I really wanted to do. My plans were far from clear, because I was still hedging my bets. What I *was* clear about was that I wasn't going to take on work that didn't inspire me, and I wouldn't allow any entity (including Hollywood) to shake my conviction that I was *built* for a career in front of the camera. When I took an acting class with the iconic acting coach Susan Batson, she told me that *I* was the character I should play, that I could work as *myself*, and that my current state was a book, a movie waiting to be seen. That galvanized me. If this woman who had coached Oprah and Nicole Kidman saw a career in entertainment for me because I had shown up stripped down . . . well, shove some singles down my G-string. I'm taking it all off!

I'm being flippant, but as I said before, change is hard, and most of us will avoid it whenever we can, or make changes when the people we admire tell us we should. But what if you never get confirmation for your dream? Are you supposed to just maintain the status quo and wait to die?

When I began to talk to people about my goal of working in TV, I received pushback. What some people refer to as "haters," I like to call naysayers, 'cause everything you say, they hit you with a "nay," as in "No, don't try it, it will never work."

One naysayer in particular stands out. When I told my dear friend Kevin Harter, a top executive at Bloomingdales, that I wanted to pursue a job in TV, he offered to set up a dinner with a woman he knew from HBO. I was so excited. I put on a fab outfit and was ready to dazzle her with my scintillating wit and Lil' Brown Bevy authenticity. Well, she took one look at me—actually, it was more than one look; she looked me up *and* down—and clearly found me lacking. She then proceeded to cast doubt on every one of my ideas, from what kind of show I thought I could be a part of (*The View*) to my ideas for shows I wanted to develop (according to her, they'd never sell). I don't even take pleasure in the fact that I proved her wrong. Okay, so maybe I take a little pleasure. (I'm still working on being gracious. You know Michelle Obama's quote "When they go low, we go high"? Well, I'm all set for that, but then Big Bev shows up and says, "Fuck that.") #WorkInProgress

When I left that dinner, I flashed back to when I was eighteen and surrounded by women who didn't look like me. Granted, there were alterations I could have done to make myself more palatable for the entertainment industry—installing a back-grazing hair weave, losing my lisp and my New York City accent, and, the most obvious, losing weight. When I started doing TV, I was a size 10, and while I wanted to lose a few pounds, I wasn't interested in trying to be the size of so many other TV hosts.

People don't believe it, but I have never wanted to be skinny. Even when I was a size 4, I had curves. I think of my hourglass shape as a blessing, as do many folks, obvi, who are out there paying good money on what God saw fit to give me for free. From the time I was in my mid-thirties, I've gradually gained weight, and although the number fluctuates, I've always felt I looked good on TV, and judging by my DMs on social media, so do a lot of other people. While writing this book, I started wondering if there were jobs in TV that maybe I didn't book because of my curves, but thankfully society's physical standards are changing. Also, I'm sure I've changed more than a few TV executives' minds about what is attractive in a host.

When I was on the set of my former TV show *Page Six TV*, with my cohost Elizabeth Wagmeister, a beautiful, smart, young blonde, I would marvel at our being on a show together, and was proud that I showed up on that set every day ready to represent a different standard of beauty. I wasn't the sidekick to the young blonde white woman. We had great chemistry, and our relationship was that of mentor and mentee, but we've added an element of bestie into the mix—Elizabeth is a true friend. I also didn't fall into the trope of self-deprecating Black woman who bemoaned not having a man and who constantly discussed diets. Folks picked up on my healthy self-esteem. Anytime I had a personal appearance or even met fans in the street, people admired my "sophisticated yet real" approach to life. They felt connected to me and to my girls, aka my breasts. Everyone wanted to know what kind of bra I wore. Well, wonder no more: Bevy's Big Busty Bras is coming to an Etsy or Instagram shop, soon*ish*!

Speaking of the girls, people also tuned in to see what I was wearing, and thanks to the show's wardrobe stylist, the divine Fran Taylor, we never disappointed. Fran "got" me. At our first consultation, I explained my background in fashion and showed her some of my favorite looks from my previous show, *Fashion Queens*, where I was styled by my bestie Renee, aka Nay Nay Billy. Renee had the budget to put me in nothing but designer clothes: Alexander McQueen, Versace, Missoni, Mary Katrantzou. *Page Six TV* wasn't about that life; they had a tight budget, but Fran and her team made it WERK. When Fran wasn't available, she left my look in the very capable hands of Ashley Miller, a young woman who appreciated my curves, never tried to shroud my shape, and was a master at adjusting my boobs right before we went on air. During the trial run plus the two seasons that *Page Six TV* was on the air, I never experienced what so many women who aren't sample size go through when doing TV, and I was never made to feel like being curvy was a hindrance to being stylish.

The first time I was a cohost on a nationally syndicated TV program just by being unequivocally me—outspoken, irreverent, comical yet compassionate, and not changing a thing physically—was a really proud moment. I'd found my red sole, my ability to be genuinely me no matter where I was or whom I was around. This isn't always easy to do. Believe me, there are still some rooms where I think I want to shrink so I don't offend anyone. Then I remember how it felt to be a follower, to not be in control, to give others' opinions about me more weight than my own, to believe their words more than facts I knew to be true about myself.

No, it's not easy being authentically you. If it were, you wouldn't see so many people out there being pale facsimiles of someone else. So, I urge you to *do the work*: ask yourself the tough questions, and answer them honestly. Unearth your core. Be aware of how you're perceived, and then start adjusting your behavior so that you're being perceived the way you see your best self.

Dare to Dream

WHAT WOULD YOU DO IF MONEY WERE NO OBJECT, IF you could pursue anything you wanted? What would your life look like? Try to answer those questions. I'll bet your first attempt won't represent your true desire.

If I'd been asked those questions at the age of thirty-three, when I first decided to change my life, my answer would have been, "I want to become a merchandise editor, someone who works with the advertising side of magazines to create and host special events for fashion clients." That was yet another job I pitched to the president of *Vibe* when I was trying to get out of ad sales. Thank God he turned me down. It's a pleasant job for someone, but not for me—it's one step away from being a salesperson, but without the commission checks, which, to be clear, are the best part. But I get why I thought that was my dream. I was hedging my bets. You see, I was new to actually having dreams. Before that moment in Milan,

I was happy just to be in a position many people envied. I certainly hadn't given myself permission to imagine "a life filled with creativity where every day looked different from the day before." Now, *that* was a life I didn't dare dream.

Now that I no longer fear what other people think about what I want to do with my life, I can rattle off a series of wildly ambitious goals. (My dreams have become *goals*.) For example, I'm obsessed with people who have EGOT status. An EGOT is a person who has earned an Emmy, Grammy, Oscar, and Tony, and to date there are only fifteen of them, including Whoopi Goldberg. When I had Whoopi on my SiriusXM radio show, *Bevelations*, all I wanted to do was talk about the EGOT life. Whoopi is the most unaffected famous person I've ever met, but she's proud of being an EGOT, and she should be. It ain't easy to gain that status. Just ask 1980s heartthrob Philip Michael Thomas.

You remember Philip Michael Thomas of *Miami Vice* fame? He played Ricardo Tubbs, he of the chocolate brown complexion and curly jet-black hair. This fine-ass man came up with the term *EGOT* in 1984 at the height of the show's success, telling a reporter that in the next five years, it was his goal to win all four awards. Now, that's a guy who dared to dream—after all, no one watched *Miami Vice* to see Thomas's acting. However, he really believed he could achieve this status, though tragically, he's never been nominated for even one of the awards that would have gotten him to EGOT status. Damn, damn, damn!

I think it's awesome that Philip believed in himself, but you've got to have a plan, a strategy.

So, here's my strategy to become an EGOT:

I will win an Emmy for one of my talk shows. (According to Philip Michael Thomas, a Daytime Emmy doesn't count, but as much as I respect him for coining the phrase, I'm going to ignore that "rule." Moving on.) I will secure my Grammy for my audiobook reading of the *New York Times* bestselling book *Bevelations*, which you are reading or listening to now. (Look at you, supporting my dreams. THANK YOU! Come on, creative visualization.) For my Oscar win, I'll take home the trophy for the *first* time as Best Supporting Actress for a riveting and moving performance that made the Academy laugh and cry. Last, but certainly not least, is the Tony, which I consider the holy grail of awards. Broadway is tough. They aren't enamored of stars—you have to have *talent*! Granted, in an attempt to woo tourists to the Great White Way, Broadway has lowered its standards by casting anyone who has starred on a hit reality TV show or been a one-hit wonder, but you still have to razzle dazzle 'em. (See what I did there? I referenced a song from the Broadway show *Chicago*, which won six Tonys during its 1997 revival.)

I'm leaving it all on the floor when I go for my Tony, and I'm going to try several angles. The easiest way would be to produce a show. All I would need is money and good taste, but I'm dreaming *big*, like bigger than my breasts. That's right. I'm not hedging my bets with a Tony for producing. I'm earning a Tony for the one-woman show *G.A.W.: Grown-Ass Woman*. It'll be my story (from Lil' Brown Bevy to Fashionista Beverly, rock star, and home again to Lil' Brown Bevy), somewhat the same story as Dorothy's in *The Wizard of Oz*, but a very fresh take (and with even better shoes), told through song, dance, and satire. It opens to rave reviews from the *New York Times*. I play to sold-out audiences during my limited run (think Bruce Springsteen's Broadway run, which was originally supposed to be only eight weeks). And by the time the Tony nominations are announced, I'm in London doing the show on the West End.

Twenty years ago, I wouldn't have dared express to you or myself that I wanted to be in entertainment—much less sing, dance, act, produce, direct, write, and host my own content. That's why

I'm in awe of people like Issa Rae and Tyler Perry who believed early on that they could buck the Hollywood system and manifest their dreams. I also marvel at folks who never had a regular job because they always knew they wanted to work in entertainment. I made it my business to befriend them. I just liked being around creatives, and I may have slept with a few of them. (Look, I told you I liked being around them!) I laughed out loud just typing that sentence, but it's true! I've slept with creatives—writers, rappers, comedians, painters—and for a few I acted as their muse.

Google the word *muse*, and lots of articles pop up on how to be a muse to a *man*. Can you believe that misogynistic, antiquated shit? In 2020, we women are still being fed information on how to service a man instead of ourselves. I can definitely relate. My creativity used to be so shut down, I thought the best way to tap into it was through a man's vision. This is embarrassing to even write. I'm cringing at admitting that I gave ideas to men I slept with instead of keeping them for myself. Musical inspiration; story ideas for books, films, articles; business strategies—and all because I didn't believe I was a creative. Ladies, stop "supporting" men and giving them your ideas for no credit or money. If you're brainstorming with your lover, you should receive more than a thank-you on social media or at an awards show. Run me my check!

This kind of BS happens all the time to women because we don't believe we have the ability or the *right* to create. Even seemingly independent and successful women have been groomed to be helpers, to take care of everyone else's needs and put their own to the side. How many of you helped your boyfriend in college with his work when you should have been concentrating on your own studies? I remember when I decreed that I would no longer help lovers with their résumés, and I advised all my girlfriends to do the same. Of course, you do hear about marriages that operate as true partnerships, but too often the men get the glory and the women get to be "the wife of" and enjoy the money that comes in through her husband's bank account. (Money which you then have to fight tooth and nail to secure a portion of, should you decide to divorce him after being his lover and secretary for decades. Not everyone ends up with half like MacKenzie Bezos, now Scott, so take heed and get official credit for your work—a bonus Bevelation.) You may not want to admit it, but I'll bet there are times when you hide your gifts or bestow them upon someone else, never daring to utilize what's inherently yours.

Before you think I'm a bitter single lady who blames men for everything, I need to mention that I'm always quick to point out when I encounter great guys, and I've actually dated my fair share of them. (I'm saving those stories for my biopic.) I've never had a relationship with anyone who tried to keep me from exploring a creative life. As a matter of fact, several of the artists I dated tried to bring out the artist in me. One lover in particular—I love the word *lover*; it makes me think of a man bringing me breakfast in a sunlit room while I recline in our canopy bed after a night of torrid love-making . . . again, dare to dream—was a rapper who was impressed by my wordplay. He told me I should rap and even brought me to the studio to work with him.

This was in my twenties, when I wasn't ready to tap into my creativity. Deep down in my heart, I wanted to do it; I had a real desire to perform; but I couldn't even imagine myself onstage rapping about sex. How could I, when at the time I couldn't even admit to myself that I wanted to be *seen*, that I had words and creativity to be unleashed. Has that ever been you? Not the part where a well-endowed, bohemian rap star offers you an opportunity to record a song. I think I'm a rare breed in that regard. But maybe someone in your life has given you a great opportunity, one you really wanted to take but didn't feel worthy of, so you ran and hid? I think that happens to a lot of us.

I have tried to be "the plug" for a few people, and they either squandered the opportunity or outright sabotaged themselves. I'm not blaming them. It's unnerving when folks see your talent and potential, but you can't see it yourself—or else your own potential scares you so much that you freeze up and opt out of the entire situation, afraid of failure or, worse, letting down those who believe in you. That clearly was me when that rapper offered me a genuine opportunity. I didn't take him up on his offer, and he never asked again—and I get it. If you can't invest in yourself, why should others? Just a FYI, I would have been a *huge* success. My raps were raunchy yet insightful, inspirational even—imagine Cardi B but with a Harlem accent and a background in marketing. (Actually, Cardi has marketing experience, too. Stripping is all about selling an unattainable fantasy, just like advertising.)

Fortunately, I have done a lot of introspective work on myself since then. Most important, I became nurturing and patient with myself, honest about what I wanted in life. I now take care of myself the way I used to take care of a lover I'd been waiting on; I cherish Bevy.

Once upon a time, I wallowed in self-doubt and hid from my ambition because I couldn't accept failure. Anything less than excellence was failure, and that failure was met with harsh words for myself and others. The old me didn't allow for mistakes, but now I fully embrace the mantra "Shit happens." And when said shit takes place, you do what you can to clean up, and you leave the rest right there, kind of like New York City dog owners do. If I'm tired, I rest. If I'm depressed, I own it and wait for it to pass. And when I do something I know I shouldn't, like eat a heavy meal late at night, I pray that I have another day to get it right.

The rapper and I are still friends; when when I see him, he tells me how proud he is of what I've accomplished since we were together, and he berates me for not having done it sooner. Another ex-lover who is quite famous recently told me that I was the most "late-bloomingest" motherfucker he knows, and that he's happy for my success. (No, I'm not naming names. I'm going to save that for my fifth autobiography, *Don't Stop, Get It, Get It: The Bevy Smith Story*. That will be published when I'm eighty-five and a lot of folks are dead—I'm going to "Quincy Jones" all you mofos!)

Speaking of being eighty-five, my number-one Bevelation is #ItGetsGreaterLater. That belief powers my goals, and I know I will be creating well into my nineties (hello, Cicely Tyson), so squelch the idea that you've wasted time or passed your prime. My mantra, "Everything is as it should be," always holds up—though there *are* rare occasions when Basic Bevy shows up and forgets all she learned from her self-help books.

Listen, every now and again, there's a twinge of "What if?" That's when I ponder what my life would look like if I had tried out for theater in junior high and high school. I think back now to how, as young as thirteen years old, I placed limitations on myself—and I'm not alone. I've met plenty of people in their late thirties and older who are just starting to move on their dreams. While conducting my Life with Vision workshops, I hear from lots of folks who feel shut down by people who want to control their lives, often under the guise of doing it in their best interest. In fact, the reason I created my workshops in the first place was because so many people had reached out to me on social media, inspired by my story of having changed my life in my late thirties and wanting to meet up for coffee, lunch, just a few moments to "pick your brains." For the record, if I had met with all the folks who wanted to pick my brains, I would need to hang out my shingle and become a life coach. I'm sure many of you reading this act as life coaches for your friends, so I've got advice for you. If you're so good at it, get paid for it; go get certified and start charging folks, because that's a skill and it's draining, so you deserve a coin. Sharing your story while receiving others' emotional baggage, helping them sort it out, and all you get is a thank-you, a hard scone, and a watery coffee? No, ma'am, secure the bag.

With my Life with Vision events, fifty to sixty of us come together in fellowship. I share my story, but we are all ACTIVE participants in this together. I don't sit on high, an all-knowing guru. I insist that *you* help *yourself.* I encourage my guests to find co-conspirators at Life with Vision; that's what I call folks with similar dreams. Everyone who attends sends in their résumé, but they are also asked what they aspire to do. I then place folks with similar aspirations at the same table in the hopes of sparking an exchange of information and hopefully a collaboration. I try to foster alliances, not competition. The good news is that just by reading this book, you're ahead of the curve. In fact, you've answered the three important Life with Vision questions in the last chapter: Who am I at my core? How am I perceived? How would I like to be perceived?

In those seminars, I found out that I wasn't the only one who didn't dare to dream for a very long time in life. Seminar participants have tearfully told me about teachers who crushed their aspirations and spouses who laughed at them and told them it could never happen, and of course, parents. Parents who outright don't believe in you, who can list all the reasons you will never realize your dreams, are the most damaging of the naysayers. Whether it was your parents or your bitchy best friend who loves to point out your failures (see Molly and Issa in season three of HBO's *Insecure*), these critics can do real damage to our ability to dream. When we're young, fairy tales tell us that it's outsiders—a wicked stepsister, a witch—who will tell us we aren't pretty or smart enough to go to the ball, so we're prepared for *that.* But what do you do when it's your own flesh and blood, or a person who has vowed to help you, who doubts you and feeds your existing insecurities? Or maybe it's even deeper than that. What if no one even cared enough to ask you what you dreamed of being?

There are so many ways our goals and aspirations can be crushed. How many of you are in the career you dreamed about as a kid? Now let me up the ante and ask: how many of you can even remember what you dreamed of being as a kid? My childhood dreams were buried deep, and it wasn't until I decided I was going to change my life that I began the excavation process.

Remember that when I sat in that hotel room in Milan at the age of thirty-three, I had no idea I wanted a career in entertainment. I was merely hiding out, as I mentioned earlier. I thought my "dream" was to become a fashion merchandising editor for a magazine, and even that was a big stretch for me at the time. Then, when I realized I had to change my life, I still didn't really want to do anything drastic, and I continued to seek permission (from men, a recurring theme for me).

It's tempting for me to call myself stupid or a loser because I didn't act on my dreams sooner, but what would I gain from that? Anyway, that would be in direct violation of the first of the Four Agreements, "Be impeccable with your word." Would berating myself encourage me to start where I am *right now* and not worry about yesterday? Nope, it sure wouldn't—and you know it wouldn't, but I'll bet you're guilty of inflicting painfully negative criticism on yourself. If so, please stop! You live and, hopefully, learn, so don't anguish over what's in the past. *Just be mindful of your past mistakes and try not to repeat them.* And know that you're not alone in this journey of discovery—if you were, there wouldn't be an entire self-help section in bookstores!

Society's rules don't help us dare to dream. Instead, they set us up to follow the well-trodden path of least resistance. We're told that being unique, standing out, is for other people, for someone special—and who gets to anoint who is special? People in power, usually men, and usually *white* men, with their own biases and blind spots. So, if you're not deemed "special," what should you do? Society grooms so many of us from a very early age to believe that the key to having a good life is to go to school, major in a field so you can find a good job—it doesn't matter if you're interested in the profession or not—get married, have children, and that's it. You've got it made! And that "dream" is even more linear and doesn't allow for many adventures and certainly no exploration of "finding yourself" if you're from a lower-income community. Many of my childhood friends went straight from high school into city jobs. College wasn't even an option, due to lack of finances coupled with having no one to guide them through the college application process. None of my friends had helicopter parents willing to pay millions and Photoshop them being a member of a rowing team so that they could gain a slot at a prestigious school. (Can you believe Aunt Becky is a crook?) Instead for many of us, our "hookup" was a parent, an auntie or uncle who told you in advance when the aptitude test for a city job was happening and told you what to study to pass the test. Upon passing, you received a uniform, joined a union, and started counting the days until you could receive your pension. That's not a bad life. To be able to provide for yourself and your family is always an accomplishment, especially in today's society, where folks might work two or three jobs and still need government assistance.

But what if, at that point in their lives, after they've been at their jobs for thirty years and they're about to retire with a good pension, it's their time to dare to dream? Every time I'm out in my neighborhood, I encounter people who tell me they'd like to be a writer, actor, or comedian, to have a profession in a creative field, and that seeing me succeed—someone from their community, someone who is just getting started in her fifties—inspires them, tells them that maybe it's not too late. Their dreams weren't encouraged to blossom when they were young, and maybe yours weren't, either, but please believe me: even if you think you're late, you're actually right on time because, as I said before, *everything is as it should be.*

When I was a kid, around eleven years old, one of my dreams (or so I thought) centered on securing a job as an executive assistant. This stemmed from my watching late-night movies—*Gentlemen Prefer Blondes* and *Valley of the Dolls* were two of my favorites—where young, smart, beautiful, well-dressed women, women who worked in gorgeous midcentury modern offices, were in service to powerful men. This "dream" was also shaped by my reading too many old issues of *Cosmopolitan* with cover lines like "How to Get Your Married Boss to Leave His Wife" or "How to Please Your Man Each and Every Day." Now, because I believe in the sanctity of marriage, I was never interested in seducing a married man, but I *definitely* bought into the "please your man" part.

In my "dream" life, I was married to a man with a "good job" he didn't like but was good at it. He made about $150K, and I made $125K—even in my "dream," I made less than a man (damn patriarchy)—which afforded us a very nice lifestyle in our neighborhood. We had two children, who attended parochial school. We had a co-op in Harlem and a time-share in Florida—that's where we vacationed *every year*, although for my fortieth, he took me to Paris. And I had a Bergdorf Goodman charge card, which I used semiannually for my spring/fall shoe and handbag purchases, for special occasions, or whenever I was depressed. (Even in my "dream" life, I was a shopaholic.)

When I discuss my "dream" life, I'm aware that it sounds satisfying to many people. It's comfortable, perfectly nice (ugh, there's that term again)—and most important, it appears secure. Security is a basic need, number two on Abraham Maslow's hierarchy of needs, just above food and shelter. However, if I had pursued that "secure" life, it would have been a disservice to who I was born to be. Holding on to security and daring to dream don't work in tandem.

That version of me would never have realized her potential. Had I stayed on that path, nothing I am today would have come to fruition.

I never would have published articles in national magazines, much less written this book. Do you think the woman my eleven-year-old self dreamed up would have traveled to six continents—many of them on solo trips? Hell, no! Yes, her husband would have taken her to Paris at the age of forty, but "world traveler"? Nah! Would she have become an entrepreneur who built a business that sustained her and her parents? Not likely. Having a career in television or radio also would have been off the table. The me who dreamed up that version of herself was so stunted that she would have never attempted to pursue a career in TV. (Please believe, TV as a livelihood is not for the risk averse.) Yes, when I was a kid, I saw the beautiful, Brown, and sophisticated Kiki Shepard standing on the stage of the Apollo Theater hosting "Apollo Amateur Night," but I never imagined that could ever be me. Today, I've stood on that iconic stage and hosted several events, including interviews with rapper/actor Common (BTW, he's almost an EGOT; all he needs is a Tony Award) and Olympic gymnast Gabby Douglas. Even those moments pale in comparison to just being there on the stage, tapping into Lil' Brown Bevy, who used to watch Kiki Shepard rub the legendary Tree of Hope (an Apollo tradition). I feel blessed just to be following in Kiki's esteemed footsteps.

◆ ◆ ◆

I know I'm blessed because I dodged a life that would have *never* satisfied me. However, I want to pay homage to the assistant I would have been. The assistant who is the boss of all the other assistants, the one whose desk everyone comes by to spill the office tea. She's excellent at her job, constantly receives bonuses, and runs her office and the boss.

Do you recognize that assistant? Maybe that's you, and if so, you owe it to yourself to step out of your comfort zone and explore a hidden desire. You obviously have something, that "it" factor that makes folks gravitate to you, so take a public speaking course and look into becoming a life coach—you're always giving advice anyway! Whenever I encounter gregarious folks in offices, I'm compelled to give them a mini Life with Vision seminar. I advise the funny office manager to try stand-up in her spare time, take a comedy class, do improv, anything to share her gift. When I meet the IT guy or the accountant with the incredible voice at the holiday karaoke party, I tell him he should, at the very least, be singing in some church choir or making a few extra bucks at weddings and funerals. I believe the world will make room for your gift, even if the "world" is Sister Jenkins's homegoing.

All this boils down to *daring to dream*. But to do this work, you have to get *brutally honest* about which areas of your life are dissatisfying. Often that means disrupting the system. Disruption is challenging the status quo, and folks don't like that, especially those who benefit from you staying stuck right where they placed you. Come closer; here's some insight, a Bevelation: When you decide to buck the system, there will be people in your life who won't support you, even though you've always supported them. They'll be angry that you're not there the way you were before. They got used to you playing a role in their Lifetime movie, wearing a bad outfit that no longer fits. Isn't it time that you stop playing a supporting role in someone else's life and become the lead in yours? You at least deserve to, say it with me, *dare to dream*!

Okay, maybe disruption sounds like a bit much to you. Maybe it's more of a remix that you're seeking. I urge you to reject being shackled by others' perceptions of a dream life, even if you're the one who created yours. Give yourself permission to shift, to remix that life that worked so well before but now just doesn't do it for you.

A friend of mine had a child on her own while in her forties. She had a very good life, not rich but never wanting for anything, and she had freedom. She's a writer and a damn good one, too; her gift is always in demand. Her life was one that I looked upon with admiration. She would spend about half of the year out of the country, living in foreign places that interested her. She'd come back to the USA to work and replenish her bank account and visit her family, which sounds perfect to me. Having a home base but being a global citizen, #Goals. However, she decided that she wanted a child and so she utilized her research skills and applied the determined focus that makes her a great writer/editor and now she's a mom. She remixed her dream, but didn't abandon all parts of it. Nope, she won't be sitting in one place raising her baby. Instead she's planning to continue traveling the world but this time with a tiny, adorable companion. I love that she wasn't shackled to that perception of who I and probably many others thought she was. She remixed her life and dared to dream anew.

This can be tough, though. Admitting that your "good" life isn't what you want it to be means you're an ingrate, right? Wrong! You can be grateful for everything you've been blessed with, every accomplishment. Take a look at your gratitude list (if you don't have one, please create one). There are people who would envy a few things that you've listed, #Blessed. However, it still doesn't mean you can't want more. It doesn't mean you can't dare to dream!

I know a few of you are reading this chapter and saying, "*Yaaaas*," but battling with your ego that's saying "*No fucking way, we are not about to blow up this persona, lifestyle, brand we've carefully curated for the gram.*" Tell the truth and shame the devil, how many of you are doing the damn thing just for the gram? Or tossing and turning at night feeling stuck, not knowing how to get out of your own way?

During the coronavirus pandemic, so many people with successful careers that have *nothing* to do with entertainment or are behind the scenes in the industry began creating Instagram Live shows. I'm talking about folks who do well financially, are highly respected in their professions, and in April 2020, between trying to find Clorox wipes and toilet paper and binge-watching *Tiger King*, created *whole* weekly Instagram Live shows, complete with a producer, celebrity guests, and theme music. Now that just proves to me that for so many folks, no matter how good their lives look to the outside world, there's something missing, and for many that was being a talk-show host on Instagram. Who knew?! I'm glad that folks ventured out of their comfort zones, but if this global catastrophe has confirmed anything, it's that tomorrow truly isn't promised and we'd better start living for today.

Many folks who started these IG shows probably wanted to be in entertainment as a kid. I want you to look back and try to remember what you loved as a child. I was a voracious reader; I loved adventures, even if they were only in my head; and I was obsessed with travel. James Bond films were my favorites because of the exotic locales, all the beautiful clothes, and the heavy drinking. (Even back then I knew I was a cocktail hour kind of gal.) As a teenager, I would style my friends, with no idea that styling was an actual job. I put them in the latest fashions, and I'm proud to say I was the first girl on my block to wear spandex dresses. Take that, Fashion Nova. I enjoyed being the center of attention even if it was just within my small group of friends.

I hesitated to put that line in, and I'm actually still mulling over taking it out. (Is it too late to pull the book from the printer's?) Admitting that I wanted to be the center of attention could be construed as conceited and not humble. However, it took me a long time to get here, and I'm not interested in being humble if it means dimming my light. (By the way, have you ever noticed that it's rarely ever men who use the word *humble* as an example of a redeeming characteristic?) No one wants to be around a blowhard or braggart, but I think there's a happy medium between forcefully yet respectfully stating what you want, being acknowledged for your talents, and being true to yourself, *and* being a pious, "Who, *me?* I don't deserve this" kind of martyr who actually wants it all but can't admit it. RIP to Little Richard, the *king* of telling people anytime and anyplace that he was the architect of rock 'n' roll and that everyone from the Beatles to the Rolling Stones stole from him. If more of us had the gumption, the confidence of Little Richard, we wouldn't be in this mess of having to relearn to dream. We would have taken life by the balls and shouted "A-wop-bop-a-loo-mop, a-lop-bam-bom" until we got what we wanted.

Thankfully I cleaned up my mess and actually mastered how to dream, tapping into my childhood fantasies of traveling the world, wearing fab clothes, and drinking martinis—my life actually resembles that today, except my drink of choice is tequila. I also loved writing and telling stories, and as an adult, I've written for magazines, penned this book, and I tell stories for a living on TV and radio. For twenty years, I made a career in fashion; later on, I also became a fashion editor at large and styled quite a few celebrities. I haven't quite conquered the singing and dancing as a profession, but I *have* appeared onstage in a professional hosting capacity and sung various parts of songs. I was always trying to sing on any TV show I've ever hosted, but due to copyright laws, the producers rarely allowed it (or so they say; I think they were trying to block my dreams, damn them). I've also been known to do a high kick and a two-step onstage, as I'm obvi revving up for my professional debut singing and dancing. All things considered, I'm actually doing many of the things I was passionate about as a kid, and those are the same passions I quit my job to pursue. Come on, full-circle moment!

Whenever I tell stories about how I went from advertising to being a TV/radio host, the first thing people say is that it's not that easy for everyone. "Easy" and "living your dream"—yeah, that's not a word combo you will ever see in play. None of it has been easy, but it's also not easy living a placeholder life.

One morning in July 2004, while I was still working at *Rolling*

Stone but had only a few more months before I quit, I woke up and wrote this in my journal:

> Dearest Beverly,
>
> I know sometimes you doubted yourself, didn't see all the things you could achieve, but look at you! Just by stepping out the tiniest bit with acting, photography, travel, look how much happier you've become. Look at the new things you've added to your repertoire.
>
> You must continue to push, sing, you are musical, so SING! Run, you want to move fast, unencumbered, do it whenever you can. Write a one-woman show, do music chronicles, do Englewood Cliffs [hip-hop's version of *Sunset Boulevard*], go to church, praise Him, feel all your emotions.

My journals are filled with pep talks like this one. They helped align and motivate me. Being able to write out my dreams was the first step toward manifesting them.

Join me. Sit down in a quiet space, don't go on social media—I don't know about you, but the first things I reach for during "downtime" are distractions; my top three are food, drink, and social media feeds—put down the Moscow Mule and macaroni and cheese, stop watching your chiropractor's IG Live show, and push yourself to write out your wildest, most outrageous people-will-think-I'm-crazy dreams. Remember, you don't have to share them with anyone. Just dream about what your life would look like if you didn't have insecurities or obligations (familial or financial). See what comes up, and then—here comes the challenge—look at how you can start instituting tiny bits of those dreams into your life. My friend Lisa Bonner is a lawyer by trade, but on the side she's a travel journalist who has been all over the world *for free*. My son/friend

Wardell Malloy is a music publishing executive but he's always had a passion for photography. He started taking lessons, bought lots of expensive equipment, and began shooting friends for fun. Well, you know the photo on the front cover of this book? Wardell, aka Warren White (his photography pseudonym), shot that photo. He received that opportunity because he invested in himself but most importantly, he dared to dream.

Are you obsessed with makeup tutorials? Maybe you've gotten so good at it that you blend your own colors to get a highly pigmented eyeshadow or the perfect gloss on your lipstick. Well, that sounds like multi-millionaire Supa Cent of the cosmetic empire The Crayon Case. Raynell "Supa Cent" Steward is a single mom and former waitress from New Orleans who rose to social media prominence just by being herself—funny, down to earth, and raunchy, but always relatable and inspirational. She also loved makeup, and in 2017 she created The Crayon Case, a brand that caters to novice makeup artists. Her line made $1.37 million in just *one hour* on Cyber Monday in 2019. My sister is a fantastic home cook and the first person everyone calls when they need good food for potluck. Well, guess what? She's turned her gift and passion into a business! She's catered meals for several TV productions, including shows I've been on, and hosted holiday pop-ups, where she sells cakes so good, folks have risked running up their "sugar" (diabetes) just for a slice. Her business is named Miss Lolly's Kitchen, after our mom. Awww, all the feels!

Here's a Bevelation: Once you receive payment for an endeavor, you've gone from amateur status to being a pro. #SexWorkers OfTheWorldUniteAndUnionize.

Please believe when I tell you that I started changing my life in small increments, and I'm a size queen, so it wasn't an easy transition. I expected and wanted it all, even if I had to stretch to accommodate it . . . are we still talking about daring to dream? Anyhoo, it still took *four years* to quit my job at *Vibe* once I realized I needed to change my life. So, don't badger yourself or allow anyone else to. Go at your own pace, and don't compare yourself to anyone else—especially not on social media. There's a lot of catfishing that goes on, so always do a background check before making some stranger's life your goal.

Run your race and remember, there's no reason to go out and blow up your entire existence. I didn't do it, so I won't advocate that you derail your life. That works only if you've got a wealthy and supportive husband or a trust fund. If you have either one of those things, put this book down and start your business *immediately*. But if that's not your story, I urge you to examine your list of dreams and see where the entry point is, what you can do to move a step closer without doing something drastic like quitting your job because you've read this book. That's it (for now)! Take that class, volunteer for an organization with a mission you're passionate about, go in to work and lead that meeting, wake up early on the weekends (before the kids, your spouse, Twitter) and write, try something new that has always intrigued you, but that you convinced yourself wasn't for you. Well, after reading this chapter, you know it's all for you—if you *dare to dream*!

My first trip to Paris, I was accosted at the Tuileries.
I wonder if he was after my goodies from Colette (RIP)
or my goodies in those jeans.

Broke but Blissful

'LL ADMIT IT: I WAS DELUSIONAL WHEN I DECIDED TO PURSUE a career in entertainment. Folks usually think of optimism as the nectar of youth. Yet, I was thirty-eight years old and you couldn't tell me I wasn't going to have a TV show within a year of quitting my job.

I'm not surprised if you're reading this in disbelief. My current self is incredulous as well. If I could go back in time, I would probably ask past me, "Really, lady? You believe that some TV executive is just waiting for a thirty-eight-year-old Black woman with no TV experience to come on the scene so they can give her a job?"

But I believed it so much that I would not make alternate plans in case it didn't work out the way it was mapped out on my vision board. I had no plan B (condoms are cheaper) because I believed a backup would signal to the universe that I didn't believe whole-heartedly that I could change my life.

I admire the chutzpah of the woman who told her boss at *Rolling*

Stone she was quitting her job to do "whatever I like," that she was going to "write, act, sing, travel, do photography, deejay, paint, be a fire eater, and maybe even juggle." When I walked out the door of 1290 Avenue of the Americas having committed to do all the above—okay, I never made it to juggling or fire eating, but there's still time—I had a good chunk of change in savings. I won't tell you the exact amount, but I had enough to put a down payment on a pre-gentrification Harlem brownstone. (I decided to opt for betting the bank on a dream life versus my dream home.) I actually thought it was enough money to last until my big break.

It's important to note that my confidence was on a Kanye West/Trump level. I really thought I would secure a TV job within a year; we now know that that level of confidence also veers into delusion. Here's a Bevelation for you: Confidence is good, but it doesn't pay the bills.

Seven years—*not one*—after leaving *Rolling Stone*, I was hired to cohost *Fashion Queens* on Bravo. But before that call came, I had to go through an entire journey, one that forced me to find out exactly what I was made of. Turns out: strong stuff. It seems I'm nothin' if not resilient. It also showed me what I could do when my back was up against a wall. When I decided to write this book, I chose to be *incredibly* honest about my journey. To some, it may seem like I decided I wanted to do TV and then . . . *voilà*! There I was on the screen, opinionated and busty. But the real deal is that getting to my dreams took sacrifice on myriad levels.

I speak to so many people who believe that because they "tried" to pursue their dreams and it didn't happen according to their time frame, they felt they'd done their part and should go back to the regularly scheduled programming (i.e., the life they didn't like). Here's the thing: I get it. The fear of judgment holds you back from stepping out and announcing you're going to do something new. There will be people who'll whisper behind your back that you're crazy, and a few bold ones will say it directly to your face. This will probably cause your confidence to waver. I know. There were many days when I had to write positive affirmations to combat what I'd heard from other folks about my pursuing my dreams. I get you and your shaky self-esteem. I get that proclaiming that you're going to pursue a goal and change your life is a big step—but honestly, that's just step one. As I learned, the big test comes when the money runs out.

For me, the first two years of my journey went according to plan. I was writing for *Paper*, *Interview*, *Glamour*, and *Essence* magazines. I was appearing as a panelist on shows like E! Network's *The Fabulous Life of Paris Hilton* and similar series on BET. In the early 2000s, folks were obsessed with being fabulous and obvi my new life fit the bill—but my wages didn't allow me to pay bills. I was so euphoric when I was assigned to write a Rihanna cover story for *Paper*—that is, until I was told it would pay only five hundred dollars. With wages like that, I realized no one was going to be chronicling the *Fabulous Life of Bevy Smith* anytime soon.

And that was okay—until it wasn't. My finances took a major hit when I lost my gig as fashion editor at large at *Vibe*. That's right. About six months after leaving *Rolling Stone*, I went back to *Vibe*, but this time, I was on the editorial side. The editor in chief, my ride-or-die bestie Mimi Valdés (who has continually employed me throughout my life-changing journey; get yourself a Mimi), and Bob Miller (one of the owners of *Vibe* at the time) realized that all the luxury fashion advertisers had pulled out of the magazine when I stopped working there. So, when *Vibe* found out I'd quit *Rolling Stone*, they wanted me back.

I had already decreed in my journal that there was absolutely no way I was going back into an advertising or marketing job, even temporarily. I was on a creative path, but I was also used to making coins. I wasn't so sure that I wouldn't get lured back into my old life; old habits die hard. So, I negotiated the fashion editor at large position. It was a dream job: I wasn't required to come in to the office daily, I selected which celebs I wanted to shoot for the editorials I oversaw, and I still traveled to Europe for fashion shows, but this time as an editor, so there were no needy clients to babysit. The annual salary was $80,000, less than my old expense account budget. I was making far less than I had as an ad director, but I was able to be far more creative, and that was my goal for my new life.

OMG! I was actually doing a job I had dreamed of: I was working in fashion on the editorial side. No more selling ad pages. Now I had the opportunity to work with some great celebs. I shot Zoe Saldana for a spread and took the rapper T.I. to Milan Fashion Week, expeditiously! And my name was appearing in print because I also wrote an advice column, called Bevy Says, for *Vibe*'s female spinoff magazine, *Vibe Vixen*.

That fab situation ended abruptly—and dare I say, tragically?—in the summer of 2006, when I was laid off because of management restructuring. I went from having a small but steady paycheck to none. In this one case, I will agree that size had not mattered. Something was better than nothing. (I would never admit that to a man I'm dating, so please don't share.) Still, I didn't panic. I had a few dollars saved and had started taking public transportation— much to the distress of my neighbors.

There was a barbershop on the corner of my block, and when I was living the high life, the barbers would see me getting in and out of town cars with luggage from my exotic travels or shopping bags (aka my medication). One of the best things about Harlem is that we have many public transportation options—I tried to keep that a secret, but the gentrifiers caught on—and right across from my building is a bus stop. So, in an effort to squeeze out my remaining coins, I'd take the bus. One day, I stepped outside and one of the barbers from the shop called me over with a concerned face. He asked, "Are you okay?" I replied, "Yes, I'm good. Why?" And he said, "Well, I'm so used to seeing you dip in and out of cars. Now I'm seeing you take the bus a lot. Are you sure you're okay?"

For a lot of folks, that would have been an embarrassing moment. So many of us are ashamed when we go through financial difficulties. However, I had absolutely no shame in my game. As a matter of fact, I felt proud that I was able to go from riding in town cars exclusively to taking the bus. See, I knew it would make for a good story in my journey. Also, I had made this choice, and while I didn't expect to find myself in *such* reduced financial circumstances, once I was in that position, I kept it moving. My bank balance would not define my journey. I was truly broke but blissful.

That's not to say I didn't gag when it first dawned on me how broke I was. And of course it happened during the Christmas season. (The holidays will always let you know how financially challenged you truly are.) There I was, putting together my tiny shopping list, and checking it twice—you know the drill: robbing Peter to pay Paul—when I realized I couldn't pay any of the P's because I had totally run out of money. The money I'd stashed away had dwindled down to a couple thousand bucks. Savings evaporate quickly when you're giving your mother an allowance; helping to pay your parents' bills; pursuing your creative life by taking expensive classes in photography, acting, improv, deejaying; plus taking trips to LA to network and mingle with anyone who will take a meeting with you.

◆ ◆ ◆

It had been a little over a year since I'd left *Rolling Stone*, and though I get an A for effort, for actually creating a budget, I earned a major F, as in *fail*, as in *fuck-up*, for not being a better steward of my money. I really believed I had been living low to the ground. When I examined my expenses, it didn't seem I had a lot of monthly bills. But what I'd missed in my "Take This Job and Shove It" euphoria was that I had an entire *lifestyle* I was not accustomed to supporting financially.

My mistake: I didn't alter my behavior to match my new reality. Like many single people who live in big cities, I continued to go out to dinner almost every night—except that I no longer had an expense account. Back when I did, those dinners at fab, chic restaurants where the tab was, on average, two hundred bucks per person weren't being paid for with my money. I also now had my own cell phone. Before I started working at *Vibe* in 1998, I didn't even have a cell phone. When I took my job there, the company purchased a phone for me and paid the bill. So, when I quit, it didn't even dawn on me to calculate my cell phone bill into my monthly expenses. Ditto when I traveled overseas for work: back in the day, I would simply tack on a vacation while I was already in Europe on business. For example, if I was in Milan for fashion shows, I would hop over to Rome or the Amalfi coast, or maybe Switzerland. True, while I was officially on vacation, my company didn't pick up my meals or other expenses, but I saved thousands by not paying for airfare.

Then there were the little perks of working for a music magazine that I hadn't accounted for—like never paying for concert tickets. I love live music, but I started loving it less when I realized that sitting in the first five rows at a Jay-Z show will cost you at least five hundred bucks, and that's not including the premium booze and free-range chicken tenders. (What? I should sit there thirsty and hungry while listening to Jay-Z rap "Hard Knock Life," actually experiencing said hard-knock life? I don't think so.)

I'd never really given much thought to those kinds of perks. When you're in that life, those extras are just a given. But those "good" jobs, they suck you in and start to define you—not just to others, but to yourself. I didn't necessarily believe I needed all the trappings. I thought I was prepared to scale back on them, but I had no idea I would be completely forced off the scale.

I was under financial duress, but that didn't affect my popularity in the fashion scene. During the holiday season, invitations to all kinds

of chic parties and dinners poured in. Most magazines and big fashion houses host decadent events, glittering parties where everyone
dresses up to maximize the holiday cheer. I might have been broke,
but I still had my garments, shoes, and bags. So, I "shopped my
closet" and put together looks that belied my cash-strapped existence.

And at one of those chic holiday dinner parties—the best kind:
where you get a full meal versus just appetizers—I became an
accidental entrepreneur! This party happened to be a Hugo Boss
Christmas dinner at Nobu. Now, if you don't know Nobu, let me
fill you in. It's a sushi restaurant where dinner can easily cost three
hundred bucks per person. It's also a celebrity haunt and partially
owned by Robert DeNiro. It's *fancy*, and Black women are always
welcome there. (Hey, Bobby!) It had been a minute since I'd been
able to afford Nobu, so I walked in the door dreaming of black
cod, creamy rock shrimp, and lychee martinis. But when I arrived,
I realized I was the only person there with no job. I had no cre-
dentials. I wasn't Bevy from Rolling Stone or Beverly Smith from
Vibe. I was Bevy Smith from . . . *nowhere*. I also realized, though,
that I was *still in the room where it happened*. And that's when it hit
me that people liked me, they really liked ME! That is, they hadn't
invited me because of what I could do for them as a fashion editor or
a fashion advertising director. They had bought into BEVY SMITH.

At that moment, I decided that things weren't as bad as they
seemed. After all, likability is major social currency. The drinks were
flowing, and I was consuming them like it was my last time ever to
have a lychee martini, which technically could have been true. (Those
tasty cocktails run about twenty bucks a pop, and I was slurping
them down.) As I was about to leave, I had to make a choice: take
a twenty-five-dollar cab ride home or ride the rails, aka the subway.

Now, remember, I was dressed to the nines, including a fur, stilettos, and a cleavage-baring dress. On a sober day, that's not great
attire for the subway. And even after about eight drinks, I still had

my wits about me enough to know that this could end terribly on the 2 train! So, I chose the taxi option and committed to being on a budget even tighter than my dress—what? I had been eating carbs due to my limited funds—for the rest of the week.

As I was staggering outside to find a cab, I heard someone say, "Bevy!" It was Omarion, formerly of the boy band B2K. I'd styled Omarion when I was a *Vibe* editor at large, dressing him in a Dolce & Gabbana suit that he loved so much he asked to wear it to his birthday party, where he had a dance-off with a not-yet-famous Chris Brown. I was impressed by what a lovely young man he was, and I'd enjoyed working with him. Now I was so happy to see him! He was just embarking on a successful solo career, which is why I said to him, "OMG, I was just at a dinner with the top fashion editors for *GQ, Esquire*, and *Men's Health* . . . You should have been there!" As I said it, a lightbulb went off: there's no way Omarion would get into that room unless I escorted him in! At this point, fashion hadn't yet become democratized (i.e., they weren't interested in diversity like they pretend to be today). Yes, the designers loved Puffy, Mary, and Lil' Kim, but if you weren't a multi-platinum artist with crossover appeal, they wouldn't lend you their clothes or extend a discount to you, and fashion magazines wouldn't include you in even a small story.

I was reflecting on how hard it was for Black artists who actually shape pop culture to gain access to the fashion industry. I had a lot on my mind that night, including hoping that the cab meter wouldn't clock a dime over twenty-five dollars, because if it did, I'd have had to jump out and run home—thus proving thousands of cab drivers right that they should not take people to Harlem. Once the meter started going, it became clear it was going to be less than twenty-five, so I relaxed and started thinking about all the dinners I used to host in Milan: I'd invite representatives from the top fashion brands and introduce them to the top Black music stars we'd brought over for Fashion Week. Heading uptown, I thought about bringing that concept stateside and starting a business where I'd host dinners on behalf of music artists. I'd invite fashion brands and editors to meet them in the hope of getting the two sides to collaborate (i.e., get the Black celebrity media coverage or a check).

A lot of people keep their ideas close to their vest for fear of someone "stealing" them. That's a philosophy I've never bought into. Here's a Bevelation: Anyone can come up with an idea; they're like the following cliché—a dime a dozen. But can they execute the plan? Strategy and execution are what manifest a dream into a reality. I'm all about using my resources to make things work. Which is why the next thing I did in that taxi was take my eyes off the meter and call Cara Donato.

I'd mentored Cara when she was an intern at *Vibe*. Afterward, she joined Atlantic Records as the PR director. (She's now an executive VP at one of the largest record labels in the world.) I asked Cara if she thought record labels would be interested in paying me to host dinners to get their "urban" artists more exposure in the fashion world. Not only did she immediately say yes, but she added that she was pretty sure Kevin Liles, then president of Atlantic, would love to do a dinner for the Grammy Award–winning artist Musiq Soulchild.

Most people in my position—getting paid to host a dinner for a major company—would also be focused on doing everything themselves, so they wouldn't have to split the money. However, that's being penny wise and pound foolish. Which is why, after talking to Cara, I teamed up with my bestie, and now business partner/publicist, Aimee Morris.

Details aren't my thing, and if I had attempted to put together the dinner all on my own, things would have fallen through the cracks. The key to being a successful entrepreneur is repeat business, and you don't get repeat business if clients aren't pleased with the services rendered. It's all about execution. So, I needed Aimee on my team. Not only was she a godsend because she's incredibly organized, but she is also very tough with clients. For one thing, Aimee made sure the record labels we worked with paid us up front. She had worked at record labels and explained to me—and not so patiently, BTW; that Aimee is a taskmaster—that because we were two women with a small business, we would be at the bottom of the totem pole when it came to sending out checks. If we didn't insist on payment right away, we might have to wait months for it. Y'all already know I had buses to catch. I needed my money ASAP.

The first "Dinner with Bevy" happened at the end of January 2007. We hosted about ten editors and fashion influencers at a restaurant in Manhattan's Meatpacking District. I had wanted to do the dinner in Harlem, but even though Bill Clinton had his offices on 125th Street, folks acted like they'd need a passport to get there! "Dinner with Bevy" wouldn't make me rich, but now I knew I could make money on my own as the "Accidental Entrepreneur." I call myself that because I'd never previously thought of working for myself. Creating "Dinner with Bevy" gave me much-needed reassurance that my sales experience was transferable, proof that I knew how to sell a product, especially if that product was me.

Dinner with Bevy, LLC, was conceived as a quick fix to my temporary financial struggles, but it has been so much more. For years, it became my calling card, upping my profile in every regard, from garnering me publicity (the *New York Times* called me a "noted hostess") to securing me TV work. I appeared on my friend's Bravo show *Chef Roblé & Co.*, finally hosting a dinner in Harlem for my fancy downtown friends; to this day, people gush about the show, saying that it was the first time they ever saw me on TV.

All that from running into Omarion at Nobu while I was drunk! That's why I always keep an open mind when it comes to ideas. You never know where an idea will take you. So, get drunk and hope to run into an R&B star!

Dinner with Bevy started off without a hitch, and by spring, Aimee and I were hosting two dinners a month on average. The average rate for each dinner was three thousand dollars—if you're thinking of booking a Dinner with Bevy, please know that the rate has increased; add at least a zero—which didn't include the cost of the dinner. That was just my fee, from which Aimee received a percentage.

So, I had figured out a tiny revenue stream that allowed me to continue pursuing my career as a TV host while developing new relationships with celebrities. (To this day I book guests on *Bevela-tions*, my radio show, because of how many celebs know me from my dinner parties.) Yay, I'm an entrepreneur now! All my problems are solved, right?

Sounds good, but before we start popping sparkling wine—for bus-riding Bevy, champagne wasn't remotely in the budget yet—this is what the reality looked like: I definitely could have made six thousand dollars (minus Aimee's percentage) a month work; it was a fraction of what I'd made just a few years ago, but I could have skated by—except I had more than a few past-due bills, so a lot of that money was used to play catch-up. Dinner with Bevy wasn't a lifeboat so much as a life preserver. I wasn't going to drown, but I still might die from hypothermia. (Y'all know Jack could have fit on that door, right?)

Still, also at this time, I started making real progress with my burgeoning TV career. First, I found two mentors, Alec and Monique Chenault, who groomed me for TV. Monique was the executive producer of *Access Hollywood*, and for two years she hired me to do celebrity interviews for the TV One version of the show. She also managed to get my interview included on the main show, which was hosted by Shaun Robinson. Monique taught me how to ask the tough questions but still be likable, a crucial skill to have when you're a celebrity interviewer.

Monique and Alec, through their production company, Mac-vision Entertainment, even found a way to incorporate Dinner with Bevy into an episode of *Access*. I hosted an entire weekend getaway with fashion insiders for the rapper T.I. in Atlanta, and it was filmed for the show. We took fashionistas who travel to Europe on a monthly basis out to the best soul food and strip joints in ATL, and to this day, my high-flying fashion friends ask me when I'm doing another trip like that. Alec and Monique *saw* me, the real me. They didn't just think of me as their fashion girl; they valued my broad knowledge of pop and lifestyle culture. And it was through Macvision that I got the chance to interview Denzel, Natalie Cole, and Gladys Knight and conduct the interviews for BET's Whitney Houston memorial special, *BET Remembers Whitney*, on camera. On camera is an important distinction to make; the next time you're watching an entertainment show, especially a red carpet segment, you'll see that often the interviewer is off camera, unseen. Having Alec and Monique in my corner meant that I was always *on camera*, even when the networks they worked for didn't "get it"—get *me*—including Black networks. (Black networks really had a problem with my ample cleavage. Alec and Monique spent a lot of time convincing the powers that be that this dark-skinned, forty-year-old woman's breasts weren't offensive. Oh, the joys of the glamorous life of TV hosting!) They advocated for me and I wasn't about to let them down. I was a prepared interviewer; I wasn't going to squander the opportunity or jeopardize their credibility. Like I told you, as Black folks in white work environments we get one chance, if that, and if we fail that means the next person won't even get in the door. The Chenaults always took chances on new talent, Black talent, and they are a cornerstone of my TV career and the first time I ever had Black mentors. My fashion/advertising mentors taught me so much, but never underestimate the power of having mentors with shared experiences.

At the same time I was working with the Chenaults, I began working with BET directly on various projects, including covering New York Fashion Week (for no pay; I had never in my life worked for free and I never will again) on the network's now-defunct entertainment show *The Black Carpet.* On that shoot, they sent a green but smart producer, Leigh Davenport, to produce the segment. I got the feeling that they didn't expect much. Clearly, they had underestimated me and Leigh, because between my knowing everyone in fashion, many of the stars sitting in the front row, and Leigh's hustle, we created entertaining and informative fashion segments.

My TV bookings were starting to manifest, but they weren't attached to checks. Thankfully, I was also booking corporate speaking engagements for brands like Morgan Stanley and Boost Mobile, jobs that entailed speaking on panels. But I really started making my mark as a public speaker when I got booked by HBO to host its Short Film Competition at the American Black Film Festival. Before that gig, I had never hosted a public event. But early on during my career change, at a Housing Works meeting, I met Dennis Williams, a young HBO executive. We hit it off, and I told him about my dreams of being a TV host. A few weeks later, Dennis called to ask if I was interested in hosting the film contest in Miami. Of course, I was! But the decision wasn't his alone. He could get me in the room, but I had to impress his boss, a delightful, full-of-life, keep-it-100 Dominican woman from Washington Heights. I went in and met with Lucinda Martinez, and she decided that Dennis was right, I would make a wonderful host. Dennis and Lucinda took a chance on me and now, for the past fourteen years, I've been the host for HBO's ABFF Short Film Competition, and we are family.

❖ ❖ ❖

It was those wins that let me know I was on the right track. I was actually achieving the goals that only a few years ago I had hoped for but had no concrete strategy to accomplish, had been afraid to even dream of, including writing for national magazines and appearing on TV. My career was on the upswing, but I still wasn't making enough money to maintain my greatly diminished lifestyle.

Let me count the ways my lifestyle went from champagne to malt liquor: I had to cut premium cable, disconnect my telephone landline (which actually made me look like an early adopter; only boomers have landlines), and you already know I was Bus-riding Bevy on the regular. All this cost cutting made a difference, but . . . not enough to keep me out of housing court.

Now, I was aware that I was behind in my rent by two months, but I also knew I was only temporarily "not liquid." (That's what rich people say when they have no cash.) So, I was quite outraged when an eviction notice was slid under my door! I mean, how could Charlie, the building's maintenance supervisor, do this? I'd tipped him at Christmas! Where was the loyalty? Filled with disdain, I looked at the notice and realized I was going to have to make the dreaded trek to housing court. It's like forty minutes on the subway or forty dollars in a taxi (so you know I was on the subway), and then when you get to court, there are lines that stretch out the courthouse doors. Once you're in, you run the risk of being fondled by surly police officers as they check you for weapons. My, how the fab had fallen!

This eviction notice was particularly alarming because I had a New York unicorn: a rent-stabilized apartment. (Rent stabilization means that no matter what is going on in my beloved Gotham— which is rife with gentrification and cries of "The rent's too damn high"—*my* rent never increases by more than 3 percent from year to year.) My apartment was a saving grace that I was not about to lose.

Oftentimes people look at those who are single and believe they have no obligations to anyone other than themselves. Well, I've found that not to be true. I know very few peers who aren't helping someone—for many Black professionals, philanthropy begins at home; when we make it, often we have to reach back and help others in our families. Maybe it's their parents, their grown-ass spoiled kids, or extended family. Another Bevelation: When you're trying to soar, you can't have folks holding you down. Find a way, if not to cut ties, then at least to loosen them a bit. You have an obligation to take care of yourself, your school-age children—that doesn't include your twenty-eight-year-old daughter who's on her third graduate degree in ornithology—and your elderly parents. However, if you're taking care of able-bodied adults to the point where it's putting you in a financial bind and you can't pursue the life you want (and I'm not telling you anything you don't already know, but just don't want to face), CUT THEM OFF! I know Lil' Brown Bevy is supposed to be incredibly empathetic, but she's also nobody's fool. Thankfully, I don't have family that expects me to support them. Even my parents understood. When I tightened my belt so much it could have been a waist trainer, they never complained about the loss of perks, although they did get nervous when the landlord slipped late-rent notices under their door.

Faced with covering my own rent and making sure my parents weren't homeless, I started selling my clothes, bags, and, of course, shoes. I took inventory of my stash and realized there was *gold* in the Goyard. My dear friend Fred Jackson took my bags, placed them on his eBay account, and took a small commission on each sale. Selling those things went toward a few months of rent, mine and my parents'. Remember, I told you buying those three Goyard bags during one shopping spree would come in handy! (The shopaholics reading this probably feel vindicated—well, don't! Admitting that you have a problem is the first step!)

Through it all, my faith kept me going. I was always able to look on the bright side and know that "this too shall pass." Which brings me back to housing court. Although I had to make that trip about five times, I was always able to figure out a payment plan with my landlord and was never evicted. One of the few good things about living in NYC is that the landlord/tenant laws are beneficial to the tenant (at least for now).

So, I avoided eviction, but I couldn't avoid being recognized.

Thankfully, this was a time before social media. Now, if you are on TV and riding coach on an airplane cross-country, people will call you out and plaster a picture of you in a middle seat eating your small bag of peanuts, just to mock you. Imagine what Twitter would have done with a photo of me in housing court. Yikes! At the time, I wasn't mortified when I was recognized. In fact, I took it as a good sign. I wasn't a regular on any TV show, yet people remembered me! My interpretation? I'm on my way! I *told* you I was a glass-half-full kind of girl.

Time for another Bevelation: When trying to change your life, finding GRATITUDE in all things is essential, even being recognized in housing court. On my way down to court I would listen to my gratitude playlist I'd made, replaying "Be Alright," by Mary J. Blige, over and over. "Trouble don't last always," she sings, and I kept repeating that to myself as I took the subway to avoid being evicted.

The best thing about my broke-but-blissful journey is that I was again reminded that the love I received had nothing to do with my job title. People genuinely supported me. Many folks will tell you that once you don't have a prestigious position or status, your phone stops ringing, and that people who once picked up for you on the first ring won't return a call for months. That wasn't my experience, but as my dad, Smitty, always says, you can get out only what you put in. I think back on my career, and I see that I put *a lot* into my work—but I put even more into my relationships. I have so many friends who started off as clients.

And those same friends came through when I was transitioning into a new career. Billy Paretti hired me to be a Hennessy brand ambassador, a job with a $2,500-a-month stipend, plus a case of Hennessy, which made me quite popular at house parties, baby showers, housewarmings, and cookouts and with sundry lovers. Hey, I was an ambassador! My friends Kim Hastreiter, Mickey Boardman, and David Hershkovits allowed me to write whatever I wanted for *Paper*, and they handled influencer marketing for Target. So, when that retail behemoth opened its first-ever Manhattan store in Harlem, Kim selected me to be a Target ambassador/influencer! This gig not only paid me a few thousand dollars, but more important, it garnered me my first-ever written mention in the *New York Times*. That Target connection also allowed me the opportunity to host a Dinner with Bevy for Pharrell at the iconic Château Marmont, with Usher, Charlize Theron, Cameron Diaz, and many other A-list stars.

It seemed that I had help every step of the way and in every aspect of my new life. My dear friend/hubby Stan Williams edited each and every magazine piece I wrote during the early days, when I will still unsure about my voice—and he never charged me! My friend Shavon (aka Shay of #The80sLadies) would take me out to dinner every single week, sometimes a couple of times a week. We would go to local restaurants in Harlem and eat really high-caloric food and drinks. Sometimes I would feel guilty, and Shavon would tell me to shut up and eat my hot wings! Having a friend like Shavon, with whom I could just blow off steam, was a real godsend.

It's also important to have friends who are going through similar struggles. Many of my friends with corporate jobs didn't understand why I didn't just go back to work in an office. So, I had to stop hanging out with them. I didn't need anyone messing with my vision, having me second-guessing my life choices. Thankfully, I had two friends from my *Vibe* days in the trenches with me: Ali Muhammad, aka Mr. Muhammad, and Damien Lemon, aka D.Lemon. (Interesting that we all have aliases.) We had all worked in marketing and advertising before deciding to pursue more creative lives—D.Lemon as a comedian/actor and Ali Muhammad as a content creator, producer/director, and professional storyteller. We would meet up for a cheap lunch and take turns giving one another pep talks. We each had a different level of stress in our lives. Ali is a husband, a father of three, and the owner of a brownstone in Brooklyn that some hipster would just love to take off his hands should he foreclose. (They'd probably turn it into a commune that makes vegan honey potato chips, packaged in bags made from recycled condoms; Brooklyn hipsters wear me out!) D.Lemon was entering the highly competitive field of stand-up comedy, a business where young Black men are expected to have a "you know what I don't like about white people" joke in their repertoire. But D.Lemon's comedy wasn't that. He was droll, sardonic, and a bit of an asshole (only onstage), so we nicknamed him The Black Larry David (as in Larry David of *Curb Your Enthusiasm*). Damien was breaking the mold. As I write this, I'm happy to report that we are all currently making money and working on projects we love, ones based on our passions, our dreams.

I have so many wonderful stories about my generous friends, but there is one in particular who enabled me to cross the finish line into being a bona fide TV personality. As an entrepreneur, you will have slow periods throughout the year. Traditionally I'm not just slow with freelance work between September and November; I'm stagnant. (For years, I was broke on my birthday, November 2. Send gifts!) And that one particular broke-but-blissful season—five years after quitting *Rolling Stone*, that season when Bus-riding Bevy had to go to housing court—I did the math and realized I needed a few thousand dollars to tide me over, since it would be a few months of no checks. Tallying up how much money I didn't have, I felt a little tired.

I was keeping the faith, but also keeping it real. Showing up at housing court works only if you can see a light at the end of the tunnel, also known as a check on the horizon. But my horizon was flat, dry, barren, very *Grapes of Wrath*. I would wake up from nightmares, thinking I was at my parents' apartment because I had been thrown out of mine. Psychologically, I was beginning to get as frayed as the golden-brown mink coat I wore in my early *Vibe* days. I had done a few TV pilots that hadn't gotten picked up, and signed a few development deals that hadn't taken off. I was beginning to think that maybe I needed to get a job, a real high-paying job, to get back on my feet.

Thankfully, because I let my friends and family know all along my journey that I was financially broke but spiritually abundant, I didn't have to hide or feel ashamed. I spoke honestly to them, expressing to them that unless I received a lump sum, my five years of striving to become a TV personality would be coming to an end. In my spirit, I didn't believe that I was going to have to give up my dream, but I was pragmatic enough to know that I couldn't go on walking a financial tightrope. Finally, it was my dear friend, my sister Cheryl Calegari, who was the catalyst for my being able to sustain long enough to manifest my dream.

Cheryl and I met when she did PR at Tommy Hilfiger and I was at *Vibe*. She was a crazy Italian American girl from Connecticut who worshipped Mary J. Blige. We hit it off through work and became *real friends*. She came to my sister's house for a cookout, and you know how tight you have to be with someone to invite them to a cookout. We weren't industry friends; this was *real love*, just like Mary sings about it. Through the years, Cheryl's career continued to soar, and she began doing international marketing for major brands. She was based in Shanghai when I was changing my life, always cheering me on from afar and always taking me to Barney's for a fancy three-hour lunch when she came to town. Cheryl also bought me a Yves Saint Laurent bag when I mentioned I hadn't had a new handbag in years. I still have that bag. I carried it almost exclusively for several years, and I will never get rid of it because it represents a special time in my life, when I was broke but blissful.

I was at my wit's end, and I realized that as much as I thought I had humbled myself by letting folks know about my financial difficulties, my trips to housing court, and my taking the bus when I used to be in and out of town cars, none of that compared to the moment when I had to call Cheryl in Shanghai and ask her for a loan that I had no idea when I could pay back. Cheryl is that friend everyone needs—she's easy to talk to, doesn't judge, and is laugh-out-loud funny! She has also always supported my dreams, so when I called to tell her I was broke and if I didn't get a loan, I was going to have to get a job, thereby ending my quest to become America's Next TV Host, she laughed and said yes immediately.

A challenge began when we tried to figure out how she could wire me money from China. After a few days of her running around Shanghai, the wire came through, and I paid up my rent for a few months, put my head down, and resolved to spend no money at all.

I knew time was running out for this vision of mine to manifest. I had been at it for almost six years now, and yes, I had had a few victories, but I could no longer go on treading water financially. I was about to be forty-five years old, and the struggle was getting even older than I was.

I cut off all spending. I also put myself on a food budget. I would buy ground turkey meat and make four meals out of that one serving. But the culinary feat I'm most proud of is what I was able to do with a can of salmon! That one can was breakfast, lunch, and dinner. In the morning, I'd make salmon croquettes using an egg, onions (Vidalia preferred, but sometimes a yellow onion from the bodega would have to do), bread crumbs, and Old Bay seasoning. Mix it together, lightly pan fry in olive oil (if I was flush, but if I was really down on my luck, good old vegetable oil), and voilà! You have six hefty salmon cakes. Pair them with eggs for breakfast, French fries for lunch, and a leafy green salad and rice for dinner. A can of salmon will cost you about four dollars. To put that in context, I used to spend *two hundred dollars* on one meal.

A big test happened during my season of salmon croquettes. I was hanging out a lot in Harlem because I couldn't afford to go downtown, so most of my leisure events were an eight-dollar cab ride away from my home (versus twenty-five if I'd gone to Midtown). Hanging out in a local bar, I met a man with a designer clothing store. He was a fan, and he asked if I would host a Dinner with

Bevy for him for ten thousand dollars cash. He desperately wanted to attract a celebrity clientele to his store, and he knew about my dinners. Now, at the time, I was stretching a four-dollar can of salmon, so ten grand would have been a windfall. However, the man had some shady business dealings, and I realized that as much as I needed the money, I needed my brand unsullied even more.

Here's a Bevelation: All money ain't good money, and sometimes taking money from the wrong people will cost you more than you can truly afford to pay back. That was certainly the case with the clothing store owner: later on, he was involved in a stabbing at a club. Had I done that dinner for him, my name and, more important, the Dinner with Bevy brand would have been linked to his. I dodged that bullet—or that shank!

It was also during salmon croquette season that I called my friend, the professional storyteller Ali Muhammad. As I mentioned, Mr. Muhammad and D.Lemon would often meet me for lunch to commiserate and chop it up, but on this particular day, I called Ali for a solo lunch and announced that I was "Last Chance Bevy," meaning, if things didn't work out in the next year, I was going to throw in the towel, take a bow, do the whole swan song, *shut it down*. Still, I had an idea that Ali would be the perfect creative to follow me around docu-series style and film my last year of struggle. Either I would emerge a winner or pack away my dreams and get a real job.

We never did the docu-show, but I wish we had, because the next year, Dinner with Bevy rates catapulted due to major press coverage. I started working with even bigger corporate clients, with larger budgets—and I landed *Fashion Queens*, a weekly show on Bravo, and my first regular paycheck in *seven years*! You know that one of the first things I did was pay back Cheryl Calegari, right? And goddess that she is, she asked, "Are you sure you can?" #ShesABlessing

On *Fashion Queens*, I, along with two gender-fluid hairstylists from Atlanta, critiqued celebrity style. Seven years, and rewarded at last! It felt serendipitous. The number seven represents divine completion in the Bible. And getting that show definitely felt like a gift from God. We live in a world where folks want their wins instantaneously. I get it, but I'm glad that I'm a patient person. I know that when building something that's meant to last, it's all about what's in the *middle*, what binds the beginning and the end. It had been a hard but glorious journey, and that's because of my outlook, not because I didn't have struggles that tested me. I savored every win, every check, every job, no matter how little, seeing each as a sign to keep going, that I was on my way to fulfilling my destiny.

I know it's a cliché and I hate to be sappy, but in true Lil' Brown Bevy spirit, I'm a sentimental gal, so here goes: in life, it truly is the journey, not the destination. At every turn, I found happiness, meaning the five-hundred-dollar check was celebrated just like the fifty-*thousand*-dollar check. (Though, obviously the fifty-grand check was a far more exorbitant celebration.) Running out of money had forced me to become an entrepreneur, creating a business that in turn was a godsend beyond money. That business helped me build a brand that no one can ever take away from me. I own Dinner with Bevy and all its intellectual property. And I plan on revamping the brand and creating merchandise (including Dinner with Bevy meal prep, Dinner with Bevy tabletop design, and Dinner with Bevy pots, pans, mixers, etc.) so I can earn money while I sleep. (Come on, next level, passive income!) It also taught me that I have the ability to eat what I kill, and I actually gained confidence in knowing that I can go out and make money representing myself, not someone else's brand. These are valuable skills for anyone to acquire but especially for women and people of color. Oftentimes we have to create our own opportunities just to get noticed. When I chat with people who are newly unemployed and they start talking about trying to find a job, I always say, "In the meantime, why don't you find some money?" The challenges that I endured when I didn't have a steady paycheck taught me that if nothing else, I know how to make a way out of what seems like no way. I'm resilient and creative. As a Black woman in particular, I feel empowered that even through hard times, I stayed the course and created a life that I'm proud of. That's why I was broke but blissful.

Me and "Dr. Cherrie" on one of her rare trips back to the US

The Manhunt

I F YOU HAD ASKED ME IN MY TWENTIES IF I WOULD BE SINGLE IN my fifties, I would have responded, "*Hell* no, I will not be an old maid!" Welp. I guess you should hand me a mop and a broom because I'm definitely single.

Back when I was twenty-eight, I went to see *Waiting to Exhale* with my new boyfriend. Afterward, I walked out of the theater feeling so sorry for those women in their mid-thirties. They were single and middle-aged—when you're in your twenties, anyone over thirty-five is middle aged. Ah, youth! I was filled with concern and sympathy for those fictional characters. I was also positive that that *definitely* wasn't going to be me. Unlike them, I had a plan, and it began and ended with getting this guy to marry me.

Now, he wasn't the first man I'd thought about marrying. My first boyfriend, my first *everything*, gave me an engagement ring when I was seventeen. And my second boyfriend, five years later, gave me a ring as well. What's interesting about both those relationships is that I never really intended to marry either one. We never even set a date. The whole thing was ego based: I just wanted a ring. I was just elated that I got "chose." In my mind, which was shaped by rom-coms and women's magazines—with the exception of *Ms.*, Gloria Steinem would never—if you were in a committed relationship, to really prove his love, he had to want to marry you, right?

Listen, before you scoff at this thinking, look at Elizabeth Taylor and J.Lo. These lovely ladies seemed to have married, or at least been engaged to, everyone they ever had sex with, so there are precedents. From fairy tales where Prince Charming rides in on a white horse and saves the day (or at least a damsel in distress from being a spinster), to *Coming to America*, where Lisa becomes a queen from Queens, the world tells us that women are essentially born to be wives, so why wouldn't that have been my #LifeGoals?

The problem with this concept is that, based on divorce rates in America—40 to 50 percent of married couples—having marriage as a singular goal probably isn't a great idea. But what's a girl to do? Develop interests and passions outside of being the "wife of"? What are you, Oprah? Maybe if *O Magazine* had been around when I was in my twenties, I would have pursued fulfillment outside a relationship, but I didn't have a *What I Know for Sure* template to follow. Instead, what I knew for sure was "If I can just get married, it will be my husband's job to *make* me happy." Can anyone else relate to that idea, or is it just me and every person in a combative relationship who has appeared on *Divorce Court*, *The Maury Povich Show*, and *Iyanla Fix My Life*?

Have you ever heard of an MRS degree? A popular story line in movies from the 1950s or *The Marvelous Mrs. Maisel* series is a woman attends college not for a higher education but to find a husband. The phrase "She's getting her MRS degree" was most commonly used in the early twentieth century, when white women were allowed to attend universities, but weren't allowed to actually do anything with their degrees. Now, working outside the home wasn't something most Black women and certainly not the women I grew up around in Harlem had to fight to do. If anything, the women in my neighborhood probably looked at movies centered on bored suburban wives and thought, *I'll gladly trade places with you.*

For a long time, I did think the MRS degree life would be a good look for me. I never wanted to move to a suburb, but I definitely looked admiringly at Weezie Jefferson and Helen Willis of the seventies TV show *The Jeffersons.* Living in their deluxe apartments in the sky, "working" (i.e., volunteering) at the Help Center, Weezie and Helen made me think, *Now* that's *moving on up!*

I dated my fair share of corporate types, with the understanding that my career in advertising and my having attended New York University were all the trappings I needed to get an MRS degree. Yes, I was setting a "trap," trying to ensnare some nice gentleman with a hefty corporate job. And why not? I was not only an advertising executive but also an "around-the-way" girl, someone who knew her way around the Pool Room at the famed Four Seasons restaurant and could be equally comfortable at a pool party in Queens hosted by your frat brothers. I was the best of both worlds! You could take me to your work events, where people would be impressed by the clients I'd had (everyone is in awe of the glamorous world of high fashion), and then we could go home, where I would perform sexual favors like an adult film star (I'm double jointed). I was attempting to lure a man into my trap by presenting myself as a good catch, but I had every intention, once wed, of doing a bait-and-switch by morphing into a lady who lunched, who needed a daily housekeeper and a nanny to help care for my 1.5 kids. (The .5 is my very small dog, Peaches, who is more fashion accessory than pet.) I can own my conniving ways now, because Lawd knows I've changed and have rebuked my sophisti*rachet* ways.

If my "best of both worlds" scenario sounds remotely like you, please know that I'm not judging, but I am warning you. On the one hand, kudos for having a plan and seeing it through. But I wouldn't be a good auntie, big sister, or best friend if I didn't task you with examining whether you're really satisfied with your life. Maybe your life *looks* like you've always envisioned it, but what does it *feel* like? In the words of Prophetess Beyoncé, "Are you happy with yourself?" Part of my breakdown in Milan was centered on this question, not just professionally but personally. I cried that day because I realized I wasn't satisfied with the life I had created, and I had no clue as to what would satisfy me.

There's an old song by the Marvelettes, "The Hunter Gets Captured by the Game." It plays in my head on a loop whenever I think about the last man I dated in the hope of marrying. By my late twenties, I had done it up real big. I'd gone through my Big Bev from Uptown stage, attended the best parties, had "situationships" with some of the hottest guys on the party scene, including celebrities, and made it out with my reputation largely intact. (Again, *thank God* there was no social media then.)

At the same time as I was closing out my stint as Big Bev, I was doing incredibly well as Beverly Smith, advertising executive. My career was taking off—five-star business trips, promotions, raises. #MommaIMadeIt! Even so, my restless spirit had a creative urge to do something else. Now, at the time, I thought that "something else" was not working myself but living off the hard work of someone else, aka my future husband.

I was aging out of being a party girl. I had been partying at the hottest clubs since I was in my early twenties. That's the peak age to do it, and here's why. Men know that a woman is the perfect storm of beautiful, sexy, and naïve yet legal for only a limited amount of time—guys used to call girls like that "young, dumb, and full of cum." We really needed Tarana Burke and her #MeToo movement back then. Women were/are looked upon as disposable.

It's not that men can't find incredibly good-looking women in their thirties, forties, and even fifties in search of a good time, but the "problem" with those women is that men can't just tell them anything and get them into bed. Experience is the best teacher. I saw it with myself. Around age twenty-five, I started becoming very discerning, giving guys the side eye, analyzing and poking holes in anything and everything they said. A Los Angeles–based hip-hop titan/bully/menace (who is currently incarcerated) who was a part of the Bloods actually threatened to throw me out of a window because I dared to challenge him when he told me and my friends to forgo attending the MTV Music Awards because he was going to have a cookout at the Four Seasons Hotel in Midtown Manhattan. Sir, there are no barbecue facilities at the Four Seasons. The only wieners being served at that event would have been this guy and his entourage, and from the looks of his roid rage, it probably would have been more like a Vienna sausage.

But even before my mid-twenties, I saw through a lot of the malarkey the guys were handing me—but what the hell! It was fun, an adventure I could later recount in a book (not this one). When you're twenty-six, you realize that while you're still attractive, you're no longer one of the hottest chicks on the scene. You still like to go out and party; that's just who you are in your spirit. But then you realize that your competition is you—well, who you used to be: that young, bubbly, vivacious girl who laughed at everything, even when the joke was on her. And you have mixed emotions toward her: resentment, because she's the Ghost of Clubbing Past, and compassion, because even then she was dispensing lessons, schooling the younger girls. ("Stranger danger! Don't do it, girl. He's broke [that's his friend's car], has an STD or a wife, or all three!" True story.) But when you start feeling more resentment than compassion, it's time to take a bow. You've had your run. Now it's another young girl's turn, fumbles and fucks included. Go do something else with yourself. Take up a hobby or get a hubby.

I chose the hubby route, which leads us back to the Marvelettes song "The Hunter Gets Captured by the Game." In the nineties, dating a rap music executive was like dating a legal drug dealer. I knew lots of guys in the music biz, and I liked the fact that they had corporate jobs (expense accounts, benefits, offices, and six-figure salaries) as well as swagger. They were the living meme of "Get you somebody who can do both." I was a perfect fit for those men because most of them came from backgrounds similar to mine, and like me, they were striving to make a way in a new world. By the time I was twenty-eight, I was fully matriculated in what it took to make it in corporate spaces, and I was truly a catch because I had a career working in the glamorous world of fashion *and* was still video vixen fine.

How could I lose with the stuff I was about to use? Well, here's how you can lose: in the words of Sister Lauryn Hill, "How you gonna win when you ain't right within?" I was lying to myself, and I was definitely entering into my personal relationships with a selfish spirit. I literally wasn't interested in what my partner wanted. It was all about what I thought I desired, about having someone else be in charge of my happiness.

The guy I went to see *Waiting to Exhale* with, my new boyfriend at the time, was a music executive. He was a nice man, but not a pushover, which was a surprise to me. When he did things like dictate to me how I should dress, I thought he was just trying to assert his masculinity. As you can see from the photos I've included, I wasn't shy about showing some skin, and by "some," I mean lots—of cleavage, leg, and a peek of a butt cheek. In the olden days (aka pre-Instagram), most guys didn't want their lady showing the world what was supposedly all "his." But nothing could have prepared me for when, maybe a year into our relationship, he chastised me for wearing a bikini *on the beach* in front of his six-year-old son. WTF? His kid couldn't see my toned tummy? *Really?* I balked a little, but I still purchased a one-piece bathing suit to appease him. Looking back, I see that I relinquished my power, but I felt sure that eventually, with my looks, sexual prowess, and charm/manipulation skills, the natural order of things would be restored and I would have him wrapped around my finger—along with a very expensive diamond ring.

Reader, I underestimated him. Plot twist: this guy had a backbone *and*, more important, a huge ego, which I didn't recognize until later. Granted, I also had an ego, so it was a constant battle, with lots of arguments and no one wanting to give in. This should have been a red flag, except I had one goal in mind: to get married.

In spite of our issues, I gradually fell in love with him. When we weren't arguing, we spent most of our time together at his apartment, listening to music (he had phenomenal taste), cooking, and playing video games. Now y'all know I must have been trying real hard to secure a ring if I was playing video games. I'm so embarrassed; the thirst was real. However, what wasn't embarrassing is that he loved the core of me, who, though she wasn't defined as such back then, was Lil' Brown Bevy. With him, privately, I could be my nerdy girl self. We spent hours together in the same house not talking, just enjoying each other's company: me reading, him playing music he knew I loved, a real bond. And in many ways, our relationship was such a relief; I felt like I could exhale. Which is why I'd left that movie feeling smugly superior to Angela Bassett's and Whitney Houston's characters—I was going to end up with a man who loved me. I wouldn't need to set fire to his possessions or have my momma say to me, "He's a good man, Savannah, a good man.

He's just in a bad situation right now," while trying to convince me that a married doctor just needed time to work out a few things, like his current marriage. (If you don't get the reference, please go watch *Waiting to Exhale*, and get your entire life.)

As he and I started getting serious, I let him know my misguided hopes and dreams, which at the beginning consisted of being a stay-at-home mom with help. To his credit, he never strung me along. He immediately said that that didn't work for him, that it was an antiquated lifestyle and that we would need my salary along with his to have a truly amazing life.

Ladies, how many times have you dated a guy who told you something but you were convinced that what he said didn't apply to you, even though he said it directly to you? Well, that was me with this guy. I had my own ideas about what our life could look like if only he cooperated with me.

One of the things I adored about him was that he wasn't some average guy. He worked with some of the top stars in urban music and therefore, in my mind, had the potential to make the big bucks. My idea was that *he* would work incredibly hard, and I would help him create strategies to ingratiate him with his higher-ups. This would garner him promotions and, voilà! He'd be running a music label and making a million dollars in no time. He appreciated that he could take me into any room and I would dazzle folks, his bosses and coworkers loved me, we made a great team . . . but sometimes he thought I was doing a little too much. He began to refer to those moments as "The Big Bev Show." People gravitated toward me, and he appreciated that—it made him proud that his lady could hold her own, but only to a point. I believe he would have preferred it if I charmed folks and then let him take over. And for a time, I tried to do that.

When I turned thirty, we had been dating for almost two years, were practically living together, and were talking about marriage.

But the troubles weren't over for us. Toning down my risqué outfits was just the beginning of what he required of his woman. There was also a battle over my cooking versus our dining out. When we first started dating, he wined and dined me on his expense account. I was used to men spoiling me, indulging my fine-dining habit, so this was nothing new. What *was* new was when he flipped the script and notified me that his boss had flagged his expense account, saying he was overspending. So, he suggested very strongly that I begin to cook. Okay, I love to cook, but I'm a very specific kind of cook. I'm not giving you a "Big Mama's Soul Food Feast"—you'd better take this protein, vegetable, and starch. You won't receive a buffet banquet from Bevy. He liked my cooking, but he complained that the meals were bougie. He also said that whenever I did cook, I turned it into an event, going on and on about how hard I'd worked. I won't deny it, he was right. I *was* definitely looking for applause, and I believe all women who work full-time and then come home and run a household deserve a standing ovation.

Although I had a warped idea of what a relationship was supposed to be built on, it was rooted in traditional roles. (Men are breadwinners; women are homemakers/bread spenders.) Of course, I put my spin on it with my dream of being a homemaker "with help." And I had no intention of cooking every night, or even five days a week. Look, when I was growing up, my dad cooked for us five days a week, and my mom made a huge Sunday dinner. It seemed perfectly logical to me that my preparing a meal should be met with great appreciation and excitement. When he began to complain about my not cooking often enough, I balked at the idea of becoming Julia Honeychile.

And that was when I realized that the hunter had been captured by the game. (You know I was going to find a way to tie the Marvelettes back in.) I'd started this relationship with the idea of having my way with him. Then I woke up when I realized that it was beginning to be his way all day. I fought the good fight, though. I didn't automatically acquiesce to his every request, but by the time I had this realization, I loved him and (say it with me) was trying to get married.

Early on in our relationship, I let him know that I was unhappy with my job and told him I wanted to quit. He asked a logical question: "To do what?" My answer was "I don't know." As our relationship continued, what I did know was that he wasn't making me happy, and I had no idea why. I asked myself, and then I began asking him, "Why aren't you making me happy?" Ugh.

To make matters worse, I was a nag, and a hysterical one at that. Granted, there were times when he didn't come home from the recording studio until 4 a.m., and there were business trips to Miami and Los Angeles for video shoots and awards shows that I wasn't "allowed" to attend. So, yes, I was jealous, and I thought I had good cause. Looking back, through the prism of maturity, I see there's never any reason to be so insecure in a relationship that jealousy is a constant source of conflict. If I had been good with who I was, if I had been *happy* with myself, I would have addressed those matters that made me feel I wasn't fully a part of his life, and either things would have changed or I would have left. Yet I wasn't at that point in my journey toward self-awareness. So, instead, I cried, threw tantrums, threw plates, and made scenes any- and everywhere—I was cute, but my histrionics were not!

Now that I've done the work on myself and no longer feel that that younger me was a victim, I've realized I can't look at what he did or didn't do and place blame. I can only look at myself and say what *I* did, examine how *I* was culpable. I could have left anytime I wanted if the relationship wasn't working. And for a long time, it wasn't. But we really wanted to salvage our relationship, and thinking it could help, he told me I needed therapy.

That turned out to be a game changer. I started going to therapy for *us* and ended up finding out that *us* wasn't going to work, and that there was only one thing I needed to focus on, and that was *me*. We didn't break up immediately; therapy isn't a quick fix. Instead, we dated off and on for five-plus years, with varying degrees of commitment, before it was finally done. When we at last broke up, there were no fireworks; it was more like a fizzling out. Over the years, we had done the dance of break up to make up, and then one day, the music just stopped. I think both of us simply felt we had run our course. I realized that the fantasy I had had in my head about him taking care of me, allowing me not to work, was just that, a fantasy, and honestly not one that in my core I really wanted.

Had we gotten married, I imagine the scenario would have been: I'd have continued in my advertising career, making a mid-six-figure salary, commuting from a beautiful, well-decorated home in Westchester, where we lived with our two kids. It's pretty much an upgrade of the "dream life" that I hatched when I was a kid. And that was the problem—that dream hadn't evolved much, and truthfully, it wouldn't have fulfilled me. I would have loved my kids, but I know plenty of women who love their children and their husbands, but also resent what they had to give up personally for their "perfect life." This isn't to down women who are wives and mothers. I know many who are incredibly happy. But I don't think that was my calling, not my ministry. When I reflect on why I even wanted those things, I see that I thought that's what I was *supposed* to want. Back then, there were literally no role models, no examples in films or on TV of women who were single, childless, and happy (even Willona from *Good Times* adopted Penny). We were then and in many ways still are pariahs, looked at with derision and pity, even by other women in the same circumstance (allegedly, there are millions of us out there). Society is trying to change the narrative from old maid to PANK (Professional Aunt, No Kids), and it's cute, I guess?! I would rather just be Bevy instead.

But I digress, *again*. I have no regrets about the time I spent with him. I look back fondly on our relationship; it helped me unearth Lil' Brown Bevy. He just wasn't meant to be my husband, but I feel blessed that I can call him a true friend. However, before we got to that space, I had to learn that I was enough and that it wasn't his or anyone else's job to fulfill me. Being happy with yourself is a constantly evolving solo project.

When we consciously uncoupled, with no more "maybe we should try again" scenarios, I was thirty-four, heartbroken, and overall, not in a good place mentally. (My Milan breakdown had happened just the year before.) Plus, there was lots to get used to. To begin with, I hadn't expected to be single ever again. This relationship was supposed to have been my ticket to We and Us. There were lots of adjustments to make, but one of the most painful was realizing I had to live at my apartment. We'd spent most of the relationship at his, a huge space where we were able to be together without being on top of each other. Coming back home to my apartment was downsizing, literally, and a reminder of what I had lost. I didn't feel at home there anymore, so I decided I would travel. (Now that I'm typing this, I feel like it is turning into a Terry McMillan novel.) At first, I found friends who were willing to take trips with me, quick weekend romps, nothing exotic. Those trips helped me to not dwell on being single. Then I started wanting to get away every couple of months, and my friends couldn't go, and that is how I started traveling by myself.

At this point, I've traveled all over the world alone, including to Australia, India, Indonesia, and South Africa. But once upon a time, I was afraid to go to the Grand Bahamas without anyone else. That's right. My first solo vacation was only three hours away from Harlem, and I was petrified—so much so that as soon as I arrived at the hotel and realized there was no one to talk to, I was ready to leave. Thankfully, this was a time when dinosaurs roamed the earth, and there was no such thing as online booking for travel; you had to call the airline directly. After being on hold for an hour, only to find out there were no flights available for the next two days, I realized I had to figure out how to be okay with being alone. I had just started journaling daily, so I did that, writing about my desire for a new boyfriend and being very bitter and mean-spirited, tearing my ex down so I could feel better about not being with him. After three days of consuming sugary alcoholic drinks and fried bar food while sunbathing and journaling hateful letters to my ex, I was happy to head back home.

However, when I arrived, I immediately had that same feeling of sadness. I wanted "home" to be his space. So, I booked another trip back to the Bahamas, but this time I visited Nassau, Paradise Island. They say "it's better in the Bahamas." Clearly, I was out to see if that was true. When I arrived, I felt the pang of loneliness again and attempted to leave on the next flight out, but the cost of the ticket change was prohibitive, so again, I decided to stay. One major change was that I actually left the resort this time, and let's just say, Stella got a little bit of her groove back!

Now, before you think this actually is becoming a Terry McMillan novel, he wasn't a Winston and I wasn't smitten enough to invite him back to the United States to live in my home and eat cereal on the sofa while I worked. I was clear that my fling was a vacation thing.

After that escapade, solo personal travel got easier. My first international jaunt beyond the Caribbean was to Vancouver, and that's where I truly began to appreciate trips taken with just myself. My chic boutique hotel was at the base of Stanley Park, which made it simple to hike every day. I was trying to figure out my life, reimagining it after the breakup and the epiphany I'd had in Milan that something had to change. Hiking represented that—it was something I had always wanted to do, so I gave it a try. It didn't fit any of my adult personas—not MC Bev-Ski, not Big Bev from Uptown, and certainly not Fashionista Beverly Smith. But spending time outdoors, communing with nature, with the water, while walking the seawall and hiking through the rainforest, I was reconnecting with Lil' Brown Bevy—although, at the time, I couldn't have articulated this. All I knew was that I felt free, unencumbered by having to be fabulous or "on."

After going hiking two days in a row, I decided to see other parts of Vancouver and took a ferry to Granville Island, an urban renewal project that boasts food markets, local vendors, and small theater groups. It was the middle of the week, and I had the boat pretty much to myself. When I got off, I roamed around the food stalls trying various treats. As the sun began to go down, I saw droves of people carrying wine and cheese from the stalls heading in the same direction. I followed, and what I saw that evening changed my life.

That group of men and women were sitting on the dock of the bay (come on, Otis) just watching the sky. It was at that moment that I had a Bevelation: There were many different ways to live well, and having a mandate to watch the sunset with a glass of wine seemed like a pretty solid version to me.

By the time I returned to New York City, I had a newfound lease on life. I knew I wanted a free lifestyle. I wanted to romp, play, take off, and go watch a sunset. I took myself on "artist dates" courtesy of Julia Cameron's *The Artist's Way*. For the first time in a long time, I didn't think about *him* or any other man as the way to build a happy life. Something in me had clicked, and I started dating men while holding no ulterior motive, but simply because I was attracted to them. I wasn't sizing them up for their marriage potential. I had an affair with a man ten years my junior. (Before you think about calling me a cougar, he charged after me, so I was more like a sultry house cat.) I dated a very talented but not famous rapper (i.e., he was broke), and that was really exotic for me—not a fancy meal to be had during the entire affair. My friends remarked on that relationship that I really had changed. I was very happy dating this financially challenged and promising rapper. I was finally focusing on what I really wanted, intimacy, and not thinking about securing a ring.

I've had various lovers over the years, but in the words of George Benson and Whitney Elizabeth Houston, "learning to love yourself is the greatest love of all." Once I stopped focusing on outside relationships, my mindset changed, and I began tapping into life to find out where my joy might come from. I began pursuing Lil' Brown Bevy's interests: pleasures I had buried a long time ago; simple, solitary pursuits like getting a library card and withdrawing books weekly, romping in Central Park, visiting museums. I started to realize that I hadn't truly cultivated any passions or interests of my own because all I had been interested in was finding a husband.

By the time I quit *Rolling Stone* at age thirty-eight, two years after my Vancouver sunset, I had a few lovers on tap. None was serious. My friends didn't even meet them. However, I still have fond memories of each, because they were there when I was changing, morphing into the woman I've become. I wasn't seeking their approval, so I was able to open up to them and share my dreams of becoming a TV personality, with no fear of their judging me. What did I care if they thought it was crazy? I showed one of them my #MalibuBevy vision board (complete with beachfront home, fire pit, breakfast nook, and a silhouette of a toned Black woman with natural hair doing yoga). He laughed and said it was the dumbest thing he'd ever seen, cutting and pasting photos in the hope that they would manifest into reality. And guess what? I didn't care what he thought. I no longer needed to contort myself to fit into a vision that a man had for me. I had agency over my life, my very own Life with Vision! It was a nice full-circle moment when, years later, he texted me after seeing a TV commercial for *Fashion Queens*, simply writing, "You did it." Yes, I did, and I'm incredibly proud that I didn't need a man to cosign my vision to believe I could achieve it.

Folks often say you can't have it all. I don't know if you can. (I hope so.) But I do know that I couldn't have forged this new life if I had been consumed with a relationship. I know a lot of people are able to search for a new job and a new man at the same time, but that wasn't me. I needed to be devoted to me, I needed to be truly selfish and think about what *I* wanted. That's a hard sentence to write, even now, because I don't want to be misunderstood, and women are always judged when they choose themselves over others. However, it's important to put it in the book because I know a few of you are feeling that way. Well, I'm here to give you a Bevelation: Being singularly focused on yourself at some point in your life is a luxury—and luxury is *always* a good thing. I'm talking "self-care" beyond a bubble bath and a shopping spree.

Very early on in my new life, my independence was put to the test. Although I'd stopped being a party girl, I had morphed into a "gal about town," which is like a senior-level party girl. Instead of hitting the clubs, you attend galas and hobnob with the elites (usually in arts and culture). Well, at one of those events, I met someone who was in the creative arts. He was somewhat successful, and also older, which was nice. I had gotten used to dating men who were younger and not as successful, so being with him was a bit of a flashback to the old me. But uh-oh! He was a grown-ass man, and he had very definite ideas about his "woman." Now, I wasn't sure I wanted to be his woman, but he was charming and knew how to romance. He wrote me sonnets, mailed me illustrations he'd drawn of me. (BTW, we lived in the same city, but he used a stamp to seduce me. Swoon!) And bought me books, including a history of the colony of Malibu after I mentioned that my goal was to become #MalibuBevy. I mean, is that sexy or what?

What wasn't so sexy was the way he was controlling and a bit manipulative. It started off innocently enough. We could have dinner only in restaurants of his choosing. At the time, I thought, *Well, this is nice. I don't have to make decisions.* What wasn't so nice is that we had to go to dinner for the early bird special; a 7 p.m. dinner reservation was late for him.

He had a studio/living space that was huge and cluttered with art, quite a lot of it with sexual themes. There was also a big dog. Now, you guys know about Peaches, my imaginary small dog, but this dog was no Peaches. It was huge! An enormous, lumbering, shedding, hairy, gigantic thing. What wasn't gigantic was the man's "thing." He had so many huge phallic symbols in his space, but his wasn't. Perhaps that art was a form of psychological foreplay or wishful thinking, I don't know. I will say this—he was a grown man about his situation, and he not only acknowledged his "shortcomings," but he tried to compensate with romantic gestures, heavy foreplay, and toys. I made allowances because he was romantic and catered to me in bed, and it was nice to date a successful grown-up, even though at times he seemed like a cast member from the 1993 film *Grumpy Old Men*.

With his thriving creative career and my burgeoning one as a writer/TV personality, I thought we could have some fab dinner parties in his huge space (if we locked up his dog and if he could manage to stay up past eight). Well, that fantasy came to a swift end. We had been dating for a few months when he saw a clip of me on a VH1 show discussing some celebrity. He felt like my language wasn't very ladylike, and I immediately went on the defensive.

I chafed at being told to act like a "lady." Imagine the chafing of thick thighs encased in Daisy Dukes made from raw denim and worn in hundred-degree heat—that's how irritated I was by the reprimand. The "lady" he had in mind was an antiquated paradigm designed to place limitations on women's behavior. No, Feminist Bevy had no interest in being a lady; a woman with agency was my goal. Plus, I had learned from my prior relationship that I didn't want a combative life with a lover. My intention moving forward was, and still is, not to let anger fuel my emotions. It was my goal to be a softer Bevy, and if my guy hurt me, instead of reacting with a "I'm not having it" attitude, one filled with vitriol and histrionics worthy of an Erykah Badu opus, I would respond with the most honest and vulnerable words you can say to a lover: "You hurt me, and this is why."

Unfortunately, I wasn't that advanced yet. I went straight to my "Call Tyrone" zone of anger and cursed at him. My Scorpio venom shot out, and I let him know I wasn't interested in being a lady. I was a woman. Furthermore, if he wanted to be somebody's daddy, he should stick to dating silly, impressionable young girls! The daddy job in my life was already filled by Smitty!

Words have power, so let me be clear, now that I'm firmly in the life I imagined, I do want to be in a fulfilling, committed relationship, but that no longer necessarily means marriage. I never expected to be single this long, but there's obviously some lesson in it for me. Anyway, I firmly believe #ItGetsGreaterLater. Now, because this is a safe space, I can tell you that if I wind up a ninety-seven-year-old crone who never experienced a great, passionate love, I will be asking for a do-over in the romance department in my next life.

But for now, I'm very pleased with the way my life is going. I've become a better person not just where romance is concerned, but also as a friend, a sister, a daughter. Transparency and the ability to tell it like it is have been hallmarks of my personality. But I'm now less biting, not so caustic in my approach. Having a rift with one of my oldest friends, Micki (of the '80s Ladies), taught me that being a friend is not a one-size-fits-all proposition. Micki is my "sensitive friend," and when we bump heads, I must keep that in mind and temper my approach, because I *value* our friendship. Probably the thing that has made the biggest difference in all my relationships is that I'm no longer so quick to give my unsolicited opinion.

As in #GirlMindYourBusiness and #IfYouLikeItILoveIt. I've also developed patience. I no longer allow myself to be railroaded into a relationship because we spent one great weekend together. I'm affectionate but not clingy, and the best part? I'm celibate for long bouts of time, which means I no longer depend on sex to attempt to build a relationship or to self-soothe. That also means that whoever I share my vagina with is getting it refurbished, and with a tight guarantee.

I'm happy with myself! My work and my personal life have melded. I've created a fine template for living my best life (one that I share through my Life with Vision seminars). I'm a media personality, entrepreneur, writer, and world traveler. I've visited every continent except Antarctica, and I'm leaving that for when I'm ninety—if the polar ice caps haven't melted by then. (Come on, Greta! Save us from ourselves!) I've hosted four TV shows, including a nationally syndicated talk show. I have my own radio show, titled *Bevelations* (a full-circle moment with Andy Cohen), and my relationships are better than ever. I get it now, that if you love someone, you have to show up for them, and not just in lingerie while lip-synching "Private Dancer" (although, that's a bonus). I know that to receive love in any relationship, you actually have to give love, which is probably a simple concept for y'all, but for me, it took a while to comprehend. On my radio show, I like to speak honestly about what I want out of my life—and now I will end this chapter with this public vision board for my love life. (Given that, as of this writing, I'm still single, I want to make sure that the universe knows I want to be in a healthy, loving relationship.)

My guy will be a warm, loyal, compassionate, financially stable, secure, brilliant man capable of love; a man who openly and readily displays that love. I will recognize him because in him, I will see the best of me, and vice versa. I finally understand you can get out only what you put in, and I intend to put in LOVE, to radiate it until I take my last breath. Now let the church say AMEN!

"Three the Hard Way": *my sister, Stephanie,*
supporting me and Renee at a party we promoted.
This is the epitome of Big Bev.

Booked, Blessed, and Busty

GROWING UP, I WAS FLAT CHESTED. YES, I KNOW YOU'RE probably shocked. You thought I showed up at grade school with double Ds in my overalls, didn't you? Well, you're wrong. I was bony, and I took great pride in my non-shape. Being skinny and double-jointed meant I was able to squeeze into small spaces. I would show off to my small group of friends my ability to fold my rail-thin body into a pretzel. I was doing yoga moves and didn't even know it!

In my community, many kids went through puberty early, starting at around ten years old. I know that, according to books about preteen angst, I should have been envious of them, but I liked still being a skinny little kid. Author Judy Blume's famous line "I must, I must, I must increase my bust," from her book *Are You There God? It's Me, Margaret*, didn't strike a chord with me. I wanted no part of those grown-up body parts. I realized early on that to have *bawdy* meant unwanted attention, not just from lecherous men but also from envious, less well-endowed girls. I used to see my mom get catcalled on the streets of Harlem. It was shocking to realize that complete strangers thought it appropriate to say hello to her while staring deep into her cleavage. I also noticed that neighborhood women were disdainful of her. Now, that could have been because she didn't socialize; she went to work and hung out with friends who didn't live on the block. My sister and I were aware that when our mom stepped out of 2813 Eighth Avenue dressed in lovely garments and high heels, highlighting her shape, she didn't want to fit in. All this didn't exactly endear her to many of the women on the block, who rocked wardrobes similar to their daughters', jeans and sneakers. Between her fab outfits and her seemingly haughty demeanor—let's just say she wasn't exactly the belle of the block. Watching all this, I was in no rush to have puberty bring that kind of drama to my life. Instead, I clung to my Lil' Brown Bevy persona and body.

Standing out is a gift and a curse, and it's tricky to know which one will win out, especially if you're the kind of girl who is looking to fit in and not make waves. As a kid, I kept my active dream life to myself, never letting on that I had gifts that could have made me the center of attention. I honed the popular-girl skills I needed, but, still, I felt I had to be careful. If you were too vocal or showy and drew too much attention to yourself, the popular girls could decide they didn't like you. My mother didn't seem to care that none of the neighborhood women chatted her up, but I wanted the approval of my peers. As I discussed earlier, I was a girl who had been bullied, so I learned to keep a low profile and not give the popular girls a reason to pick on me.

At around thirteen years old, puberty hit. And no, I wasn't one of those girls who went to bed flat as a board and woke up with D cups. Nope, my boob journey was slow and steady. For a while, a regular-size training bra was enough to keep my girls under control. However, it was around that time that I began to want a little attention, not a lot, but I had been studying the popular girls since sixth grade, and I knew what it took to fit in.

Thanks to Black Twitter, I realize now that what I was yearning to show the world was my particular brand of Black Girl Magic! Unfortunately, that term hadn't yet been coined in the early eighties, though the magic was very real. The street-smart, witty, popular girls I went to school with were imbued with it. I stood on the sidelines of early teen life watching and cheering them on, while secretly wanting to show the world, or at least the block, a few of my tricks. But what if I tried and failed? Imagine jumping into a snapping session, and no one laughing. Back then, I wasn't familiar with the street philosophy that nothing beats a try but a failure. Like most people, I feared failure, especially in front of the people I had to see each and every day. I wasn't willing to take that chance, so I sat on my dreams like they were a splintered school bleacher. Ouch.

By the time I got to high school, I had a cute bawdy on me. I'd sprouted nice-size breasts (34C) and a cute booty. And I took a chance by changing my narrative, combining all my natural talents—sharp wit, good intuition, innate sense of style—with a fake-it-till-you-make-it brand of confidence.

Once I was popping on all cylinders, I became popular, and I never looked back. And my popularity continued to grow—from high school to college to my professional life. The dreams Lil' Brown Bevy had of showing folks her Black Girl Magic had become a reality.

However, when I was thirty-three and trying to figure out what would come next after my Milan meltdown, though I was still bodacious and busty, wearing a double-D bra, my dreams had shrunk to training-bra status; I had begun to be afraid again. But instead of being afraid of being the center of attention, like in junior high, I was afraid I had reached my peak. Sure, I was confident in many aspects of my life. I knew that my personality attracted people to me. I knew that I was good at my profession—my checks confirmed that, and I was highly respected in my industry. But I'd realized that what I wanted more than other people's approval (i.e., popularity) was to lead a creatively fulfilling life. And I wasn't confident about my creative ability. As an avid reader, a lover of history, and a patron of the arts, I hold artists, writers, comedians, and actors in high regard. So, when I started having an inkling that I wanted to do something where success wasn't rooted in money, it was jarring. Succeeding financially was my comfort zone. I knew how to make money. At this moment of adult fear, instead of moving toward what I truly desired, I began to talk myself into opting for a happy medium.

Bevelation: Finding a "happy medium" is settling, and the only time settling is good is when it concerns a facelift or ass implants; then you want things to settle. Otherwise, it's not a good thing. If you're currently living a life where you are not fulfilled, but you figure "At least I have a good job," or "I just bought a house," or any number of things we tell ourselves to be able to deal with the mediocrity in our lives—SNAP OUT OF IT!

In my journals I kept praying for a sign, a way out of just treading water in my perfectly nice life. Thankfully, the universe heard my cry—as did Kenard Gibbs, the president of *Vibe* magazine. *Vibe* had created an awards show, *The Vibe Awards*, produced in conjunction with Queen Latifah and celebrating the best and the brightest of our culture. The company had secured a TV deal and hired Fonzworth Bentley to host the red carpet. Kenard, whom I'd been petitioning for a new job, came to me and asked if I would like to host with Fonzworth. Now, at the time I hadn't yet given any thought to being on TV. However, I knew it was an opportunity to do something other than sell ad pages, so I said "hell, yes" and started thinking about my outfit.

I was thirty-seven years old and although I had just begun to put on a little weight, I felt at the height of my sexy. Remember, I was cavorting with younger men at the time. Ladies, if you ever need an ego boost, sleep with a man a few years younger than you. They'll worship at your throne as if your initials were HRH!

Fonzworth, who had made a name for himself by being Puffy's valet, is a man of impeccable style and manners, a bona fide media personality, and celebrities loved him. I knew that to stand beside Fonzworth on the red carpet, I was going to have to look smashing, dripping with designer labels, and be quick with commentary—or I could easily be overshadowed. I was up for the challenge. After all, I had been training for this moment since my high school days, "coming to the stage, MC Bev-Ski!" To get my look right, I called in my "son" Terrell, a celebrity stylist (and the first person I ever officially mentored), and he styled me. I wore a pink Missoni dress and Giuseppe Zanotti shoes. I had a long hair weave that I thought was glamorous but upon reflection made me look like every other girl on the red carpet. It was an on-trend look.

Following Fonzworth's lead, I hit that red carpet, using all my undercover Lil' Brown Bevy gifts. I danced with Fonzworth, joked/flirted with all the male celebrities, and engaged in friendly fashion banter with the women who stopped for interviews, a precursor to my career as a red carpet fashion commentator.

By the time the red carpet segment was over, my feet were hurting and I wanted an In-N-Out Burger in the worst way. (This was before Seamless and Uber, so you had to drive to an actual drive-in to secure one. The inconvenience and indignity of it all!) I may have been hungry, but that night on the red carpet, my spirit was nourished. I knew I had found my calling: I wanted to be in entertainment; I wanted to be on TV.

Okay, you think that should have been the end, right? I had found my "calling." She's booked, blessed, and busty, right? Not that easy, hunty! "Life for me ain't been no crystal stair." (Come on, Langston!) In fact, getting to this point in my journey has been more like climbing to the top of stadium stairs (the ones with the openings in the slats) in a six-inch heel, wearing skin-tight white jeans and juggling a twenty-ounce subpar margarita and nachos while trying to look cute. No part of my story is easy. My trajectory was often harrowing, almost as dangerous as pairing cheap tequila with Cheez Whiz nachos knowing there's only three stalls in the ladies' bathroom. I had begun to envision myself as a creative and I had stopped thinking that I had to play it safe, but it turns out that when you're recalibrating your life, an epiphany is often the beginning, not the end.

Often, too, the dream is born out of pain. One dream I still have came straight out of physical pain. Thirty-five years old and frustrated with work, I was on my way to Hawaii. It was a solo trip on New Year's Eve, which was quite daring then as now. You guys know I love to travel alone, but there *is* something especially brave (yes, we can use the term *brave* here) about spending New Year's Eve alone. I was sleeping almost exclusively with younger men at that time. Not so young that they could pass for my nephew, but they were definitely in their late twenties and thought of me as a wise older woman who could teach them something. Anyhoo, one younger lover I fancied quite a bit was a very talented West Coast rapper. (Don't try to guess who he is and stop being so nosy, the details of my love life are for another book!)

In an effort to buffer the occasional waves of lonely that I predicted would happen during a solo New Year's Eve trip, I decided to do a long layover in Los Angeles and see my rapper. He lived nearby (Inglewood is basically in the backyard of Los Angeles International Airport), so he picked me up from the airport, took me to get Mexican food from a hole in the wall, and then we went to his apartment. We proceeded to have sex, lots of it. Now, he was younger, but he wasn't the most adventurous when it came to sex. He liked me on top, him on top, a little doggy style, but no wheelbarrow, stand and deliver, pinball wizard, or champagne room. I tend to be a little more adventurous when it comes to the bedroom, but he was a Pisces, sensitive, and he preferred love-making over acrobatics. Big Bev from Uptown would have found him boring, but the Lil' Brown Bevy in me enjoyed sharing light caresses versus getting *playfully* choked out (with a safeword, of course). After our sessions I never felt like I had been rode hard and put away wet (a common occurrence when you're indulging in sexual rodeo tricks), but as he was taking me back to the airport, I felt a little discomfort in my rear area. I didn't think much of it. After all, we hadn't done "The Kinky Cowgirl." (You ever notice lots of sexual acts are western-themed? The West must truly be wild.) Once he dropped me off, though, I ran to the wheelchair-accessible bathroom stall and, with my makeup mirror, tried to see if anything was awry down there. Between the small mirror and my big ass, suffice it to say I couldn't see much.

Now, I'm far from a hypochondriac, but my ass was throbbing like techno music in a Miami nightclub during spring break, so I contacted my doctor, Dr. Cherrie (aka Cheryl Calegari). Remember? The Cheryl who loaned me money all the way from Shanghai? Just so we're clear, Dr. Cherrie has no medical license, but she knows all about prescription meds, so she was my go-to. Dr. Cherrie tells me it's probably hemorrhoids and prescribes hot soaks, a doughnut cushion to sit on, and Preparation H.

Later, I eased into my faux first-class seat—can anyone explain why Los Angeles-to-Hawaii flights don't have proper fully reclining seats? Hello! It's a five-to-six-hour flight! So there I am, asking for those lovely hand towels they give out in first class. They're supposed to be used to clean your hands before a meal is served, but instead I'm using them to soothe my thumping bum. (If you're a flight attendant and you're reading this, don't worry. I took them with me and disposed of them off the plane.) Thanks to an unlimited number of vodka cranberry cocktails and those hot towels, I was able to make it to Honolulu.

When I checked into the hotel, I was happy to see that I had not one but two bathrooms, including one with a bathtub big enough for a small orgy. Clearly, sex was the last thing on my mind, but I ran that tub for a party of one, trying to ease the literal pain in my ass. I grew up fantasizing about Hawaii, but what no one ever tells you is that while much of Hawaii is beautiful, Honolulu can resemble Coney Island on the Fourth of July: crowded and congested, the beach packed with bodies, including lots of kids wreaking havoc. Talk about a pain in the ass!

I stayed at an oceanfront hotel. Yay! However, the hotel was on a public beach, which meant it was clogged with tourists like Times Square. But I made the best of it. I took my iPod and my journal and I began to write down what I wanted my life to look like. And while I looked out at the Pacific Ocean's waves from that crowded beach in Honolulu, with an anus pulsating with pain in random waves, Malibu Bevy was born.

Malibu Bevy is the epitome of Booked, Blessed, and Busty but it's all on her own terms. She lives on the ocean, has natural hair, a fit body, a well-hung and caring lover, and *loads* of money. As Malibu Bevy, I have a midcentury modern–esque home with a breakfast nook complete with a window seat from which I can enjoy the sunrise while eating my healthy breakfast of berries and oatmeal in the winter and berries and yogurt in the warm months. (I realize Malibu doesn't have four seasons but I'm a New Yorker at heart.) My home has four bedrooms, enough for visitors to stay during the holidays, but not so many rooms that people feel like they can overstay their welcome (this ain't a sorority house). The hub of my home is the deck overlooking the ocean. It has a retractable wall and a full kitchen where my lover and I make dinner together every night (a grilled fish/fresh veggies kind of vibe) while we watch the sun go down and he goes down on me. We make THE LOVE—it's so special that it deserves capitalization—also on our deck, with our fire pit roaring, warming our bodies while the ocean breezes blow. I'm up every morning for sunrise. I journal and exercise, and afterwards I take a proper bath, in a Balinese bathtub big enough for four but just for me, where I also paint my feelings onto a canvas. Then I'm ready to start my day. I no longer work on a daily basis. I have an art/architectural consulting business, helping people who have recently found themselves with money add décor which appreciates (art, wine collections, first-edition libraries) to their homes. (No more *MTV Cribs* style. Sir, a garage with millions of dollars in cars shouldn't be the best-decorated part of your home.) That business brings in a few million annually, which I donate to charity. The lion's share of my income is from my TV and film production company, BS Productions, which focuses on telling stories that are REAL and UNFILTERED, with lots of BS (Bevy Smith), but NO BULLSHIT.

Malibu Bevy rarely goes out to nighttime events. First of all, after more than thirty years of schlepping around in fancy garments, I've done enough. Mutha is *ovah* it! On the rare occasion you do see me out, it's for a great cause, my philanthropic work for LGBTQIA youth, my foundation for underprivileged children and the arts. I used to raise money for HIV/AIDS awareness, but that virus was eradicated in the early 20s, as in 2020s! (We are manifesting that eradication into fact by writing it in this book.)

I also come out when friends are being honored—Andy Cohen's Lifetime Achievement Emmy ceremony, Miss Lawrence's star-on-the-Walk-of-Fame event, my sister Stephanie's book being adapted into a film (which BS Productions produced). This is the level of importance that has to be in place for me to come outside and have my hair and makeup done. Once I'm at an event, I'll do my photo ops, have a few perfunctory hellos, and about two hours in, just like a seventy-year-old Cinderella, my cherry red 1966 (the year I was born) Mustang will turn into a pumpkin and I'll have to go. It's a stupendous life filled with passion, my lover, my family, and work that is spiritually and financially rewarding.

Clearly, I was in my Zen Bevy mode in Hawaii, to be able to conjure up a dream life so beautiful even though I had a horrible ass ache. Happy New Year!

I celebrated New Year's Eve with a quiet dinner at a restaurant, complete with champagne, but it was cut short due to my angry anus. When I hobbled back to my hotel room, I took a warm bath and chatted with my LA lover. We made plans for my return, another layover so we could *lay up*. We had so many good chats while I was in Honolulu, and he kept saying how he couldn't wait to see me. I felt the same way, except I wasn't sure I would be able to walk, much less run, into his arms. However, I'm a trouper, so I popped some pain pills, got on the plane, and headed back to LA. When he picked me up, he asked if I wanted to go get Mexican. Now, with the problems I was having, do you really think I needed to eat beans? I declined, saying, "I'm not hungry," and he took that as an indication that I just wanted to go back to his place and have sex. Back then, I wasn't the evolved woman I am today. I was still into pleasing men and at any cost, so I said, "Sure." The me of today would have told him what was going on and had him take me to urgent care! I rationalized that the show must go on and I figured I wouldn't further damage myself, especially if we did his favorite position, missionary. However, in an effort to make sure we had time for only one round, I lied and said my layover was only hours. And before you knew, it was time for me to get back to the airport.

On the plane, I called my bestie Aimee and let her know the severity of my anal pain; she insisted on taking me to the emergency room the next day. Turned out I had an anal fissure, and they operated immediately to stitch it up.

They say you have to go through pain to get to pleasure. I don't know if I believe it, but I do know that oftentimes to really get to where you truly are meant to go, you have to go through some thangs. From anal fissures to failed romances to TV pilots you're convinced are going to series but instead never see the light of day, there will be trials and tribulations in life. But wherever you are in your journey is exactly where you're supposed to be. Eventually, you will know when you've outgrown a situation that feels stifling and redundant. I've done it with relationships with friends and lovers, and this whole book is about my moving on throughout my career.

For now, I've manifested Malibu Bevy on a smaller, New York City level. I have outdoor space with my two-bedroom, two-bathroom apartment. (If you know anything about Manhattan real estate, then you know that's considered a lot of space.) I've already started saying no to more events than I say yes to. On weekends, I have my natural hair out, and on Sundays, I make myself a healthy piece of fish for dinner and I'm in bed by 9 p.m. My Malibu Bevy dreams *are* manifesting.

That's it (for now)! Oh, yeah. One more really important note: don't *shrink*. I show up with a Booked, Blessed, and Busty mindset. I won't play small, not for anyone—although, could I really? When I show up as I am, my physicality, my race, my outspoken opinions all signal she's here and that's a good thing, now. I had to grow into being comfortable with being seen, and now it's the way I approach my life. YOU WILL SEE ME!

*I was ready for my close-up, my first TV appearance,
hosting the red carpet of the* Vibe *Awards.*

Brand You

WHAT'S YOUR PERSONAL BRAND? IF YOU DON'T KNOW, that's okay. Many people don't. I had no idea for many years my damn self. Of course, when I was coming up, these weren't questions folks asked themselves. But now, thanks to social media, Andy Warhol's adage "In the future, everyone will be world-famous for fifteen minutes" has never seemed truer, and people that you would have never imagined are going around professing to be a "brand." Sir, you are a dog catcher, now explain to me how that makes you a brand worth following?

When you look up "how to build a personal brand," the top questions you are prompted to ponder are Who are you? and What makes you unique? Fortunately for you, you've already read the chapter "Red Sole Proposition" and answered the three questions "Who am I at my core?" "How am I perceived?" and "How would I like to be perceived?" So, if you skimmed over that chapter, go back and revisit it. It's a crucial chapter for anyone who wants to create an *authentic* personal brand.

Okay, now that you've figured out your red sole, let's get to work. One of the fastest and cheapest ways to build a personal brand is through social media. In my early days on Twitter, I thought, *Oh, I'll try to engage So-and-so and befriend him on the platform, and hopefully he'll follow me, and then I'll gain followers.* I tried that a few times, to no avail. My follower numbers stayed flat. So, I went back and studied that person's feeds again and found the answer, a real personal brand game changer. I discovered that real thought leaders on Twitter rarely if ever join anyone else's conversation. They traditionally always start their own. Sometimes they post articles from magazines or quote famous people, but they have their own thoughts, and the more outrageous or funny the thoughts, the more engagement they receive, and they establish themselves as experts in their current profession or in a space they're hoping to pivot to.

Most social media experts will advise you to tweet about something you're already an expert in. For me, the obvious choice would be fashion. Still, as I think you guys probably know by now, I have no interest in being or doing the obvious, so fashion was only a small part of what I tweeted about. I discussed books, art, pop culture, politics, social issues, and I was hella BLACK with it. My feed was very Lil' Brown Bevy–centric, eclectic, and diverse. Folks began following me and, more important, retweeting me. But the real breakthrough came when I started live-tweeting *The View*. That was my social media moment.

I have always loved *The View*. In my opinion, it's the perfect show because it provides a venue for an all-female cast of hosts of varying ages, religions, and races to talk about wide-ranging topics, from politics to pop culture. There are so many different opinions at the table that it makes for great debates and the occasional meltdown. Many people started following me on Twitter from seeing me on various shows on VH1 and BET, but once they visited my Twitter feed and saw the way I broke down *The View*, they stayed. For several years, Monday through Friday, I live-tweeted *The View*. Followers would come on my feed daily and ask, "Bevy, are we watching *The View* today?" So, it was indeed a full-circle moment when I guest cohosted *The View* in June 2014. Even though I was no longer live-tweeting the show, many of my Twitter followers remembered my live-tweeting days and sent beautiful messages to cheer me on. For many people who had been following me for years, it felt like their win as well.

So, what did all this mean for my brand? Well, thanks to my live-tweeting of *The View*, people began to look at me as a pop culture aficionado, business-savvy best friend, and auntie. Those tweets of mine had garnered tens of thousands of followers and helped build my personal brand. A #MommaIMadeIt moment!

Soon, brands began to pay for *my* brand. I'll bet a few of you are reading this and thinking, *I hate social media. It's a shallow, fake popularity contest.* Okay, you're right, and I won't try to convince you otherwise. However, that shallow, fake popularity contest can help you build your brand much more cheaply than hiring a publicist or a manager. It can also put money in your pocket. I know for a fact that, for me, my Twitter popularity solidified my speaking engagements, my social media ad campaigns, and my radio show. That's right. When Andy Cohen approached me about being on his SiriusXM channel Radio Andy, I told him I didn't want to do a show exclusively about fashion. And he said, "Oh, no. I was thinking it would be like your Twitter feed, with politics, fashion, pop culture, and self-help." And just like that, *Bevelations* was born!

Past successes helped fuel my Twitter success. I recycled the strategies I'd learned as a fourteen-year-old girl and remixed them with my marketing know-how. Had I not done any research and simply gone on Twitter hoping to make "friends" with the popular people, I would have wound up as a fan just like twelve-year-old handmaiden follower Bevy. Be clear, there's nothing wrong with being a fan, but I didn't want to be in servitude to someone else's message. I wanted to share my own.

When I started doing self-awareness work through therapy and by reading my favorite self-help books (*The Artist's Way*, *The Four Agreements*, and *Creative Visualization*), I identified the first personal brand I ever built, MC Bev-Ski in high school. That was the first time I took charge of my narrative and created a persona. Back then, the only brands I knew about were blue-chip brands. Iconic brands like Procter & Gamble, IBM, and Kellogg's were names I'd grown up with, and they were brands that had earned my trust over decades. Every great brand has tenets that you can identify with and rely on. Over the years, TV producers have come to know that when you hire Bevy Smith to discuss fashion, she's going to be fully knowledgeable and her take on pop culture is going to be rooted in her honest opinion. Many times, that opinion will coincide with what most people at home are thinking, and with what many people are too afraid to say. Producers know that I'm going to wear a bright, pretty dress—and yes, more often than not there will be cleavage.

◆ ◆ ◆

Nobody can be you but *you*. But there's a gap between knowing this and understanding how to craft your unique brand philosophy.

Let's start with what makes you you.

1. Who Am I—No, *Really*?

If you did your work in the "Red Sole Proposition" chapter, you have the answer: who you *really* are is you at your core. Take what you learned while identifying your red sole and write down a few of the attributes you'd like to align with your brand. That's right. Stop reading stories about me for a minute, get out a piece of paper and pen (or your computer or whatever it is), and think about yourself for a few minutes.

What words do folks mention time and time again when describing you? Mine are: *funny, blunt, transparent, savvy, real,* and *down-to-earth.* One of the things most of my friends and even clients say about me is "You can tell people things that others just couldn't get away with." The first few times I heard that, I didn't acknowledge it as a compliment—and honestly, I think some meant it as a backhanded compliment (folks can be so snide and shady). But now I accept that I have a gift for being outspoken yet inspiring, and I go right ahead and use it to my advantage, especially on TV. I've become aware that with a certain inflection in my voice or if I insert a pithy phrase right before or after I say something that goes against the grain, folks will receive it in a positive manner. Keep in mind, I didn't start making forthright comments, being comical, and sharing my truths in an effort to build a brand. It's *authentically* who I am.

In order to build a personal brand that will *stick*, you have to take advice from Willie Shakespeare and "to thine own self be true." I know I keep saying it, but you have to be authentically you, or eventually the persona you built will become a prison—and Kim Kardashian West won't be there to help you receive clemency. The actor, rapper, and all-around good guy Will Smith was on a radio show, *The Breakfast Club,* and he spoke about painting himself into a corner with the Will Smith persona. As many of us do, he had also created characters that would "protect" him in the world. On air, Will talked about those personas winning a few things for us, but also about how, when a persona stops working because it's not true, because it's not who you really are, you have to kill it off.

Sound familiar? It does to me. After that meltdown in Milan, I knew deep inside, at my core, that I was going to have to shut down some of my old personas in order to build a life, a brand, I could truly be happy with. But the old you is a lot to give up, especially if, like Will Smith said, you've experienced some meteoric success by draping yourself in that character. It's much easier in the short term to keep offering what the folks have been buying. But if you know better, you have to do better, once you acknowledge that you have been locking away the best parts of yourself. And yes, your current incarnation (who hid those best parts) has garnered you some wins, but if that's not the core of who you are, if it's not how you want to be perceived, that's a recipe for an inauthentic life. I was able to get folks to see Lil' Brown Bevy by showing up and being vulnerable, of letting them know that, yes, I have feelings and sometimes they get hurt. This was in direct contrast to the decades I spent being a take-charge, boss of a woman. Letting go of those other personas so Lil' Brown Bevy could have room to flourish meant losing the ego and asking for help when needed. I also began to tap into my natural gift as a connector and mentor, offering help unprompted and appreciating but not expecting reciprocity, just like Jeff McKay did for me decades ago.

My advice on your "fifteen minutes of fame" persona? Be like Elsa and *let it go*! I'll bet you love that persona, are wedded to it, and (as with most weddings) maybe even broke the bank to create it. Is it shiny, popular, and feels untouchable? If so, that sounds good, but isn't that a big part of the problem? People are looking for brands to connect with, believe in. My friend DJ D-Nice became a global superstar during the early days of the coronavirus pandemic by hosting a virtual party he titled "Club Quarantine." He spun records for *hours* in an attempt to lift not only his own spirits but his friends' as well. And guess what? Club Quarantine wound up attracting over 150,000 people each night, including celebrities from Halle Berry to the Obamas, and spawning a myriad of copycats. D-Nice solidified his brand simply by doing what he loves and inviting people to share his joy and passion for music.

Your brand must be true to who you are, leaving room for subtle changes, upgrades, and shifts (aka brand extensions), of course.

Remember, this is an interactive exercise!

2. Why Me?

Now for your second step: put away your humility and get to boasting. Tell me why *you*—why should someone buy into *your* personal brand over someone else's? Okay, I'm sure you're shy about what makes you so epic, so I'll go first. Brands hire me because I've spent the past fifteen years earning respect in a lot of different realms. I have a pedigree—a lineage of doing good work, going above and beyond what is asked of me, and collaborating with brands versus just taking a job. I'm also not cheap, but you'll also get more than what you pay for, because I only work with brands I connect with on some level. These are the building blocks with which I created my brand's ethos.

In my quest for outspokenness and transparency—which are also part of my brand—I'm hoping that the blank lines that follow, which are intended for you to write your list on, will count toward the word count my publisher requires. Namaste.

_____

_____

_____

_____

_____

_____

_____

_____

_____

Put Some Respect on My Name

I'm sure that, unlike me, most of you are not particularly interested in changing your name for branding purposes. That's fine. Keep your dry name. (I *kid*.) I'm sure your name is marquee ready. Still, keep in mind that your name is not the only way folks identify you. You're also identified by how you're described when you're not around. Once upon a time, if you worked as a fashion stylist, that was your descriptor, and there wasn't much room for creativity. Now I meet folks who perform jobs that certainly make them sound like stylists, but instead they call themselves "style architects," "fashion mavericks," or "design innovators." Some people consider that extra and unnecessary, but I understand these fancy labels. Stylists who are also creatives are thinking about the long-term value of their brand. Remember, they may just be pulling clothes and putting them on clients today, but five years from now, when they're collaborating with designers and creating lifestyle extensions like home furnishings, the title "stylist" simply won't do!

When building a personal brand, you have to be clear from the outset how you want to be perceived both now and in the future. When I created Dinner with Bevy, people would say to me, "So, you're an event planner" or "You're a publicist" or "You're a caterer." Now, there is truth in each of those descriptions. Using the Dinner with Bevy brand, I certainly had created events, garnered press, and fed folks. But I understood that what I was doing was an amalgamation of all those things, and at the heart of that is hosting people, inviting them into a world that I've curated.

True story: as a kid growing up in Harlem in the seventies, I would go with my friend to see her dad in the Dunbar Tavern. It was a dimly lit bar with red accents and the smell of scotch permeating the air. To this day, I love a dimly lit spot, especially a dive bar. (Dear Men Who Want to Date Me, a perfect date is a fancy dinner followed by a make-out session at a dive bar). But even more than the environment, I loved the characters who frequented and ran the joint. The people I was most inspired by weren't the ones with the most money, either, like the hustlers; they were the women behind the bar, the barmaids. They had all the clout; they were the conduits, the connectors. Plus, they were incredibly stylish, from the top of their elaborate wigs to the bottom of their metallic platform shoes. I was in awe of the way they commanded respect. They were pillars of the community, too, always there with a helping hand, organizing clothing drives, giving hungry winos plates of food, telling my friend's father to stop being such a cheap ass and give his daughter a dollar for snacks. Whenever I'm hosting anything, whether it's a dinner party or a TV show, I'm tapping into my inner Harlem barmaid. Those women were the ultimate event hosts, and the bar was their stage.

For now, my stage, my brand, is centered around me being a host, engaging folks whether it's in a conversation on radio or TV or hosting a Dinner with Bevy. I can't foresee a time in the future where I will chafe at being a host, because I know even when I'm a celebrated actress and running a successful production company, being a host paved the way for all my success. It's an innate part of me.

Please Recycle

Reduce and *reuse* are tenets of recycling trash, but they can also apply to recycling within your life and building a brand. Instead of discarding whole chunks of your old life, you can reduce the parts that no longer serve you and reuse or repurpose the aspects that still hold value.

That's how a former fashion advertising executive/salesperson became a TV personality against all odds at the age of thirty-eight. It happened because I took the twenty years I was working pre-television and kept the pertinent skills that could help me succeed in my journey.

The most valuable gift I kept from my life as a salesperson— besides a few handbags, a numbered David LaChapelle print of Tupac in a bathtub, and a now depleted 401(k)—was my ability to handle hearing the word *no*. As a salesperson, you can't be afraid to hear no, because every single day someone is going to say it to you—even when they should be saying *yaas*! You know what other industry is like that? Entertainment. As the talent, you are constantly putting yourself out there, and you can't fear rejection. No matter how good you are, some TV exec with an antiquated notion of what Middle American (i.e., white) viewers want to watch will try to shut you and your good ideas down. Oh, and if that sounds personal, it's because it is.

You know, it took time for me to build up my self-confidence and not shrivel at the first sign of disapproval, which is what a no feels like. I considered my constitution too delicate to withstand rejection, but I was tougher than I thought, and so are you.

Sales was the best training ground for entering the world of entertainment. As a salesperson, *no* was just the beginning of the negotiation.

At that time, fashion and luxury brands didn't believe *Vibe* or any magazine catering to Black and Brown people was the right place to spend their big money—we'll get to the reasons in a minute. And honestly, people who worked at *Vibe* didn't really believe I would be able to secure luxury brands. When I started there, the person I replaced said I would *never* break brands like Gucci—he said they wouldn't even take a meeting. That made no sense to me, because I didn't just study the culture, I *was* the culture. So I knew that Black and Brown folks were not only consumers of designer fashion, but that when we wore it, we remixed it and made it better. At *Vibe* we were competing for ad sales against fashion magazines like *Vogue, GQ, Harper's Bazaar*, and *Esquire*, whose readers looked like the customers that luxury brands wanted in their stores, people they weren't compelled to have followed by security or check the validity of their credit cards. Brands claimed that our household income numbers for *Vibe*'s readership just weren't high enough—even though the purchasing power of *Vibe*'s readers often rivaled that of the magazines those brands advertised in. Research wasn't going to secure the deal; I knew I couldn't just show up with a PowerPoint presentation and win the business. I had to illustrate *why* those brands needed to advertise in our magazine. They were certainly enamored with Black artists, from Usher to Lil' Kim. The brands loved the music and even occasionally loaned runway looks to A-list Black stars. Unfortunately the treatment of *Vibe*'s celebrities was the exception to the rule.

Gucci was actually the first designer brand I booked on my own. (Tom Ford was a fan of *Vibe*'s fashion director and later editor in chief, the visionary Emil Wilbekin.) Many fashion people are sheep—and at that time Tom Ford was the herder—so once I broke Gucci, I started booking lots of luxury brands. Unfortunately, while I was working in the space, our stars never received any endorsement deals. Why? Because even at the apex of hip-hop taking over the charts, luxury brands didn't envision Black stars selling luxury items. The cultural bias and systemic racism that exist in the fashion and beauty industries have ultimately cost those brands a lot of money. Today, beauty brands are scrambling to offer makeup in a wide range of shades, all based on the hundred-million-dollar success of Rihanna's Fenty Beauty in just a few weeks. They had a head start that spanned decades, but they didn't think women of color were worthwhile consumers. Well, now they're playing catch-up.

Knowing that those brands were convinced that people from various backgrounds couldn't identify with Black people prepared me for TV auditions. I took the tenacity I'd honed in fashion ad sales and recycled it. Please believe that in 2005, I was not what casting agents and producers thought of when they were looking for TV hosts. (I may not be what they're looking for in 2020, either, but here I am, still working!) But my sales background had prepared me to go in there and win over the hearts, minds, and ultimately the checkbooks of those who thought I didn't belong in that space.

Whether it's a pitch for a TV show or an endorsement deal, I lead with my Harlem upbringing, just like I did when pitching *Vibe*. And I reused the strategy I'd applied to bringing luxury fashion advertising into that magazine—going beyond the numbers, looking at the real people and who they were influenced by—to get myself onto television. Folks are no longer looking for a pretty talking head to read a teleprompter and smile. TV is now driven by *personalities. Hello, lover!*

◆ ◆ ◆

Time to Marie Kondo your Brand You. For example, there are elements of my old life as a fashion executive and a salesperson that still "spark joy," so I'm keeping them. There are always a few vintage lessons learned along the way that can help you refresh your life.

Building your personal brand, Brand You, means getting to know yourself. Your *genuine, no imitations accepted* self. We've already gone over that in "Red Sole Proposition," so now you can begin building a brand that will last you throughout your various incarnations. Please believe that when I move into art and architecture curation—oh hey, Malibu Bevy!—and producing my own content, all my brand tenets (my hostess-with-the-mostest, tell-it-like-it-is persona; my accessible-yet-aspirational approach) will travel right along with me.

#MommaIMadeIt

HI, I'M BEVY, AND I'M COMMITMENT-PHOBIC. LIKE FRANKIE Beverly and Maze said before Beyoncé masterfully remixed it, "I gotta make sure I'm right before I let go." This kind of commitment phobia is how I ended up a single lady of a certain age, but it's also how I've dodged more than a few shoddy career moves. Considering that a number of those relationships fell into the category of inadequate offers, it seems that being a commitment-phobe isn't completely bad. After all, if I hadn't been fearful of commitment, if I had just gone around saying yes to everything and everybody, I could be the thrice-divorced star of Bad Bougie Bitches Fight Club or some other tawdry reality show instead of the single yet romantically optimistic woman with a thriving career as a media personality that I am today.

Thankfully, my commitment phobia doesn't spill over into mundane areas of my life. I'm not the kind of woman who takes hours to buy a dress or spends thirty minutes mulling over a menu trying to decide whether she wants the chicken or the fish. Nope, my fear of commitment centers on contracts, on paperwork that has consequences should I change my mind. I once delayed signing a holding deal with a television studio because Mercury was in retrograde. Luckily, it was an LA-based company with crystals all over their office, so they were very understanding. However, the honest truth was Mercury's being in retrograde had only fed into my existing anxiety over having to sign.

The only time I've felt good about signing a contract was for this book, and that's because I felt sure I could deliver what was promised in the agreement. Also, this contract is for only one book, so once I'd delivered it, I would be done, free to explore other opportunities. Again, I'm such a Scorpio. I like to keep my options (as well as my legs) open—you may not end up "exercising" them, but just in case.

To my mind, entertainment contracts are stifling. They restrict movement. They are the ties that bind you to a bed of nails for five to seven years, with 3 percent annual increases and 1 percent net of merchandising. Listing the terms makes them sound a little too close to sharecropping for comfort. Of course, if I had a multi-year contract for *The Bevy Smith Show* and the terms were favorable for me, then yes, I would be ecstatic to sign on the dotted line! However, in my fourteen years of pursuing a career in entertainment, I've never been presented with a contract that didn't make me feel trapped. Not even with my beloved *Fashion Queens*.

Dear Andy,
        Don't get me wrong. *Fashion Queens* changed my life, and for the better. But I wasn't looking for it, and when you told me about it, I wasn't especially excited.
Signed, Your Bevy

Now, if you're a *FQ* fan, I'm sure you feel like I'm being blasphemous. Please forgive me, Father, but I'm living my truth. Here's the thing: I thought I was *done* with the fashion industry at that time. I saw leaving *Rolling Stone* as my swan song to the whole dog and pony show. But like what the Mafia did to Michael Corleone, just when I thought I was out, they pulled me back in! You know I'm a dreamer, but I'm also a practical gal; I realized that whenever I went on auditions or took meetings, people were enthralled by my fashion background. It didn't matter how rich or powerful an executive was, they were all in awe of the behind-the-scenes stories of the fashion business. Granted, I didn't exactly stray from the Fashionista Bevy persona, especially once the film *The Devil Wears Prada* was released. It was then that I saw that the quickest way for me to get on TV as an expert/authority was through my fashion knowledge. So, even though I was out of the game, I took the cards I had in my hand and I played to win. I started doing those red carpet interviews during Fashion Week for BET (did I mention that I worked for free?), and loved it.

Yes, I was covering fashion, but I was now a TV personality who talked about fashion, not a fashion person who occasionally appeared on TV. To some this seems like semantics, a distinction without a difference, but I understood the nuance. I was officially "talent" now, with TV credits on major channels, and when I started getting paid for my opinions/commentary, you really couldn't tell me nothing about how good my old life was.

Now, back to *Fashion Queens*. Despite my lack of excitement over the prospect, I took the job because *seven years* had passed since I quit *Rolling Stone*, seven *jobless* years, and while I'd managed to ward off eviction for both me and my parents, I was in my midforties. Honestly? I needed a break like Nell Carter. Also, seven is the number of completion in the Bible, and I felt I had completed my penance for quitting my job without a solid plan and had even gone broke to prove just how sorry I was!

I'm going to share a real solid career tip/Bevelation with you: When someone *gives* you a job—as in no audition, no chemistry test, and very little haggling over your fee—and the show is on a major cable network and doesn't require you to splash a drink on someone or make up a fake boyfriend, well, you should say yes and *thank you*! Now don't say I never gave you anything.

In March 2013, we launched the show, and it all happened so fast. I mean, one minute I'm on *Watch What Happens Live with Andy Cohen* as a bartender, and a month and a half later, I'm moderating a new show on the same set! (We traded out Andy's tchotchke-filled bookcases and replaced them with a glittery cubby filled with shoes and accessories.)

I was cautiously optimistic, and my reservations about the show were rooted in facts—and I wasn't just being a commitment-phobe. I was afraid that social media would call us a bootleg *Fashion Police*. (I mean, I didn't mind being compared to the legendary Joan Rivers, but I didn't want to *Single White Female* her!) I was also nervous about my costars . . . actually, about one of them. I knew, loved, and had mentored "Little" Derek J., but Miss Lawrence was the wild card. I'm not the biggest fan of reality TV, but *The Real Housewives of Atlanta* is a crown jewel in Bravo's tiara. I didn't really watch the show; however, I knew that several of the women were friends with their hairdressers, one of whom was Miss Lawrence. I thought that because he was on a show where wigs were pulled and drinks were thrown, he would show up on set ready to rip the "Gilda" off my head and douse me with a "Bevarita" (my version of a margarita, but with a splash of champagne and fresh lime juice versus margarita mix, *hello* tequila endorsement!). I had no interest in starring on *The Battle of Real TV Personalities, NYC vs. ATL.*

My relationship with Miss Lawrence is a prime example of why you should never make assumptions, because he's now one of my best friends and most trusted confidants. Instead of snatching wigs, he always checked my appearance (including my weave) before I went onstage, and made sure I had a cocktail on set. Yes, I was wrong about Miss Lawrence—and I was also wrong about *Fashion Queens*.

Throughout this book I've been talking about dream jobs, lovers, scenarios, and lives not meeting my expectations. Well, *Fashion Queens* was the exact opposite. I entered with low expectations and within the first month, I had a feeling of being home that I hadn't experienced since working at *Vibe*. We started with a three-week test run, the television version of throwing shit up against a wall and seeing what sticks. Well, we stuck. It turns out that all those Bravo-aholics wanted to quench their pop culture/fashion thirst every Sunday at 11:30 p.m. with three queens—although I was the only one with a vagina. (Can you believe that was my catchphrase during the first season? Clearly the show was outrageous.) We were instantly green-lit into a series, and I remember being half-excited and also just a little leery of what being on this show would mean for my career. It was never my intention to become a full-time, on-air fashion expert; I was still concerned about being pigeonholed. So, I figured the shorter the gig, the better. Essentially, I wanted to do the three-week test, collect my check, and wait for the next opportunity.

Thank God my concerns weren't warranted. Not one of them. *Fashion Queens* took me from "Aren't you that woman on TV?" to "Oh my God, my mother and I watch you and the boys every Sunday!" It felt so rewarding to be a part of a project that people not only looked forward to watching every week but stayed up past their bedtimes for. We were a late-night show, *and* we aired on Sunday, the Lord's official day of rest. I like to go to bed early on Sundays, to mentally prepare for the week—meaning, I was one of the stars of the show, and sometimes even I struggled to keep my eyes open to catch it. Suffice it to say, we weren't exactly in a prime-time slot, but our lead-in was Andy's *Watch What Happens Live*, and most of the Sunday evening programming on Bravo consisted of shows centered on Black women, including *The Real House-wives of Atlanta*, *Married to Medicine*, and *Blood, Sweat & Heels*. Some people accused Bravo of ghettoizing Sunday night because the programming consisted of Black women fighting, two fashionable, gender-fluid Black men, and what some would describe as an outspoken—okay, maybe they described me as boisterous and opinionated; okay, maybe they said I was loudmouthed, bossy, and showing too much cleavage; don't forget, it's important to know how you're perceived—Black woman.

To those critics, I say this: while I can't speak on the reality shows that came before us, there is absolutely nothing we did on *Fashion Queens* that I was ashamed of airing. I'm so damned proud of that show. We were ahead of our time. Truly inclusive and diverse, we introduced ballroom culture to the audience on a weekly basis, and when it comes to unscripted shows, we represented for the Black LGBTQIA culture like none before us and none after. We were also the only fashion commentary show helmed by Black people on a "general market" network, and that meant our critiques were unique. We were like Black Twitter brought to life on your TV screen. We not only embraced but *encouraged* body positivity. How could we not? I was curvy, and the boys were from Atlanta; they *worshiped* bawdy. And while we liked a long, lean model like Gisele, we also applauded the thick girls who graced the red carpet. And we celebrated older women who looked amazing: Cicely Tyson, Jane Fonda, Christie Brinkley, and Bethann Hardison. Our outlook on beauty meant that we gave red carpet kudos to women whom other fashion shows willfully ignored for years. Now, of course, all shows that discuss red carpet style are careful to celebrate different body types, ethnicities, and ages, but we pioneered that concept.

And perhaps most important, we weren't mean. Could we be shady at times? Yes. Did we throw in a zinger if someone decided to dress in a monochromatic outfit that matched her complexion perfectly, making her look like a Band-Aid on a thumb? Yes. But we tried to keep our critiques on the clothes. We didn't go personal and make it about the women and men wearing them. We did that—two gender-nonconforming men and a curvaceous woman in her forties, all Black and proud. We started as a curiosity and ended up gaining a cult following.

One of the biggest blessings I received from being a part of *Fashion Queens* was the honorific of *Mutha*. My babies, Miss Lawrence and Derek J., began calling me that on set, and soon many of our gay fans, young and old, began referring to me as such. *Mutha* coming out of the mouths of a community that has always supported me and I've always tried to support right back—it's a true honor to be considered family by folks I love and respect. I'm also called Mutha by a few talented and handsome men: CJ (my very own "Creative Jenius") Terrell, Moochie, Kiwan, and Wardell are my "sons," and I'm so thankful that they are successful, because they *spoil me*! "Come buy Mommy dinner, send Mommy champagne, Mommy wants to go on a trip"—yaas, it's good to be Mutha when you have stellar sons, and I take pride in spoiling them in return and always being there with a word of guidance. On the other side of the family tree, it took a while for me to be okay with some people calling me Auntie, because a lot of y'all try to use it as shade, an insult, a pejorative term about our age. However, the fact is that I am a *proud* Auntie to five incredible humans (Melvin, Domonique, Damien Jr., Donovan, and Darius) and great-aunt to a beautiful boy named Cyrus. I take pride in being their cool-ass Auntie who takes them on trips abroad, buys them frivolous gifts, and helps out with college. *Yaas, auntie.* Of course, now the term is used by folks who aren't your family. But as I mentioned before, folks watch me on TV and I feel familiar to them—kind of like their fly auntie who still gets it in on many levels—and I'm good with that descriptor! There is an exception, though: I only allow people who are under thirty-five to call me Auntie. Like film director Ava DuVernay tweeted when the great "Auntie" debate of 2019 was raging, "For the record, I happily respond to: 'Hello, Ms. DuVernay,' 'Hello, Sis,' 'Hello, Queen,' 'Hello, Family,' 'Hello, Ava' (safest bet)." So if you're in your forties or older, I ain't your Auntie, but I'd love to be your Bestie, love you, mean it!

As the honorary Mutha of the show, I was quite pleased by the end of our third season. *Fashion Queens* was becoming a part of the pop culture zeitgeist, with people referencing our segments, "The Gag Award," "The Reading Room," and Miss Lawrence's favorite, "Is That a Read?" We were all improving as hosts, and season four was going to solidify *Fashion Queens* into the mainstream pop culture consciousness.

Or so we thought.

We always had a few months off before it was time to head back to the studio to tape the new season. I'd use part of my time off to splurge in my favorite way: with a trip. Now that I had begun to become financially stable again, I decided it was time to take flight and hit an exotic locale or ten. After the show's third season, I went to Bali. Now, here's the thing, once you get to Bali, it's relatively cheap. However, getting there and staying in luxury ain't so cheap. But none of that bothered me because I had a TV show with good ratings and a million-plus viewers, the buzz was building, and damn it, I was a Bravolebrity! I deserved to travel first class like a Housewife! So, I booked a trip worthy of a top-notch Housewife like Kyle or Kandi, and it was a spiritual cleanse. Chic, posh, and relaxing, the kind of trip where you can set an intention for your next dream.

I had been back from Bali for a day and was already booked to appear on *The Wendy Williams Show* to do fashion commentary on the *Billboard Music Awards.* I was feeling grand, vacation-rested, and happy with my own series on a top-notch cable network. #MommaIMadeIt.

And just like that, life reminded me that it has a way of slowing you down. After taping *Wendy Williams*, my fashion industry son, Terrell, picked me up, and we drove to City Island, an island in the Bronx with restaurants that serve fried seafood of every variety and frothy, sugary cocktails packed with Hennessy. It's downmarket to some and bougie to others—just like me! We were driving in his luxurious BMW, listening to ratchet rap music, windows down, feeling like it was 1988 and I was a drug kingpin's girlfriend—except I didn't have to worry about him pressuring me for sexual favors—when I received a phone call from Deirdre Connelly, the showrunner for *Watch What Happens Live* and *Fashion Queens*. Deirdre, who had become like a sister to me, is a smart, funny, independent, compassionate leader. One of the reasons I loved working on *FQ* so much was because of the family unit she fostered on set. There was no hierarchy. Everyone was important, and we all got along famously.

When I saw her name come up on my phone, I picked it up very chipper and just a tad bit tipsy from my Hennessy Colada with a floater of 1800 Coconut Tequila. I was thinking she was calling to ask about my Bali trip. Instead, she said, "I don't know how to say this, so I'm just going to say it. *Fashion Queens* isn't coming back."

Come again?

Everyone handles bad news differently, and I'm the type who takes it in quickly and immediately tries to find the bright side. I told Deirdre, "Wow, well we had a good run," and then I thought of my babies Miss Lawrence and Derek J. Not only did they love the show, but it was also a glimpse into another type of life for them. At this point, both were still working in their own hair salons, and if the show had continued for another season, both were thinking about giving up the salons and becoming talent full time. I instantly worried for them; Deirdre told me she was calling them next.

I turned to Terrell and told him what had happened, and we instantly went into positive-thinking mode. He may have been the first person I ever officially mentored, but he had become someone I could turn to for a good prayer and a positive word. Here's a Bevelation: If you're a good teacher, the student eventually becomes the teacher. Terrell tapped into his spiritual teachings, and I went through those top-ten lists of affirmations that appear on journals and mugs, including one of my favorites, "Everything is as it should be." And I began to feel optimistic. While I was definitely sad about *FQ* being canceled, I never looked at it as a harbinger of hard times to come. My *spirit*, and Terrell, told me that I would never go back to struggling as I had just a few years ago.

The biggest adjustment I had to make with *FQ* not coming back was knowing I had to stay in my aforementioned rent-stabilized apartment. Here's a short list of folks who have lived in rent-stabilized or rent-controlled apartments while famous: Faye Dunaway, Bianca Jagger, Mia Farrow, and Cyndi Lauper. Looks like girls just want to have fun, and by fun, I mean not pay market-value rent!

I was proud to be a part of that tribe, but I had outgrown my one-bedroom. Even with a storage unit, my books, clothes, shoes, and art were overflowing and had turned my apartment into a chic hoarder's space. But instead of stacks of newspapers à la the Collyer brothers—google them—it was designer bags, thousands of dollars' worth of coffee-table books, and art purchased from trips abroad. Sounds glamorous, but clutter, no matter how much you can resell it for, ain't glamorous!

That's right, hunty. Season four of *FQ* was supposed to have had me *moving on up*! A two-bedroom, two-bath extravaganza with all new furniture! I had started looking at apartments online, thinking I would be ready to make a move by my birthday. I was dismayed at the thought of having to stay in my cramped one-bedroom until I remembered to always give thanks, to practice gratitude no matter the circumstances. I changed my outlook and became profoundly appreciative that I had a cheap place to live. It meant I wouldn't have to worry about scrambling to pay market-value rent with limited income.

Which brings me to another mitzvah courtesy of Andy Cohen. About a month after the show was canceled, Andy called me and announced he was doing a deal with SiriusXM for his own network and said he wanted to give me a radio show. I was already doing a podcast called *Bevy Says*, but it wasn't paid; it got revenue share via ads. Meaning, in other words, I hadn't seen a dime.

Thankfully, I wasn't struggling financially, but I wasn't about to turn down a new revenue stream. Plus, Andy said my show could be whatever I wanted it to be, which soothed the commitment-phobe in me. The way I looked at it, this radio show was prepping me for my very own television show. So, I said yes and began planning for *Bevelations*.

A little backstory on the name of my radio show. In 2009, five years before the debut of *FQ*, Andy had me audition for a TV pilot he was creating called *Fashionality*. It was a panel show about fashion. Bravolebrities like Nene Leakes and Bethenny Frankel were a part of it, as were three other fashion insiders, PR diva Kelly Cutrone, Barney's department-store-window guru turned TV personality Simon Doonan, and the curator of the Museum at FIT, Valerie Steele. During the audition, I didn't do particularly well on the panel—this will be hard for you to believe, but I was pretty quiet, as there were lots of big personalities and I didn't want to get into the fray. I was trying to find my TV voice and was concerned about being seen as the boisterous Black woman. (My, how things have changed!) Even though my performance was a bit lackluster, Andy still wanted to find a spot for me, so he created a segment titled "Bevelations," where I headed outside and did man-on-the-street interviews.

The pilot didn't get picked up, but I damn sure picked up the name "Bevelations" and put it in my repertoire of "Bevyisms." When Andy gave me the radio show, I knew I wanted it to be called *Bevelations*. That word set a tone. I wanted my show to feature unique interviews with celebrities, and I also wanted to share more of myself than I ever had with the public—I wanted to give them a Bevelation or two. I was determined not to pose the standard celebrity questions—I don't really care about whom they're sleeping with, and I'm not interested in a "gotcha" interview. I never wanted guests to be afraid to come on my show. I wanted a friendly environment where guests could talk about their projects and give us a glimpse of who they were as humans, what inspired them, what they were passionate about, what their EGOT plan was.

My first guest, Pharrell Williams, created the perfect template for what I wanted *Bevelations* to be. I've known Pharrell for over a decade. He's best friends with one of my best friends, Mimi Valdés, who is also his TV- and film-producing partner. Pharrell saw me as a star from day one, always encouraged me, and basically thinks I could be the next Oprah—and he should know, since Oprah loves him. He believes in me so much that he made me a video vixen at the age of forty-seven when he had me dance in six-inch heels and a little black dress in downtown Los Angeles in the beaming hot August sun for almost four minutes for the iconic "Happy" video. I did it in one take and never stopped. Granted, I had no idea that it wasn't a rehearsal and it had to be done in one take. Sometimes ignorance truly is bliss.

Anyhoo, Pharrell did me this *huge* favor and came to SiriusXM on a Saturday to record my first interview. It was a big deal. Not only is he one of the biggest pop stars in the world, but he also hadn't done SiriusXM in years. The people who handle booking at Sirius were flabbergasted that he was not only going to do my show, but he was going to do it on a *Saturday*. At the time, I didn't know that being able to book him myself had really impressed the brass. Had I known, I would have asked for a raise!

Pharrell and I have talked one-on-one many times, I've interviewed him onstage, and I've hosted several Dinner with Bevy events for him, but I was still nervous. I had never done radio, and I didn't want to let Andy down. Plus, there were so many people standing around gawking at us—okay, at *Pharrell*. But he came into the studio just as down-to-earth and human as you would expect, and we got right into it. We had a deep, philosophical conversation rooted in his work as a pop star, and he shared with me that the first time he ever felt the impact of his music was with the success of "Happy." He also told me that he hadn't wanted to cry on Oprah's show, but when she showed him the global map of people doing the "Happy" video, he couldn't help it. I knew how he felt, because I almost cried after *our* interview. I couldn't, though, because I was going to the season two premiere of the TV show *Empire* at Carnegie Hall immediately after and I didn't want to ruin my makeup. I had to look good for Cookie and Luscious.

I believe that how you start is how you'll finish. So, I figured if I could book Pharrell as my first guest and get him to open up in a deeper way than just talking about his newest project, I knew I could get other guests to come on my show. And boy, did I ever! During the first year, I had on Spike Lee, Kate Hudson, Samuel L. Jackson, and many other amazing stars I had long admired.

The celeb guests were a feather in my cap, but what *Bevelations* really gave me was more confidence. I finally understood why so many radio hosts, like Wendy Williams, Ryan Seacrest, and Steve Harvey, make such great television hosts. Being able to entertain folks with just the sound of your voice, most times by sharing anecdotes and observations, is a valuable commodity. I learned to listen more than speak—that lesson came my first year on the air, from my interview with Grace Jones. I was so nervous. Not only is she an icon, but she's notoriously mercurial and doesn't suffer fools. I was so scared that Terrell picked up on it and said that he and Miss Lawrence (who was visiting New York) would come to the studio and sit in with me.

Actually, Terrell did that often in my first months at Sirius, mainly because I didn't know what I was doing and needed support. I was used to television, so being on radio felt like just talking with no one listening. In the beginning, I didn't have a producer crafting compelling questions or digging up little-known anecdotes. Hello, it's called *Bevelations*! I intended to give folks something *new*, a revelation.

You guys know I love to quit jobs. For a few years, I'd been adhering to the philosophy that if something doesn't make you happy, you quit it. So, for a little while, I thought about quitting; I wasn't having fun. But one of the biggest lessons I've learned from *Bevelations* is: don't quit anything on a whim. Exhaust every potential solution; quitting should be a last option, not your first thought when things don't go as expected.

Still, I had reasons other than nervousness. I felt like my concerns about the way the show was being produced weren't being taken seriously. Thank God Andy had two radio veterans working with me, Sandy Girard, whom I lovingly referred to as my Mean Big Boss, and Tim Johnson, the sweetest Aussie (although I teasingly call him "Thief," based on Australia's less-than-stellar origin story). They not only heard me, but they believed in my talent and really helped nurture it. That included fighting for me to get great guests and, when they saw that my original producer wasn't the best fit, finding me the woman who is the bane of my existence but without whom I couldn't think of doing the show, Andrea Puckett. She's a tiny, stern, no-nonsense white lady from Indiana, and I love her—so do the *Bevelations* fans.

Sticking it out at Sirius and fighting to be heard is why I have a story that very few will ever have: I've been groped by a legendary Bond girl! Grace Jones.

During our interview, she opened up about why she believes Lady Gaga doesn't have a soul—not soul, as in rhythm, but *a* soul, as in she's *soulless*; now *that's* a Bevelation! She also brought a bottle of red wine and drank it during the entire interview. Now, some folks say she was slurring on air, but I understood everything she said, and didn't say. It was from that interview that I learned to get out of the way once you ask a question. Early on, I would interject far more of my opinions, but with Grace there was no air, no time for anyone else, so I was forced to just listen, and that's why it was a juicy interview.

Speaking of juicy, she thought I was juicy and proceeded to squeeze my butt and boobs. While I couldn't have predicted she was going to grope me, I definitely thought she would appreciate my bawdy. Even with weight gain, I knew I had a good shape, just more of it. Encasing it in a Roberto Cavalli animal print dress, I knew, would highlight all my lady bumps, signaling to Grace that I, too, was a woman comfortable with being sexy—which is a big part of her image. I wasn't wrong. Grace took one look at me, then looked at my "sons" Miss Lawrence and Terrell, and instantly understood that I wasn't your run-of-the-mill radio host. She was especially taken by my breasts, but when I stood up, she was shocked to find I also had a nice rear end. If you don't believe me, please see the photo where she's attempting to bite it! I've never enjoyed what could be seen as sexual harassment so much in my life, and it turned out to be a legendary interview.

Radio was the first time Lil' Brown Bevy showed up fully engaged in my work. On *Bevelations*, I've been able to talk about being a handmaiden to the popular girls in junior high. At least once a year, I play Elton John's "Philadelphia Freedom," ramble on about my crush on Benjamin Franklin, and talk about how special

1976 is to me because I turned ten and America turned two hundred, so we both had milestone birthdays.

It's not lost on me that because I am the only Black host on Radio Andy, I have a large number of white listeners. I hope that by listening to *Bevelations*, they begin to see that Black people aren't a monolith and that they pay closer attention to things that concern Black America. As I'm writing this, America is going through a painful time. Not only is there a pandemic that is disproportionately affecting Black people, there are also protests happening across the country in the name of George Floyd and many other Black people who have been killed by the police.

Unfortunately, due to the pandemic, I'm not able to be live and take callers, and I miss hearing feedback from my listeners in real time. Every day since the protests started, I have talked about them and asked my guests about them as well. I've had meaningful conversations on *Bevelations* about systemic racism with many of my guests. Yes, sometimes it's uncomfortable, but it's necessary. If you loved me and my show before, when it was just pop culture and funny anecdotes, I would hope you wouldn't turn the dial as I express not only my pain, but also the pain of my people.

Bevelations is freedom. As a Black woman in media, it's liberating to be able to just be me, the full sum of my parts and with no apologies. What I realized from being on the radio is that people, *all* people, are looking for connections. My family is a major focal point in my life and, by extension, in the show, so now my listeners are invested in *their* well-being. My sister, Stephanie, aka Pillow, comes on and often calls in; fans love her, as does Andrea, who even created theme music for her, called "Pillow Talk." My brother, Gerry, has been a guest on "Family Music Day," and listeners got a chance to hear where I got my well-rounded, almost encyclopedic knowledge of music. On *Bevelations*, I'm the little sister when my siblings are on air, I'm the girl who played hooky from school in a library. Lil' Brown Bevy shows up on *Bevelations* in ways I could never have imagined, and she's an asset.

The best part of being on Radio Andy is that I'm able to ask celebrities about their career trajectories, not just throw out basic interview questions. My goal is to glean Bevelations.

For example, when Kevin Hart came to *Bevelations* for the first time, he was on a press junket for his film *Central Intelligence*. Hart showed up in the studio ready to answer standard questions like "What was it like working with The Rock?" and "What interested you in this film?"—the same questions he'd answered on every late-night show and blog. First, I allowed him to give me his press spiel, and then I asked him about *Soul Plane*. Now, if you don't know about *Soul Plane*, that means you're white, so here's a synopsis: it's an iconic yet bad film that everyone has seen and can quote lines from, kind of like what *Showgirls* is for white folks. The IMDB page on *Soul Plane* describes the plot as "Things get raucously funny aboard the maiden flight of a Black-owned airline, thanks to some last-minute passenger additions." Okay, that doesn't even remotely describe what a fiasco this film is. It stars Tom Arnold, Mo'Nique, and Snoop Dogg. Granted, one of those people is an Oscar winner, but even Meryl Streep playing opposite Morgan Freeman couldn't have saved this film. Still and all, Hart was the lead, and he definitely thought it was his big break.

So, when I saw an opening in between his overly prepared "Hollywood" answers to questions I hadn't even asked, I asked him what it was like to get the lead in a film believing it was going to catapult you to stardom only to have it not only flop but become synonymous with box-office bombs and ratchet air travel. With his trademark Kevin Hart high energy, he took a breath and began to talk about what that loss had taught him, what he'd learned from it, and how he had combatted the naysayers, kept going, and became a bona fide movie star. I nicknamed him "Blackpac Chopra" after that, he was so inspirational.

I'm still working on securing a TV show that will showcase my way of connecting with stars, doing interviews like those I had with Grace or Kevin on the radio. Thanks to *Bevelations*, I have a template for my show. I used to think it would be on traditional TV, but now, with streaming services and online properties, the platform matters less. What's most important is that I know I will manifest this dream.

During this time, even with all the celeb hobnobbing and being given the latitude to talk about sex, politics, and yacht rock all in the same hour on *Bevelations*, I was still auditioning for TV hosting jobs. I received callbacks for lots of shows, including *FABLife*, with Tyra Banks. I thought I had that one in the bag after chemistry-testing well with everyone, especially Chrissy Teigen and an old friend from my fashion days, Joe Zee. Even though it would have required me to commute from Los Angeles weekly, I was bummed that I didn't get that job, but it was just as well. The show was canceled after the first season.

In May 2016, I was minding *Bevelations* and my own business when my agent called me to say that Page Six, the infamous *New York Post* gossip column, was creating a TV show. Now, I'm a native New Yorker, but I've never regularly read the *Post* because it has a reputation for being politically conservative and, surprise! I'm much more liberal in my political views. I like a good piece of gossip every now and again, as long as it isn't malicious, but Page Six is a column that A-list celebrities fear being mentioned in. Even so, as an advertising and fashion person, I *had* to read it at times because it was a preeminent source for industry news.

Anyway, I told my agent I wasn't really interested. She reminded me that *Fashion Queens* had been off the air for almost two years, and informed me that Endemol Shine Group, one of the largest production companies in the world at the time, was producing the show. Well, those two things piqued my interest. I thought, *I'll get in front of those executives, and they'll fall in love with me and want to cast me in my own show, right?* Wrong.

When I met with them, they immediately wanted me to come in for a chemistry test. Long story short, in an effort to grow past being a commitment-phobe, and though this was one of those times when my instincts to run and flee were spot-on, I ended up taking a job that took a toll on my health, both mental and physical. I became a cohost on *Page Six TV*. From the outside looking in, it seemed like #MommaIMadeIt. But on the inside, it once again felt like #MommaIMadeAMess.

Strangé, aka the legendary provocateur Grace Jones—
the most memorable interview of my career

Maro Hagopian

When Bevy Met Andy

HERE'S A STORY THAT TURNED OUT TO BE A BIG BREAK AND a #MommaIMadeIt moment, just not in the way I expected. You know that saying "Your name is in rooms your feet haven't entered"? Well, it's more than an Instagram quotable; it's how I met Andy Cohen, a life-changing, big-break moment.

I met Andy through *Paper* magazine, a cool independent magazine focused on art, music, film, and nightlife not normally covered by "mainstream" publications until recently. As soon as I told Mr. Mickey (Boardman, editorial director) and Kim Hastreiter (cofounder) that I had quit my job as an advertising exec to lead a more creative life and that I wanted to write, they instantly put me to work. As a matter of fact, I wrote one of Rihanna's first-ever cover stories for *Paper* in 2007. I was elated for the opportunity to write for one of the more cutting-edge, trendier magazines in the marketplace. I thought that was more than enough—but the universe had more in store for me.

Enter Hunter Hill. At the time, Hunter was in charge of advertising sales for *Paper*. We had a warm relationship. Like me, he wasn't a traditional advertising salesperson. He was chill, laid-back, funny, and incredibly handsome. I don't recall telling Hunter in great detail what I wanted my future to look like, but then again, I told so many folks! I may have told his mailman, who then relayed it to him.

Anyhoo, one weekend, I received a call from Hunter. He said he was hanging out with a Bravo executive named Andy Cohen, who was looking for a fashionable and funny woman to be a cohost on Tim Gunn's new show, *Tim Gunn's Guide to Style*.

Upon hearing "Tim Gunn" and "Bravo," I became *very* excited. Not only was Tim Gunn a REAL fashion professional, but he was smart and sophisticated. As for Bravo, it had a mix of intelligent pop culture shows, including *Project Runway*, *Top Chef*, and *Inside the Actors Studio*. I had a serious daydream about being interviewed by James Lipton (RIP) on *Inside the Actors Studio*. Tim Gunn's show would put us on the same network.

Hunter told me to expect a call, and sure enough, I received one on . . . I believe it was a Monday—this was a long time ago, 2007, so forgive me if my memory's faulty—and I went to a studio to tape an audition. I was nervous; I didn't know what to expect. But once they began asking me questions about fashion and my overall approach to style, I became comfortable. I remember the interviewer and the cameraman laughing—here's a Bevelation: Whenever you can make a cameraman laugh, you're doing something right—and then I began to express a lot more of my Bevy-ness, a collage of Big Bev from Uptown meets Beverly Smith, Fashion Exec. I left feeling confident and thinking, *I may have a shot at this gig.*

Fast-forward two days. I was out of town on a speaking engagement at an invitation-only event for successful Black women in corporate America called the Odyssey Network Business Retreat, and I received a call saying that Bravo wanted to offer me the job. #MommaITrulyHaveMadeIt. I jumped up and down in the middle of a luxury resort, and I started telling women, groups of fabulously well-coifed Black women whom I barely knew, that I just got offered a new show on Bravo. Now, if you're ever looking for a group of people who will support and lift you up like a good bra, look no further than Black women. (They epitomize the spirit of Mutha, Auntie, Bestie.) They started hugging me, offering to take me for champagne, and just loving up on me like my success was theirs.

Then I received the contract.

As an advertising executive, I had seen my fair share of contracts, so I looked it over and realized the terms didn't seem that great. But I was a TV novice, so I contacted my lawyer and sent it over to him. Then I called my friend and mentor, Monique Chenault. I also chatted with a new friend (now part of my core group of friends) whom I had literally just met at the conference, Kim Bondy, a veteran TV producer. It may sound insane to let a virtual stranger look over your contract, but I needed help. Kim had seen larger contracts than mine, and I needed her insight. This was allegedly my big break, and that contract, if I signed it, sure seemed like it would break me. Yes, my lawyer was looking it over, but Kim and Monique, two OGs in the TV business, would give me the pros and cons of signing a contract like this, even if the terms weren't advantageous to me. Here's a Bevelation: Surround yourself with experts in your chosen field and don't be afraid to seek their counsel when needed. Oftentimes folks are so worried about "telling their business" and wind up doing bad business because of it.

I trusted Kim and Monique to give me their *educated* opinions on my contract, and they let me know I shouldn't take the deal as is.

If that wasn't enough, my lawyer also agreed. He pointed out that the deal was so financially restrictive that I would be riding a bus while an ad for the show was on the side of it. Nothing against taking the bus—y'all know I'd already made peace with the M101, which stopped directly across from my apartment. However, I didn't imagine being a cohost on a show and not only being paid very little, but having my income contractually restricted!

You see, there was a clause in the contract that required any deals I made with outside brands to be approved by Bravo first. By this time, I had started Dinner with Bevy, so I was working with all sorts of brands. I certainly didn't want to have to run it by Bravo if I wanted Don Julio to sponsor a dinner because its rival Jose Cuervo was advertising on the show. Bravo would have had the power to veto my deal with Don Julio. As a marketing professional, I felt that doing the show made sense; but as talent and an entrepreneur—oh hell to the nah! (Dear Don Julio, please accept this as a shameless gambit to receive a lifetime supply of your 1942 brand.)

There were other things in the contract that Kim, Monique, and my lawyer thought were red flags, so I instructed my lawyer to go back and negotiate. Keep in mind that Bravo and Andy didn't know much about me then, though Hunter had told them I had worked in fashion and was looking to do TV. I learned then that you always want to make sure folks know your pedigree. Even if they had known I'd once been a very successful fashion executive, it might not have changed anything. Still, many networks are able to get people on the cheap for unscripted shows because folks will do anything just to be on TV. But that wasn't and still isn't my ministry.

My lawyer went back and tried to negotiate, but there was absolutely no budging them. They wouldn't give me anything I wanted; it was a take-it-or-leave-it deal. At this point, Bravo was moving ahead as though my contract had been signed, and I was shopping at Bloomingdale's for an undergarment to wear, as I was scheduled to meet Tim Gunn that day and intended to be snatched.

So, you can imagine how my soul was snatched when my lawyer

called and said, "They won't give, on *anything*." I had just struggled to pull on a very tight, full-body waist trainer contraption, so
I knew about things that wouldn't give. With a body shaper, if you
just sucked in your gut and squirmed around a bit, you could, as
Tim Gunn would say, "make it work." Alas, that wasn't the case
with the Bravo deal. It didn't work for me.

My lawyer said, "You have no choice. You *have* to take the deal."

Well, I tend to adhere to the old Black saying made famous by
the bat-wielding Joe Clark, portrayed by a not-so-godlike Morgan
Freeman in the film *Lean on Me*: "I don't *have* to do anything
but stay Black and die." I refused to believe that not signing that
contract meant that I wouldn't or couldn't make it in TV. Here's a
Bevelation that I believe in wholeheartedly: What is for me, is for
me. No one person or entity can deter me from my destiny.

I was confident I would book another TV show because, in 2006,
I was the "Style Den Maven" on a show on BET J (the smaller,
female-driven sister to BET that was later renamed BET Her) called
My Model Looks Better than Your Model, starring Eva Marcille (who,
in an ironic turn of events, was recently a cast member on *The Real
Housewives of Atlanta*). I had been cast on *My Model* by a dear friend,
Nathan Hale Williams; he actually created the role of the Style Den
Maven for me. That show wasn't a huge financial boon, but it was
a fun and innovative spin on a fashion competition show, and the
contract wasn't at all restrictive. Basically, I rendered my services,
and I had the right to do whatever I wanted in the rest of my business. It was also my first cohosting gig, so I said yes.

But this time around, I felt like I'd already done one show without being paid much, and Bravo was going to tie my hands so I
wouldn't be able to maximize my other revenue streams. I told my
lawyer to inform Bravo that I wouldn't be signing on.

I was devastated. This was supposed to have been a major
moment for me. Still, the optimist in me told me to look at it from

a positive space. The offer proved that I was ready to be talent. I could actually have a career in TV!

And that's when I received a phone call from Andy Cohen's office. (Now, remember, back then, Andy was a television executive, *not* talent, so while he may have been well known in the TV business, from folks like me and you, his name got a blank stare.) We arranged for me to meet him and his then boss, a wonderfully warm woman, Amy Introcaso-Davis. For that meeting, I shopped my closet—my wardrobe was "Bevy-fied," consisting of colors and cleavage—and chose a sienna-colored wrap blouse by Oscar de la Renta and a long Missoni skirt with sienna, turquoise, and brown wiggling through the signature print. That skirt hugged my curves perfectly, and for added spice, it had a mermaid hem. (Sofia Vergara, eat your heart out!) I wore brown Tom Ford for Saint Laurent sandals and completed the look with an orange Goyard bag. I had on about ten thousand dollars' worth of clothes and only about a hundred dollars in my bag. You hate to see it—but then again, you loved to see me coming that day, because I looked like a party, like good energy, like someone you wanted to know more about and see on TV, the perfect foil to Tim Gunn's buttoned-up sartorial style and sardonic, dry wit.

Thank God I showed up looking like a Fashion Queen—in fact, we spent the first ten minutes discussing my "lewk." Amy loved me, and so did Andy. He told me he was sorry the deal hadn't worked out, but that he knew we would work together in the future. Well, in the thirteen years since then, Andy has always kept an eye out for projects we could work on together, from TV pilots that didn't make it to air, to *Fashion Queens*, to *Bevelations* (the radio show), and now this book. He is a man of his word, a real mensch, and a true friend. I'm eternally grateful that Hunter Hill mentioned my name in a room my feet never entered.

Fashion Queens: *the best TV experience I've ever had.*
It was like working with family, and obvi,
I was MUTHA!

It Gets Greater Later . . .

I QUIT MY *ROLLING STONE* JOB APPROXIMATELY FIFTEEN YEARS ago with the goal of being in entertainment, a TV host, an actor, an acrobat, a ventriloquist . . . a *something other than what I was at the time.* (I'm sure by now you realize that goals keep changing, and that's the point. A Bevelation: We are all continually evolving; don't get stuck in a rut.) So, when I was offered the opportunity to be a host on a daily television show, it should have felt like #YouDidThat! But, honestly, it never was a great fit for me.

And here's the thing: I felt that from the beginning—actually, *before* the beginning. I knew from the moment my agent told me there was a casting for *Page Six TV*, a new syndicated show. It *had* been a while since I'd been on a television weekly. And there were lots of reasons going for the job seemed to make sense. Being a host on *Page Six TV* sounds like a great gig: steady check, millions of people seeing you five days a week on nationally syndicated television. These are things that folks in my profession dream of, and in many ways, they're what success looks like if you're a TV host. But, remember, I'm the person who quit a "dream job" at *Rolling Stone* to pursue a life of work I was passionate about and inspired by. I don't subscribe to the idea that just because an opportunity is something that "everyone" dreams of, that it's something I should covet as well. That's probably why I've never been a big fan of the current trend of anilingus.

Meanwhile, pursuing someone else's "dream job" *could* sabotage the very real dreams I'd been making come true for myself. I had just spent a decade cultivating relationships with celebrities, first as an editor at-large at *Vibe*, and then through Dinner with Bevy and *Bevelations*. I was concerned that all that relationship equity could go out the window if I were perceived as the enemy by the very celebrities who had come to trust me. Most of my friends, who weren't in the TV business, felt that I was up for the challenge and could do the delicate dance of being on a gossip show without actually being a gossip.

This was not me being my normal commitment-phobe self. This was me wanting to stay on track with all the work I'd been putting in for over a decade. Still, I went to the audition. And the *signs* telling me why I shouldn't have begun to pop up right away.

Exhibit A: my wallet. Or, rather, *not* my wallet. I showed up at the ABC studio without mine by accident. Now, because of technology, you don't really need your wallet anymore—your phone can pay for everything, from meals to Ubers. However, when you're going into a major media conglomerate, they need to see your government-issued identification. Standing in the lobby, unadmittable and ID-less, I had to call my contact there, the creator and executive producer of the show, Michael Weinberg, and sheepishly explain why I couldn't enter the building. He graciously came down to pick me up from the front desk, and I went to the meeting.

I may not have been excited about this project, but I'm *always* excited about meeting new people, so I came into that meeting hot—literally, and a tad bit sweaty from looking for my wallet and panicking that, because I was late, the meeting might run over, which would put me in jeopardy of being late for *Bevelations*, which is a *live* show. When I'm late that means the listeners will tune into the show at 5 p.m. to hear Led Zeppelin's "Kashmir" or Isaac Hayes's "Walk on By" playing to buy me time to "skid" into the station. ("Kashmir" is over eight minutes long, and Isaac's "Walk on By" is twelve minutes.)

They call these auditions meetings, in an attempt to act as though they're casually getting to know you, but please believe they're auditions. The show's producers want to give you the old once-over before they pass you on to the next level. At the audition/meeting, you're asked to talk about yourself very much like at a normal job interview, except here it's totally acceptable to drone on about yourself. (Hence, I love an audition/meeting: *let me tell you about me!*) However, before I could launch into my origin story this time, I told the folks in the room that I needed twenty dollars, explaining that I left my wallet at home and I had no cash on me.

The room erupted in laughter, and the producers attempted to resume the meeting. They thought it was a joke.

So, I reiterated that I really needed twenty dollars and that the meeting wouldn't start until I'd secured my coin. Then an older man with a beautiful, full head of silver hair and an easy smile stood up, pulled out his wallet, and gave me a twenty. That man was Jim Tomlinson, a working-class Irish American guy who just happens to be one of the industry's most successful heads of production, working on iconic shows like *Who Wants to Be a Millionaire*, *The $100,000 Pyramid*, and *Good Morning America*. Jim is my kind of people, a stand-up guy who, although incredibly successful, has never forgotten his humble beginnings, nor the value of having cold, hard cash on you at all times. Later on, when we began working together, we bonded over the fact that it was our Depression-era parents who taught us that cash is *king*.

Anyhoo, once I got my Jackson in my hand (which should have been a Harriet Tubman; damn you, Trump!) the meeting began. Michael Weinberg introduced me to the team, and I launched into my story, which was basically what you read in chapter one. The real growth in my story is that Lil' Brown Bevy is now a part of my origin narrative, showing up first whenever folks ask me to talk about myself. I find that she disarms people. I'm aware that when I enter rooms, especially rooms full of white men, they expect the one-note comedic and direct Black woman. I won't be predictable, so I lead with Lil' Brown Bevy, a nerdy Uptown Girl surprise. I find that, with Lil' Brown Bevy, they begin to listen more intently and realize there's more to me than meets the eye. So, Lil' Brown Bevy went from being my secret to being my *secret weapon.*

To Michael's credit, he instantly got me and saw that I was much more than a fashion girl. I was cultured, a world traveler, a student of architecture, a lover of literature, and yes, of course, a quintessential uptown girl. (Harlem forever!) While he thought I would be a great fit, apparently not all the decision makers were convinced. Michael told my agent that he needed to get me on tape, recording me instead of having me perform live in front of judge and jury. They wanted to see what I looked like on camera, how natural I was when filmed.

It just so happened that this was the end of June, and I was heading out to New Orleans for the Essence Music Festival, my holy grail of all things good and Black! Because *Page Six TV* needed my tape immediately, Michael persuaded me to make a pit stop on my way to LaGuardia Airport to a casting agent in Brooklyn. In case you don't live in New York City, you should know that getting from Harlem to Brooklyn is a real hassle. Depending on the particular uptown and Brooklyn areas, a drive there can take anywhere from thirty minutes to an hour and a half, so Bevy does Brooklyn about twice a year, *period*. (For anyone reading this who is a Brooklyn resident, before you get all huffy about your borough, are you a transplant or a native? I'm asking because native Brooklyn people understand what I'm saying. Before BK became the mecca for people who make artisanal bath salts from pickle brine, if you were from Manhattan, you went to Brooklyn to visit Coney Island.)

Okay, so we've now established that I didn't relish the idea of going to New Orleans via Brooklyn. However, my agent cajoled me into going, and my Aimee thought it was a good idea, too. As an added bonus, because she lives in Brooklyn and is a bestie, Aimee offered to meet me for breakfast and come with me to the audition. She's such a great stage mom.

When I arrived, I met the divine Barbara Barna Abel, a veteran casting director and on-air coach. As I was waiting to be taped, other women came in to audition. They gave me the once-over, but honestly, I didn't care. I was just doing this for sport.

I left that taping, got on my plane, and proceeded to have a bacchanalian good time in the Big Easy. Of course, folks kept asking me what was going on, what was next for me on TV. And to all the nosy people who work in my business who feel that they are in competition with me but act like they're rooting for me, I mentioned my audition, just to make them envious because they hadn't even been called for one. Not my finest moment—clearly, "Petty LaBelle" was present and accounted for at Essence Fest. However, in life, balance is key, so I also found the time to be honest and authentic with real friends and well-wishers who are my peers in the business. I shared my hesitations about taking on a job in that space (no, I hadn't been offered the job, but I knew my audition had gone well), and my fear of being maligned as a gossip reporter. When I came back from Essence Festival on a high from daily Hurricane cocktails, fine-ass men in hues ranging from Creole pecan to deep dark chocolate truffle, and checks upon checks (the revenue I make during Essence Festival is usually in the mid five figures and I get to work tipsy while interviewing some of my favorite singers in the world; it's work that feels like play), my agent told me that the job at *Page Six TV* could become a reality.

Sure enough, I made it to the next round, the dreaded chemistry test, and that's where I met Mario Cantone, aka Anthony from *Sex and the City*, aka the best Judy Garland impersonator with a penis, an actor, singer, and all-around entertainer. During our chemistry tests, we had this screwball kind of banter that was just so organic.

During the chemistry test, it became apparent that I was a favorite of Michael Weinberg's, so I decided to confide in him about my concerns. He assured me that he was sensitive to all the work that I had done throughout the years and didn't want to ruin my relationships with celebrities. He admired my Dinner with Bevy brand and promised he had no intention of tarnishing it. He saw me as being on board to give context on the show. Since I wasn't a reporter, my job wouldn't be to go out and get the scoop on celebrities. It would be to move the stories along by giving color commentary. Hypothetically, if there were a segment about someone like Brad Pitt canoodling with women at a nightclub in Croatia, the reporters would give all the salacious details: who was doing shots, who was sitting on whose lap, who vomited into a potted plant. After the sordid details were spilled, I would add my own personal experience at said nightclub, something like "When I was at Club X, it was really chic, jam-packed with socialites, and I could see why starlet Z got sick. The drinks are really strong there, and the only food served are old stuffed olives." So, my role would be to bring the story to life beyond what unnamed sources had told the reporters.

Even with Michael's assurances, I still wasn't sure I was interested. To be clear, I still hadn't been offered the job, but I knew I was being seriously considered. Clearly, they liked the Bevy and Mario Show, and I can't say I blame them. We were a prime example of what a chemistry test is supposed to discover. Do the hosts look like they would be friends outside the show? Would they have drinks afterward, or would they simply do the job and go their separate ways? If you look on most panel shows currently on TV, you'll see that many of them are hosted by folks who seem to barely be able to tolerate each other on set, so you know they *never* hang out together. I could name names, but even though I was on *Page Six TV*, I ain't one to gossip!

As I got closer to a solid offer, I called two people in TV whom I trust, starting with Alexandra Jewett, a top executive on *The Wendy Williams Show*. She advised me that it's always a good thing to be on syndicated television. It would give me great exposure and put me in front of TV executives who didn't know me from *Fashion Queens* or my *Wendy* appearances.

The other pro I consulted was Andy Cohen. He thought it was a good opportunity and agreed with Alexandra that it was another level of TV. When I expressed concern about becoming a pariah in celebrity circles due to the show's content, he assured me that I was smart enough to navigate any minefields in my path. He also said that any celebrity who was my friend knew my integrity and therefore wouldn't be concerned I would sell them out.

The assurances of my TV consiglieri made me feel better, and I began thinking seriously about taking the job—especially when it became apparent that I would work with my partner in snarky humor during the chemistry tests, Mario Cantone.

Here was a man with an actual "craft." That was one of Mario's famous lines during the test run of the show. He would be oblivious to the Insta celebrities we were talking about and would ask deadpan, "But what is her *craft?*" It was hilarious, and because I felt the same way about so many of the people we discussed, we were able to have a wink and a nudge and not take it all so seriously. Mario and I discussed how we would navigate the minefield of working on a gossip entertainment show, and we agreed to stick together to remain above the fray and deliver snide banter mixed with benign—we weren't about to spill any tea about our celeb friends—insider commentary.

A few days after the chemistry test, my agent told me I had the job. I asked, "What if I don't want it?" Now, you should know that my agent, Ashley Mills, was and is a rare find in the entertainment business, one who actually goes out and finds her clients work versus waiting for the phone to ring with a job offer for said clients. I felt like she got me. But agents must have clients who make money, so I'm sure if I had been in front of her, her face would have been like "Ma'am, *really?*" After all, since *Fashion Queens*, I had been up for a few hosting gigs, but nothing had gone all the way, so I'm sure she was looking at this like it was a chance to put a win on the board with this middle-aged broad.

Meanwhile, I was still la-di-da, window shopping and not knowing if I was ready to commit. Well, that's when I learned that the "test deal" agreement I had signed when I consented to be a part of the chemistry test was a commitment to do the show if I was selected and it got picked up. I know, I know, I should have known, but honestly, I was filled with so much angst during the audition process that I remember not wanting to talk in great detail with my agent about it. I wanted to do the work of auditioning and then decide. Of course, they didn't want anyone on the show who didn't want to be a part of it, so certainly they wouldn't have held me to that agreement. However, turning down this show wouldn't have been a good look. Especially since Michael was championing me in the halls of Endemol Shine! I'm not a kiss-ass, but you don't want to be labeled an asshole in this (or any) business.

There's a Bevelation: Don't be an asshole!

So, despite my misgivings, I put on my big-girl thong and became a part of a three-week test run for *Page Six TV* over the summer of 2016. The cast was Elizabeth Wagmeister, a senior correspondent from *Variety*; Carlos Greer, a senior reporter at Page Six; Mario Cantone; and comedian John Fugelsang as the main host.

During the taping, Mario made it clear that he wanted to be next to me and that I was his sidekick, the Ethel to his Lucy. Now here's what you should know about me: I will follow as long as I have a strong leader that I respect. Plus, I knew I could learn a lot from Cantone, everything from comedic timing to perfecting my mugging for the camera.

The key to doing a successful panel show is staying in your lane—don't step on your cohosts' lines or jokes. I never tried to compete with my fellow panelists. Carlos is a senior entertainment reporter who, before working at Page Six, worked at *People*, the holy grail of entertainment magazines. Elizabeth works at one of the top entertainment trade papers in the world, and there's no one better at breaking down the business of show business, so why would I try to veer into their territory? That's not what I do; what I do is Bevy: the worldly, opinionated New Yorker with celebrity relationships, a social butterfly, media insider. The trial run was well received, and the show got picked up, but unfortunately Mario declined to be a part of it moving forward. I was devastated. I understood his reasons—which are not mine to discuss here; as I said before, I ain't one to gossip!

The show officially launched in September 2017 with busside advertisements and a huge billboard at the gates of the Fox lot in Los Angeles. This should have felt like a #MommaIMadeIt moment, but it didn't. I understood that it was a big deal, but I felt disconnected from it, like it wasn't happening to *me*; it certainly didn't feel like it was happening *for* me. Yes, I wanted to be on TV, and I'm not above friendly gossip, but one of the rules from *The Four Agreements* definitely flashed in my mind: "Be impeccable with your word." That's not easy to adhere to when you're discussing someone's personal life based on hearsay from a "source."

I'm not trying to garner sympathy. Really! Nobody forced me to take that job. I signed on to catch a check and for the national (you didn't need cable to watch) exposure. I took the job and I'm a damn professional, so I showed up and showed out during our press run. I smiled at every affiliate station stop, shook hands—the one good thing from the coronavirus pandemic is that I never have to shake hands ever again—traded jokes, and kissed babies, aka seventy-year-old white men with conservative political views and papery hands. (They own *every* TV station in the world, it seems. UGH.) I was a team player, a salesperson yet again, though this time I was selling myself on a TV show, not a page in a magazine.

On the show I was positioned next to John Fugelsang, a funny and astute political comedian. John wasn't interested in modern-day pop culture; his tastes veered more toward the Beatles and *Star Wars*, less Justin Bieber and The Fast & The Furious franchise. So, I went from having this *Odd Couple*-esque comedic banter with Mario Cantone to playing the straight guy for a political satirist. . . . May the Force Be with Us.

The producers tried myriad things to make the show stand out, including having us stand up for the entirety of an episode. People didn't seem to like that. (I know *I* didn't. Wearing six-inch heels while chatting about Kim and Kanye—talk about PAIN.) We also played games built on celebrity trivia and had celebrity guests on the show, including Ludacris, Jonathan Cheban (aka the Food God), a few of the Real Housewives of New York, and Trump's former White House communications director Anthony

Scaramucci, aka "The Mooch," a man who did Trump's bidding for a scant ten days before being unceremoniously fired. (Remember the "Put Some Respect on My Name" section of the "Brand You" chapter of the book? Well, this just goes to show you I'm right, what you're called/what you respond to really does matter to your brand. This guy was a total MOOCH!) For me, he was a low point for the show. I was enraged that we would give a platform to an enemy of the free press. The producers insisted that his appearance would be good for ratings, and I have no idea if it was, but I know it wasn't good for me. Scaramucci instantly read my disdain for him and tried to cozy up to me, even joking that we would be great as running mates. Now, I believe in being gracious when someone's in your house, even if he is a douchebag, so I held my tongue, but I shot him a look as dirty as his former orange-hued boss and muttered, "Not a chance in hell."

At the end of season one, John Fugelsang left the show. (Again, say it with me, I ain't one to gossip, so don't ask me nothing about the whys and the hows.) The producers thought they should replace him and went through weeks of auditioning potential hosts, but in the end, they decided to just make Carlos, Elizabeth, and me the permanent hosts. I named us the Big Three. From day one of our chemistry tests, I liked and respected La Liz and Los, but when it became clear that we would be helming the show—that's when our bond was solidified. I won't speak for them, but I didn't feel supported by the lead producers who steered the show on a daily basis, so we had to rely on each other. Our friendship is the gift that keeps on giving from doing the show. As the "older" host and the only one with TV hosting experience, I often felt like their Mutha, Auntie, and Bestie, and I loved being there for them. And the support was mutual; they were there for a myriad of my meltdowns when I felt like I wasn't being heard. We hung out in Carlos's dressing room after our morning meetings, closing the door and having full-on kikis. We also went out for drinks after especially grueling double-tape shows. Carlos and Elizabeth are more than my friends; we became FAMILY. We were each other's sounding boards for all things personal and professional, and that chemistry showed through the screen, so much so that people still contact us on social media to say how much they miss watching us together on the show and ask when the show will be returning. (Spoiler alert: it won't! At least not with me.)

There were other highlights from the show, things I'm very proud of—not the least of which is that we taped five hundred episodes! No easy feat. Working alongside Elizabeth as she was breaking the Matt Lauer sexual harassment story for *Variety*, and doing on-air stories that were adjacent to her serious reporting, including a one-on-one with just me and her, is work I look back on with pride. Being the first national show to correct the misconception that the #MeToo movement had been started by actress Alyssa Milano when in fact it was created by Tarana Burke, a Black woman activist from the Bronx—now, *that* felt like a win. Same with setting the record straight on Kim Kardashian's role in securing Alice Marie Johnson's release from prison. Yes, Kim did visit Trump to ask for clemency for Johnson, but prison reform activists like my friend Topeka Sam, who had been lobbying for Johnson's release for years, were also a part of the White House trip—though of course Kim K received all the press. I made sure to not only say Topeka's name but also put her face on camera! Those were moments that proved REPRESENTATION matters and when I used the powerful platform of a nationally syndicated TV show for my culture and community's greater good.

As had happened with *Fashion Queens*, during my run with *Page Six TV*, I connected with so many of the crew, and we remain friends today. But unlike with *Fashion Queens*, I wasn't remotely upset when we were told that the show was being canceled.

It was the end of March 2019, and we were waiting to hear

about whether the show was being renewed. The showrunners seemed panicked and were trying to come up with different ideas on how to boost the ratings. When Carlos, Elizabeth, and I were called into a meeting with Michael Weinberg, I knew. This was his baby, and if the show was going to go for another season, he wouldn't have felt the need to fly in from Los Angeles with an HR representative to tell us.

They sat us down and—honestly, I can't remember exactly what was said, except that the show wasn't coming back. The producers assured us that it wasn't the talent's fault. While I appreciated their trying to make sure we didn't feel we were the problem, I already knew that. I did the math: as talent on a panel show, if any of us had been an issue, they would have solved that by firing one of us, or some of us, not canceling the whole damn show. I'm an onward-and-upward kind of gal about most things, and the reason we weren't coming back was inconsequential to me—but I damn sure knew it wasn't because Elizabeth, Carlos, and I were stinking up the joint!

In an effort to avoid a maudlin scene, I jumped up and said, "Well, let's go tell the crew." We went to the stage and gathered everyone around, and Michael made a lovely speech, incredibly heartfelt. The producers and many of the crew looked a bit shell-shocked, and I get it. TV is so chicken today, feathers tomorrow. So, it's a goal to get on a syndicated show that can last for years, sometimes even decades. I have no doubt that many folks on the crew hoped that *Page Six TV* would become a show that could put their kids through college.

By the beginning of April, the trade papers had made the announcement that the show had been canceled but that we would continue with new episodes until September. That was good and bad news. The good news was that it gave us time to plan our next move while still collecting a check. The bad news? I wasn't off the inane gossip hook just yet. I still needed to clock in and talk ad nauseam about supermodel Gigi Hadid and *The Bachelor*. For months, I trudged along, in limbo: knowing that the run was ending, but still having to show up and perform enthusiastically. I was drained. I didn't have much of a social life, even less of a sex life. I was miserable being celibate, although I guess it was a good thing, because my body was wrecked.

I was never skinny—had never wanted to be, *ever*—but when I started *Page Six TV*, I was twenty pounds lighter and two dress sizes smaller. Yikes! I know exactly how it happened: I ate cheap sandwiches from faux European franchises for lunch and had dinners from Seamless on my sofa almost every night, sad times from a culinary and lifestyle perspective! Of course, I realized there was a light at the end of the tunnel. I would be done with the job in September. But I still felt in the dark.

Once the cancellation was announced in the press, people started calling me to express, in the best, most well-meaning way, their sympathies—which I didn't want. I tried to be gracious and explain that everything was as it should be. I was taking the high road, but honestly, I wanted to tell the truth—which was "I was over that job anyway, every day felt like a battle, and as a Black woman, I never felt heard. Even worse, Black culture, which all of pop culture appropriates, was looked at by the day-to-day showrunners as a marginal blip in entertainment that 'America,' aka white people, wouldn't understand or care to learn about, and even though I was talent on a nationally syndicated show, I had no intention of coming back for season three." Clearly, from the above rant, I had a few things to get off my chest. Still, I understood all too well that, for many people, *Page Six TV* was a dream job. So, in an effort not to seem like a less considerate version of myself, I kept that truth close and shared it with only a few friends and now you. *My friends* knew better than to call with sympathetic platitudes. Almost every single one of my close friends, including Andy, said, "But this is a good thing, right?" To that I answered, "Yes, it is, because deep inside, I knew from the moment I trudged out to the casting agent's out in Brooklyn with my luggage that it wasn't the job for me."

Why am I telling you all this? Because I believe that every challenge we face is put in our path for a reason. Me taking that job wasn't some random exercise; the universe was trying to show me something. At this point, I don't know what the hell that was, beyond "Always go with your gut." However, I know later on down the line, there *is* going to be a moment when I say, "OMG, *that's* why I did *Page Six TV*!" I will not be denied my aha moment!

Once the show was canceled, everyone on the set went into overdrive trying to find new jobs. It was like a Louboutin sample sale, with folks grabbing anything and everything available in the hope that it would fit. As for me, I again found myself approaching life's challenge like I was shopping for haute couture in Paris. I was determined to be discerning and only select work that I was enthusiastic about. I didn't want to be convinced to take a job. Mentally I wasn't ready to jump back into another job—I was burned out, beat down, frazzled, and seemingly depleted of any passion for pop culture television. Meanwhile, Carlos and Elizabeth were taking meetings with agents and networks, making sure that once the show was over they wouldn't end up watching daytime TV in pajamas versus being on it, smart move.

My approach to "what's next" was a little different.

I knew that I had been unhappy, but I hadn't realized just how much of a malaise I was in and how it was stymieing my personal life. Looking back, I see that gaining weight and not being remotely interested in dating worked in tandem. Instead of going home and logging onto dating apps, I was going home, getting on my sofa, and ordering from my Seamless app. During the three years of that show, I just couldn't rally enthusiasm for much of anything other than travel because it was an escape. I took a lot of great trips during the *Page Six* era. Cuba, Croatia, Tanzania, India—I mean, you're making coins, you can go see the world. But for the first time ever, travel didn't leave me inspired and renewed. Nope. All I could do was recharge my battery to the halfway mark, just enough to go back and do the work.

By now, you guys know I can usually rally and perform well under pressure, but this time I felt trapped, and I blamed myself for willingly putting myself in the position to be unhappy at work. I was back in a space I had vowed never to be in again once I left *Rolling Stone*.

Folks kept asking me, "What's next?" But I truly had no real idea how to respond. The truth was what I really wanted next was time to myself, just to be! I wanted to visit a museum, journal, go to the gym, make myself breakfast or lunch, or both, in the middle of the day. These seemingly little things had been a big part of my life before *Page Six TV*, and I missed them. When I quit *Rolling Stone*, it was with the idea of having freedom to explore my passions and interests. But at the time of the show's cancellation, it had been three years since I'd done anything remotely like that. Beyond even lofty goals, I had been in my new apartment for more than six months and hadn't hung a photo or even taken a bath. (Before you ask, yes, I showered and washed my legs.) I never felt I had the time to let Calgon take me away! The money I earned allowed me to buy luxury items, but I truly missed having the luxury of *time*. That's what I craved. But no one wants to hear that. In our society, "the grind" is idolized. But the only grinding I wanted to do was on a man.

I also looked at the television landscape and realized there weren't a lot of shows I would be right for as a host. With my lack of interest in babies, my sketchy relationship with pets, and my love of a saucy, racy anecdote, morning TV is out of the running. Doing an established entertainment show would be like doing *Page Six TV*, but a lighter, gentler, much more benign version of celebrity gossip, one where I would never have the opportunity to be snarky. The only show currently on air that I would love to host is *The View*, but they have a full house over there—but hey, you never know. And I do see this book as a vision board, so "Hey, *View*, I'm available!"

As I began doing some soul excavating, I realized that I didn't *need* to do TV in the way I had for the past ten years. A lot of talent gets addicted to the "fame." (Now, I'm not declaring I'm famous, but folks recognize me and ask me for photos a lot.) For a lot of talent, there is something addictive about having people know you and treat you nicely because they watch you on TV. I, however, have no fear of fans forgetting me. First off, when I was Bevy Smith with no show yet, I had enough public recognition to create businesses centered on me. Dinner with Bevy and Life with Vision. Second, being on television didn't make me; it only enhanced and amplified who I was to a new group of people.

So, there I was with all this personality and my show ending. What's a girl to do? Well, I made a decision to focus on *Bevelations*, my SiriusXM radio show, and to garner more speaking engagements while I took time to figure out what I truly wanted to do next versus just pursuing what others thought was my logical next step.

This kind of strategy takes confidence. Lots of people were advising me as to what I should do, including people who didn't believe in my vision for my life or in the certainty in my *spirit* that I was doing the right thing. Once again, I won't allow fear to order my steps. And now I very much know who I am and what I want, so I am self-assured enough to take my time to get to next. That's why this chapter is called "It Gets Greater Later . . ."

This has been my mantra for many years, and I realize now that it was initially inspired by my mom. Seeing her navigate life with so much confidence—being her own woman, never comparing herself to others, her age never factoring into what she could or couldn't do—that spirit, my mom's spirit, has been imprinted on mine. I'm fifty-four years old and I know I'm just getting started. The best part about getting older is the confidence to live bolder, to be feisty and exuberant, damn what people think. I thought I was good and grown when I quit *Rolling Stone*, but *baybee*, this fifties era really shows you what it's like to be a take-charge woman.

There are myriad "logical" reasons I should just count my blessings and become limited by the status quo. If I chose to, I could sit around and catalog all the -isms that will keep me from succeeding in a new way. Racism, ageism, sizeism—and those are just the top three. However, I've already beat the odds three or four times just in the professional space and countless times in my personal space. Instead of looking at life through a greasy prism of "Why me?" I'm focused with 20/20 vision on "Why *not* me?"

I'm allowing my passions and interests to order my steps. I want to refocus my energies on my radio show *Bevelations*. When I was at *Page Six*, I'd often leave the studio exhausted, drained, but whenever I arrived at Sirius, I felt a sense of relief. It was there in our chaotic studio—with my trusted, snarky producer, Andrea Puckett, and the handsome but shady engineer, Jay Jeter (who I nicknamed JG), who is like a wayward nephew—where I could talk about things that really mattered to me.

In 2019, Radio Andy was renewed for three additional years as a SiriusXM channel, so I guess as long as I keep doing what I've been doing, I've got this gig for a few more years. Yay! Momma's got one job, but unfortunately, unless you're Howard Stern, you can't do just radio. I love *Bevelations*, but it doesn't pay enough to sustain my overhead. All that is to say, as much as I love my

Bevelations gig, unless I want to sleep at the studio, I have to have multiple revenue streams.

When the country shut down in March 2020 due to the coronavirus pandemic, I was doing well financially, despite *Page Six TV* having ended in September 2019. I had managed to reinvigorate my lucrative public speaking/hosting career, and business was flowing. I'd even gained new blue-chip clients, including Netflix and AT&T. In the words of Lizzo, I was feeling good as hell—proud of myself for earning enough money to sustain my *Page Six TV* lifestyle while doing work that I was thrilled to do. Unfortunately, hosting Q&As for TV shows isn't considered an "essential service" during a pandemic, so that revenue also dried up, and I soon found myself living off my savings and my *Bevelations* paycheck.

This brings me to my current state of mind: gratitude with a dash of grief. Right before New Yorkers were ordered to shelter in place, I began to feel sick. I had gone on an acting audition—yes, I'm back to pursuing acting—and later that night, I started feeling like I had a bad cold. The following day, Friday, March 13, I decided to stop going out and interacting with people. I wanted to make sure I wasn't sick so my mom could stay with me during the pandemic.

Well, nine days after my first symptoms, when I realized my "cold" wasn't going away and was, in fact, getting worse, I decided to try to get tested. At this point in our country, tests were scarce and the government, federal, state, and local, was telling tax-paying citizens, "Unless you can't breathe, don't go to the hospital; we aren't testing people." My symptoms were a wet cough (initially, only a dry cough was thought to be COVID-related), diarrhea (not on the original list of symptoms), fatigue, and an intermittent, slight fever, so I didn't fit the profile for testing. Fortunately, I know more than a few doctors beyond the self-titled Dr. Cherrie, so I called a friend, Dr. Arabia Mollette, who arranged for me to get a test on March 22. Two days later, the results came back positive, and that was the beginning of my life changing forever.

At first, I hid my illness from my sister and from Terrell, Aimee, and Renee—basically from all my friends. I didn't want them to worry. I live alone, and I knew they would freak out. Plus, I wasn't running a fever, didn't have a dry cough, and had no trouble breathing (until later), so I was hoping against hope that I didn't really have it—so much so that I continued doing my radio show, albeit at home, in my small pantry. It lifted my spirits and got my mind off "What if I have it?" But when it was evident that I wasn't getting better, even with my humidifier filled with Vicks Vapo Steam and after taking Tylenol and DayQuil, drinking mint tea dosed with lemon and honey, and sipping a concoction of lemon, honey, and garlic—ooh, that sounds like a good marinade for chicken wings—I realized that I had to prepare myself, my family, and my "framily" (friends who are family) for what was to come.

Everyone was incredibly supportive. My "sons" CJ (who continually supports me on any and all of my creative projects) and Terrell dropped off food almost daily, and my brother-in-law, Damien Long, a first responder, made sure I wanted for nothing. He would get off his twelve-hour shift, at a job where he risked his life, and bring me and my mom, who was living alone because my dad was in a rehabilitation center, whatever we requested. (I know folks complained about toilet paper shortages, but my problem was finding a frozen apple pie, though Damien found me one.) My brother and sister lifted my spirits and made sure to take up the slack when I couldn't call our mother because I was coughing. (With the pandemic, I had begun calling her about four times a day.) We didn't tell my parents I was sick. Why? Well, at ninety-two and ninety-five, they would only have become stressed and worried.

After about three weeks of being sick, I began to feel better and thought, *Wow, I'm going to beat this thing! My coronavirus story will have a happy ending.* Then, my dad started having respiratory issues, and on April 11, 2020, my daddy, Gus Lee Smith, passed away.

◆ ◆ ◆

My life from now on will forever be split between B.C. (Before Corona) and A.C. (After Corona). The plans I made when this virus first hit were all placed on the back burner. And as you can imagine, this whole ordeal stopped me in my tracks. But I'm up and moving again, and I'm compelled to finish this book, to share it with you, because even if you haven't experienced a death around coronavirus, we've all been affected and forever changed by this experience. A global shutdown due to a viral pandemic tends to have that effect on people.

With the passing of my dad, it has become crystal clear that there's no going back. My dad would always quote Billie Holiday, telling us, "Momma may have, Poppa may have, but God bless the child that's got his own." Daddy, you would be proud. I've got my own on many levels, especially my mind. Damn what "they" say. I'm not placing any limitations on my life, and I won't allow others to do it, either.

Smitty's Youngest—The Baby

IDIDN'T EXPECT TO HAVE TO WRITE THIS CHAPTER—NOT IN THIS book! When I secured my book deal, my dad was there to congratulate me, and when I completed the first draft, I went to visit him to celebrate. But while I was reviewing the copyedit, he passed away. Yet this book couldn't exist without him. My life has been shaped by having such a present and loving father. My backbone and sense of self? That's my daddy's legacy living on through me. So, this book is his book—except for the salacious parts; that's all me—because I am his baby forever.

My father died unexpectedly, though you're probably thinking, *How can a ninety-five-year-old's death be unexpected?* I mean, I knew he didn't have decades left, but he died from complications of COVID-19, a virus whose presence our government knew about and whose transmission it did only the *bare minimum* to stem. By this writing, in November 2020, more than 9 million people in our country have tested positive and over 230,000 have died. So, yes, his death was unexpected. I didn't expect a pandemic to kill my dad. From old age, sure. But from contracting a virus in a rehabilitation center? Nope, I sure didn't.

As a kid, I had great anxiety around my parents' dying. This stemmed from their being ten to twenty years older than my peers' parents. So, I became acutely aware of age, aging, and death early on. I would pray every night to God to let my parents live until I reached eighteen. I didn't know I suffered from separation anxiety until my tele-therapist told me. (As soon as my dad died, I went back into therapy.) All I knew was that we were a small family, and we couldn't afford to lose one part of us.

My dad was proud of our family and always thanked my mom for giving him children. My brother, Gerald, was ten when my parents married, and my dad loved to tell the story of Gerald asking him to be his father. My sister, Stephanie, arrived next, and she and Dad always had such a special, undeniable bond. I guess that's to be expected when someone has waited his whole life to have a child.

My dad thought of himself as an orphan. His mother and little sister both died when he was eight—his mother of what Dad called "consumption," which is also known as tuberculosis, and his little sister of polio. The irony is that my father's closest blood relatives died of viruses during the Great Depression. Fast-forward eighty-seven years, and my father also died of a virus that careened our country into Great Depression–like conditions, with more than forty million Americans filing for unemployment.

Losing his little sister and his mother to deadly diseases that swept through the country scarred my dad. And just like now with COVID-19, back then the poor and Black who were afflicted were underreported, and they didn't receive the same level of care, which caused many to die. To add insult to injury, their deaths were only hastened under the sadistic Jim Crow policies of the South, which Trump is a fan of, Confederate flags and all.

My mom says Dad used to tease her and say he was going to pay someone to have him some more "baybees." I guess that's why he was such an involved parent. He *wanted us*, desperately, and we felt that love and that connection throughout our lives and never took them for granted. Not only did our dad teach us to read and quiz us on geography, but from time to time, he'd warn us little kids that there was another Great Depression brewing. I used to think he was just being paranoid, but Daddy, I apologize, you were so right. You'll be happy to know I have a healthy (or rather, unhealthy) supply of canned goods in my cupboard now.

Both our parents doted on us, but Dad spoiled us, always buying us treats—to this day, I blame him for my sister's sweet tooth. One of my fondest memories is of watermelon and sugar-cane season. When that season came around, my dad would be there when the truck pulled up in the park adjacent to our grade school. We'd watch as he picked out the sweetest produce, often sampling the sugarcane on the spot. He'd whip out his ever-present pocketknife and cut off a piece of the stalk for himself and his girls.

Many of our friends didn't have fathers in the house, but when my dad hit the block, he became the de facto neighborhood dad. He would hand out quarters to us and our friends, and we'd run to Mr. Lloyd's store and buy chips or a Sundew drink, courtesy of our hardworking Smitty. Yes, my dad was a provider. We weren't rich, but we wanted for nothing, and we even had a few things we *didn't* want. I can't speak for my sister, but I hated that we missed the big annual block party held in front of our building on Eighth Avenue and spanning about five blocks. You know why we missed the event of the summer? Disney World. That's right. We were visiting the Happiest Place on Earth, and while I enjoyed it while I was there, I had major FOMO upon our return when our friends told us about all the fun we'd missed at the block party.

Hanging on the block was something my mom frowned upon. We weren't allowed to just hang outside; we had to be *going* somewhere. Our parents took us to parks, sometimes to neighborhood parks, but more often than not, we visited iconic Central Park. Our dad would walk us around what felt like all 840 acres of the park, recounting its history (it was originally Seneca Village, a settlement of free Black people that was destroyed to make way for Central Park in 1857; gentrification has been a plague on Black communities for centuries) while still letting us be carefree kids using our imaginations to explore and play. That made us "different," and not always in a good way. To this day, I blame our playing in Central Park instead of on the block for my inability to jump double Dutch, cornrow hair, or ride a bike. Still, my sister and I can give one hell of a guided tour of Central Park!

My parents wanted to spoil us, and it was my dad's mission to make sure we had as idyllic a childhood as possible, certainly better than the one he'd had. When he was a kid, Dad was taken in by his aunt and uncle, where he was raised alongside his cousin Snooks like a brother. By the time we were born, Dad's uncle had long since passed away, but his aunt, whom he called "Mom" and whom we knew as "Grandma," was alive and well. I don't know who loved us more, Grandma or Dad. All I know is that when we visited Grandma in the Bronx or, later on, in Goose Creek, South Carolina, when she moved back there, it was unspoken but understood that we were Gussie's babies, and therefore very special.

There's so much I want to say about my dad, my Smitty. I'm torn between honoring him and wanting to keep him to myself. But then I think about how much he would have loved seeing this book with his last name on the cover. In his last years, when, in *his* opinion, it was apparent I wouldn't be getting married, he would always say, "You're the last one with the name"—my dad was also very shady in the funniest way. So, I know going into a Barnes & Noble and seeing a book with his daughter's name, *his* name, on it would have filled him with pride. He was a proud man, but humble; his whole life was his kids. He would always tell us, "I never want to embarrass you, and I don't want you to embarrass me." He held up his end of the bargain, and my siblings and I did our best to honor him in the same way.

Honor was big with my dad. He was a World War II veteran. When he was just sixteen, he lied about his age, saying he was eighteen, to enlist in the navy . . . a week before Pearl Harbor. I used to think, *What a bout of bad timing*, but he never complained about fighting in the war. He wanted to defend his country, even in a brutal world war. In September 2018, my dad was interviewed by the Instagram page BlkSuns ("Black Men in Their Words of Self-Reflection"). When asked, "What is courage?" he said, "17th Birthday I was in combat against the Japanese. Blacks couldn't have guns. We stood guard with rifles without bullets. It was Jim Crow from head to toe."

My dad fought against the Japanese in the Pacific Theater and was honorably discharged. Sadly, when he came back home from risking his life, the racism and prejudice were still in place in Yemassee, South Carolina, where he'd lived. So, he fought once again, this time against the systemic racism of the Jim Crow South, by moving to Harlem.

He lived in Harlem for the rest of his life, but he worked in Carteret, New Jersey, at the AMAX metal refinery, as a smelter and, later, a foreman—for thirty-three years, until he retired at the age of sixty. That's a long time to commute two hours each way. That four-hour daily commute consisted of a ten-block walk to the subway, then a thirty-minute ride on the subway to the Port Authority, where he took an hour-long bus ride to Carteret. There, he still had to hitch a ride to the plant. He made that trip, twice, *every single day*, in rain, sleet, or snow. I never remember him taking a sick day.

When he arrived at work, his job was even more challenging: melting down metal with temperatures hovering around 2,000 degrees Fahrenheit! He never complained, though. He appreciated having a good job with full benefits, and he was especially proud to be a union man. When he worked his way up to foreman, he took pride in taking care of his men. That's just who my dad was: a provider. Nothing would come between him and his taking care of his family. You know how folks say, "They don't make them like that anymore"? Well, that's what I think about my dad (even though my brother-in-law, Damien, comes pretty damn close).

One of my favorite memories of Dad providing for us no matter what was when the employees at the refinery went on strike. (This was prior to his becoming foreman.) When you're on strike, the union provides you with a stipend so that you can take care of your essential bills, food, and shelter. Once, though, the strike went on for so long that the union ran out of essential money. Of course my dad wouldn't let us go hungry, so he looked for other work. My mom was cleaning the house of a lawyer at that time, and she told him that her husband was looking for work. He said he could hire my dad to be a foot messenger. Dad was in his fifties then and was used to making good money through his union job, but he didn't hesitate to walk all around the city in the sweltering heat to earn a check that barely covered the rent. I guess it should come as no surprise that I have such a resolute work ethic; I get it from my daddy.

My dad was a role model and our protector. One of the most poignant examples of his love and devotion was during the 2003 New York City blackout. My parents were in their late seventies—in good physical shape, but still senior citizens. Of course, I was worried sick about them. When the city's lights went out, I had just come off a boat ride around the island with *Vibe* magazine, so I was at the southernmost tip of Manhattan, while my parents were up north, in Harlem. I called to check on them, and they told me they were fine. I told them, "I'm going to find my way up to you." They said, "No need," and I assured them, "Y'all just hold on. I'm coming up there. It may take me a few hours, but I'm on my way." My dear friend Karla Radford, whom I worked with at *Vibe* and who lived uptown, close to Harlem, offered a ride to a few of us disembarking downtown. With no streetlights or traffic lights on and with bumper-to-bumper traffic, the trip to my parents' house, which should have been a twenty-five-minute drive, took about *three hours.*

When we pulled up, my senior citizen father was sitting on the stoop outside the building with a baseball bat in his hand. I was incredulous, in absolute shock. I said, "Dad, what are you doing here?" and he responded, "Making sure my baby is okay."

Do you understand what it's like to be a full-grown woman of thirty-seven and see your daddy willing to risk his own well-being for you, for your safety? *That* is unwavering love.

I've mentioned that my dad was shady. It showed up in his often-unfiltered wit and his refusal to be easily impressed. When I got my job at *Rolling Stone*, I was so proud that I bounded into the house, thinking that when I told him about my six-figure salary, he would be in awe and proud—especially given that, at the height of his career, he might have made fifty thousand a year, at most. Now his daughter was making more than five times that number! But when I told him my salary, he said with a deadpan look, "That's good, real good. But now think about how much money you're making them if they're willing to pay you that much!"

This stopped me in my tracks, and from then on, I shifted the way I thought about what constituted a "good job." They aren't doing us any *favors* when they pay us the big bucks. Clearly, businesses are in the business of making money, so they aren't going to pay you if they can't recoup your salary many times over. My dad, with his fifth grade, Jim Crow–stymied education, understood how business worked! He was an astute observer of life who taught his kids all he knew about the world.

My dad is the reason I travel the world. Sunday mornings in our home began with him going food shopping—we rarely ate food that wasn't purchased the same day, no deep freezers or meat plans for the Smittys—and picking up the *Daily News*. He would read the articles to us, and we would all read the comics together. He'd also drill us on geography: "How many continents?" "How many oceans?" "What's the highest summit in the world?" On and on, he'd ask us questions, not just about the United States, but the whole world. Those Sundays shaped me and my siblings. I'm convinced that's why we all have a curiosity about the world, a wanderlust. Because of Dad, with maps and *National Geographic* stretched out on the coffee table, talking about foreign lands. The last foreign trip I took while my dad was alive was my annual New Year's Eve trip, which in 2019 was to Ghana and Morocco. My dad was in the rehabilitation center, and I was so worried about him, I thought about not going (separation anxiety), but my sister convinced me that it would be okay, and Dad said he would be there when I got back. I went to visit him every day leading up to the trip, including the day I left.

I have a ritual that helps me cope with my separation anxiety: I won't get on a plane before going to see my parents. The day of my trip, I visited with my dad to remind him of where I was going and promised to come back with stories and trinkets. And sure enough, Dad liked the wooden elephant sculpture I purchased in Ghana and really loved the *al-ayn aka*, or "evil eye," trinket I got for his wall. Still, what he really wanted was to chat about my trip, and he boasted to anyone in the rehabilitation center who would listen that his daughter had been to all the continents except Antarctica. Daddy, when I get to Antarctica, it will be in your honor.

I could write more about my dad, but instead I'd like you to get to know him through his own words from that interview with BlkSuns in 2018. I present to you, my beloved daddy, Gus Lee Smith, lover of rice (he's a Geechie), his country, and most of all, his family, my role model and hero:

Mr. Smith, from Yemasee, South Carolina, born 1925

Thoughts on . . .

Courage: 17th Birthday I was in combat against the Japanese. Blacks couldn't have guns. We stood guard with rifles without bullets. It was Jim Crow from head to toe.

Freedom: I didn't work for no white man.

Strength: I didn't fall in no traps.

Weakness: Got a lot of them I guess. Booz. Women.

Passion: Take care of my family.

Fears: Not much.

Regret: Not going to school.

Pet Peeve: Trump. Black Folks not thinking.

Happiness: To see people get along.

Sadness: Seeing how foolish we are with money.

Your Mother: I love her. She died when I was 8.

Your Father: Quiet man. Didn't drink. Didn't go to church.

Important Qualities in a Man: Hold himself up. Be a leader.

In a Woman: Raise her kids. Take care of them.

Love: Love is give and take.

Hate: That's a bad word. Let's talk. I'll discuss my life with you.

Life: Make something with it. Life is the most important.

Death: It's coming.

Last thing to make you . . .
Cry: Not trying to better myself. I just bumped along.
Laugh: I'll crack a joke but won't show off all my ivories.
Afraid: Not having money saved.
Courageous: I'm not brave but I'm not afraid.

What are you ashamed of? Nothing really. I wasn't a midnight rambler.
Proud of? Not belonging to a religion. I'm my own church and I preach my own sermons.
What do people misunderstand about you? It don't make me no difference what you think about me. I take care of my family. That's my community.
What was the most difficult time in your life? Right now. I can't move around like I used to.
The most celebrated? Don't think I had too many of them. My Children.
What age do you feel? I'm not a spring chicken. Like the sun I'm burning out slowly.
Present state of mind? I don't know what the world is gonna come to.
What is your gift to the world? Guiding my family.
What makes you, you? Don't know what makes me tick. I just hope I'm on the right road. I'll try to make it to heaven.

The Smittys on their wedding day in 1965.
My mom is so pretty in her pillbox hat, my dad dapper in his suit
with no tie. Good style is innate.

A Pandemic, Race Relations, Getting Comfortable with Being Uncomfortable, and Not Wearing Bottoms During Zoom Calls: 2020 in a Nutshell

'M FIFTY-FOUR YEARS OLD AS I WRITE THIS. IT'S BEEN FIFTEEN years since I decided to change my life, and I feel like I'm starting all over again. Yet, I sense that the whole world is beginning anew, that the universe has pushed a Reset button. On many days, I feel encouraged and excited about how rapidly the world is changing, because I know change'll do you good. But it's still the unknown, and the change that's happening is being ushered in, in part, by a virus that we truly don't know much about, other than that it can kill you. That's horrifying, and for about a month after my dad died, I just wanted to stay at home. I felt like that was the only way to keep myself safe. I even wondered if I would ever feel safe enough to be the woman I was B.C. (Before Corona), a woman who was called "a gal about town."

Then I had the legendary Iyanla Vanzant on *Bevelations* and I asked her about dealing with fear in the time of "the corona" (her term for the pandemic). She said that many of us had already been living with fears, that the virus had just exacerbated them, forced them out of the closet. Speaking with Iyanla and my tele-therapist, I realized that my fear is rooted in a lack of control. I'm a problem solver, and I got my first taste of taking control of my life, of my narrative, when I bucked the system and attended a different high school from my bullies. I'd gotten used to being able to identify what was wrong in my life and to fix it.

Unfortunately, there's no quick fix to the coronavirus, but I've realized that if I can cede the impulse to try to forecast what comes next, if I can truly relinquish the idea that I have to have a strategy to create the "right" outcome, I can be liberated. As I type these words, I'm moving into that space, and each day, I'm regaining belief in my mantra "Everything is as it should be."

Even the murder of George Floyd, an unarmed Black man killed by police officers in Minneapolis on May 25, 2020, with one of the police officers kneeling on his neck as George screamed, "I can't breathe."

Even the death of Breonna Taylor, an emergency room technician who was asleep with her boyfriend in her Louisville, Kentucky, home in March 2020, when police using a battering ram crashed into her apartment and shot her at least eight times, killing her.

The names of George Floyd and Breonna Taylor (and Elijah McClain, Tony McDade, and Rayshard Brooks; unfortunately, the list is long and I could go on) are just a handful of names that we know of. Their deaths and the deaths of way too many Black people have been the catalyst for real change, not just in police departments across the country but also in the real discussions and reexamining of policies around race that have finally started to take place, making many people uncomfortable, especially white people.

To that I say, welcome to what Black folks experience every day in America, although it's an iota of what we've felt since we were bought here against our will in 1619 and forced to build this country for free. We've been feeling uncomfortable, judged, maligned, objectified, discriminated against, policed at every turn, told that our BLACK LIVES don't MATTER, for centuries, but no more and NEVER AGAIN!

So, yes, everything is as it should be. This revolution had to happen. It's imperative to have no-holds-barred talks about race and, more importantly, to dismantle the systems in place that reward and uphold racism. Don't get defensive, don't avoid it, seek information from reputable sources, not conspiracy theorists—because you're either part of the problem or part of the solution. And by the way, silence is compliance, see something, say something, all the Instagram clichés apply!

I'm no stranger to being tenacious, focused, and driven, but believing that "everything is as it should be" in the face of a global pandemic and social uprising requires me to double down in my faith. I'm grateful that Lil' Brown Bevy is my core, because I need her optimism, her resolute ability to imagine a silver lining in difficult scenarios. Eckhart Tolle said, "When you become comfortable with uncertainty, Infinite Possibilities open up in your life." I'm choosing to let Lil' Brown Bevy's open heart and spirit be my guide.

By the time you read this, it will be 2021, and I don't know what the world will look like, but I think my book will be published. (Let's hope so, because I'm not giving a dime of the advance back!) In B.C. (Before Corona) times, I imagined zipping around the country (maintaining my Diamond status on Delta) to meet thousands of you in fab spaces for a reading of my book. Allegedly, this book comes out in January 2021, and at this point the most I can hope for is maybe ten people at a time in a well-ventilated space, or maybe the book tour will be virtual, consisting of Instagram Live and Zoom meetups. (If the readings are virtual, please know that I will go full glam with a beautiful top, but I will be naked from the waist down.)

So, I don't know what I'll be doing, but that's what excites me. I hope it *inspires* you.

We may as well embrace the unknown. *Revel* in it! Y'all know that old saying "Want to see God laugh? Make a plan"? Well, I'm no longer tethered to a plan. This book has been revised to include mentions of the pandemic and the protests against police brutality, but the part about being comfortable with being uncomfortable and getting rid of the idea of having a plan, well, that was in the book prior to Trump telling folks to ingest household cleaning fluid. When you're adventurous and challenging yourself, carpe diem–ing right up until the end, in search of the bespoke version of a good life, that's when you're really living. Plan all you want, but if you're doing it right, you won't hesitate to veer off down a road without knowing where it ends.

It's a healthy outlook to have no matter what age you are. Look at Cicely Tyson, winning a Tony Award (her first) at *ninety-two*; Norman Lear, at ninety-six, having a new production deal; Niecy Nash going from a reality show, *Clean House*, where she became known for wearing a flower in her hair and helped folks get their homes together, to becoming an Emmy-nominated dramatic actress in her late forties.

◆ ◆ ◆

If you have a first edition, preordered, that means you're reading this approximately a year after the pandemic began and eight months since the George Floyd and Black Lives Matter protests hit the streets. As I'm writing this, I'm embracing the uncertainty that consumes our world today, but one thing I'm sure about is that "It Gets Greater Later" is more than a slogan I copyrighted and put on mugs, T-shirts, and journals in the hope that you'd go buy them. (Don't get me wrong; I *do* want you to buy them, but that's beside the point.) I know this to be so because that's been the theme of my life. My career could have stalled at Peter Rogers. Sure, I would have worked my way up to office manager, but there's no way I would have been content at being the Queen B of the administrative staff. There's always been a fire inside me, pushing me forward even when I was complacent. Each time I hit a milestone, a "Momma I Made It" moment, where the average person would have been happy to rest and reside, my core, Lil' Brown Bevy reminded me, "It Gets Greater Later." I'm open to all that the universe has in store for me, because I'm tapped into my core. Are you?

Lil' Brown Bevy is my North Star. She's the best of who I am, of who I've always been, or at least tried to be. After decades of shrouding her with MC Bev-Ski, Big Bev from Uptown, Fashionista Beverly, and even Bevy Smith, I finally realized what Dorothy learned when she got to the Emerald City: that the Wizard was just a man working with smoke and mirrors, scared of his own shadow, trying to survive. (This isn't a judgment because, honestly, most of us are.) Everything I needed was already in me!

So, this book is also for her and for all the Lil' Brown Bevys out there in the world, no matter their gender, race, or sexual orientation. I will always love and honor Lil' Brown Bevy, who guides me each day toward a life of BODACIOUS DREAMS and BEVELATIONS, and that, my loves, is a Bevelation!

◆ ◆ ◆

P.S. When you come to the book signing (virtual or IRL), make sure *your* Lil' Brown Bevy, who you are at your *core*, shows up. That's who I want to meet!

With love, from your Mutha, Auntie, and Bestie

Lil' Brown Bevy, bright-eyed and optimistic.
I may look different but I feel exactly like her today.

Acknowledgments

My mother, the girl with the sparkly eyes, Geraldine Smith, you taught me the value of hard work, healthy self-esteem, and style being my calling card. Because of you, I love the Brown skin I'm in. You're the prototype.

Daddy, I pray you're up in heaven, looking down, showing off to the other angels the family you created. You always said, "You can only get out what you put in," and you put everything into us. I hope you're proud of the return.

My big brother, Gerald Timberlake, my role model for enjoying life to the fullest, thank you for teaching me to roller-skate, to dance like no one is watching, and to travel the world, all while looking good.

To Stephie, you always said that you may not fight for yourself, but you would fight for me. Thank you for not only fighting for me but for being my Mutha, Auntie, Bestie, TEACHER!

To my nephews, Melvin, Damien, Donovan, and Darius; my great-nephew, Cyrus; and my one and only niece, Domonique, being your "Auntie Bev" fills me with pride. I always wanted to be the "cool auntie." I hope I live up to the title.

My brother-in-law, Damien, you are a BROTHER to me, the "in-law" part is a technicality. Thank you for accepting the reins of the family from Daddy.

My agent, Cait Hoyt. Three years ago we sat in your office and I told you stories, those stories became an outline for this book, and then you brokered a kick-ass deal, THANK YOU.

Ayana Byrd, my book doctor, you helped shape this memoir from jumbled-up tales of sex and fashion into a memoir worthy of the *New York Times* bestseller list (creative visualization). You made my words better. Thank you for editing without diluting me.

To my Woady, aka Warren White aka Wardell Malloy aka my son, I always say folks who love you take the best photos, and the cover of this book proves it: you love MOMMY!

To my 80's Ladies, my original sister-friends, thank you to Aunt Diane, Nichelle, Nell, Micki, Renee, Juliette, Stephanie, and Shay for loving me from Big Bev and her "good in the hood" shenanigans to my current incarnation of Bevy Smith, Media Personality.

Jeff McKay family, Judy, Kim, Ali, and Jeff, and honorary members Nancy and Keni. I was an embryo when we worked together, and you each taught me so much. You were my first work family, and you never forget your first. I love you all.

To my *Vibe* Tribe, Emil, Fred, Karla, Ali, D.Lemon, Jeffrey Byrnes, Jeff Mazzacano, Scean, Cara, Marian, Junny, Beth, Alma, and Traceye, my co-conspirators, we helped shape Black culture at a time when it was underrated. Proud to be in your tribe.

Len Burnett, John Rollins, and Kenard Gibbs, my former bosses at *Vibe*, thank you for the platform and opportunities to shine in my career.

My hubby Stan Williams, my original editor, you've looked at everything I've ever published (including this book) and given me invaluable notes. Thank you for helping to hone my voice!

Monique and Alec Chenault (RIP), my only Black mentors, thank you for seeing this curvy, dark-skinned, over-thirty-five-year-old woman and *knowing* that she could be a TV host.

To my former TV cohosts Derek J., Miss Lawrence, Elizabeth Wagmeister, and Carlos Greer, I have nothing but love and respect for each of you. Thank you for always having my back, making me look good, and, most of all, being my friend when the cameras are off.

A Jew, a Puerto Rican/Cuban, and a Black girl walk into a bar, the start of a problematic joke—nope, it's the groundwork of Team Zany, a thirty-year-plus sisterhood with my Mimi and Aimee. Thank you, both, for always supporting every life change I've ever had, NO QUESTIONS ASKED!

Terrell, aka Relish, my original mentee, meeting you in Vegas twenty years ago changed my life for the better. The roles have reversed: the teacher has become the student, and I love learning from you.

Renee, aka Nay Nay Billy, we've run the streets, we've been business partners, and you've styled me, but what I appreciate most is the decades of real talk and friendship.

Emil, Lisa, Kim Bondy, Angelique, Lawrence, Kiwan, Moochie, CJ, Wardell, Nina, Terrell, and Tavia, from debauched family functions, hilarious late-night texts, and moments when you've all provided a shoulder to lean on, you are my Framily.

Dr. Cherrie, from dodgy medical advice to shady cross-continent loans, you are the Tia to my Sunshine. I love you, and never forget that #ItGetsGreaterLater.

Ryan Tarpley, your loving and nurturing spirit is a large part of how this book came to be. Thank you for pushing me. I love you.

To my Holt family, especially Barbara Jones and Ruby Rose Lee, thank you for guiding me on this journey. The infinite patience of getting this book finished through a global pandemic, social unrest, and me being distracted by life, I appreciate all of you.

To Andrew Cohen, thank you for seeing ALL OF ME and never attempting to put me in a box; for hearing me out, even when I'm saying something you'd rather not hear; and for keeping your promises and being a true mensch.

Thank you, Harlem, for giving me the confidence to withstand the judgmental worlds of fashion, advertising, and entertainment. In Harlem I'm celebrated, not just tolerated. UPTOWN GIRL FOR LIFE!

My teachers: my big brother, Gerry, and my sister, Stephanie.
Please note that I was twelve and flat as a board!